Winning the World

Recent Titles in
Humanistic Perspectives on International Relations

The Third Option: The Emancipation of European Defense, 1989–2000
Charles G. Cogan

Winning the World

Lessons for America's Future
from the Cold War

Thomas M. Nichols

Humanistic Perspectives
on International Relations

Cathal J. Nolan, Series Editor

PRAEGER

Westport, Connecticut
London

Library of Congress Cataloging-in-Publication Data

Nichols, Thomas M., 1960–
   Winning the world : lessons for America's future from the Cold War /
     Thomas M. Nichols.
     p. cm—(Humanistic perspectives on international relations, ISSN 1535-0363)
   Includes bibliographical references and index.
   ISBN 0-275-96663-1 (alk. paper)
     1. United States—Foreign relations—1945–1989. 2. United States—Foreign
   relations—1989– 3. Cold War. I. Title. II. Series.
E840 .N44 2002
327.73—dc21   2002072803

British Library Cataloguing in Publication Data is available.

Library of Congress Catalog Card Number: 2002072803
ISBN: 0-275-96663-1
ISSN: 1535-0363

First published in 2002

Praeger Publishers, 88 Post Road West, Westport, CT 06881
An imprint of Greenwood Publishing Group, Inc.
www.praeger.com

Printed in the United States of America

The paper used in this book complies with the
Permanent Paper Standard issued by the National
Information Standards Organization (Z39.48-1984).

10 9 8 7 6 5 4 3 2 1

Copyright Acknowledgments
Excerpt from John LeCarre, *The Secret Pilgrim* © 1991 Random House, Inc. Used
by permission.

"Everybody Wants to Rule the World." Words and Music by Roland Orzabal,
Ian Stanley, and Chris Hughes © 1985 EMI VIRGIN MUSIC (PUB) LTD., 10
MUSIC LTD. and AMUSEMENTS LTD. All rights for EMI VIRGIN MUSIC (PUB)
LTD. and 10 MUSIC LTD. controlled and administered in the United States and
Canada by EMI VIRGIN SONGS, INC. All rights reserved. International copy-
right secured. Used by permission.

For
Stephen Sternheimer
William C. Fuller, Jr.
Thane Gustafson

Teachers, colleagues, friends

It is our hearts' desire that peace be preserved, but we should all have learned by now that there is no safety in yielding to dictators, whether Nazi or Communist. The only hope of peace is to be strong, to act with other great freedom-loving nations, and to make it plain to the aggressor, while time remains, that we shall rally the free men of the world and defend ourselves and our cause by every means should the aggressor strike a felon's blow.

Winston Churchill, 1948

Contents

Series Foreword

International relations is a thoroughly humanistic subject. All its actors are human beings, or they are institutions and organizations built and controlled by human intention and maintained by daily decision-making. Individual states, which emerged as the most powerful and decisive actors on the world stage over the past 350 years, are not reified constructs with an independent will or social reality beyond human ken or volition. Properly regarded, they are wholly human constructs. All states are designed for and are bent to the realization of goals and aspirations of human communities. That is true whether those ambitions are good or evil, spiritual or material, personal or dynastic, or represent ethnic, national, or emerging cosmopolitan identities. So, too, is the international society of states a human construct, replete with its tangled labyrinth of international organizations, an expansive system of international law which creates binding obligations across frontiers, ancient norms of diplomacy and ritualized protocol, webs of economic, social, and cultural interaction, and a venerable penchant for disorder, discord, and war.

Immanuel Kant observed with acute accuracy: "Out of the crooked timber of Humanity, no straight thing was ever made." The endless drama of human affairs thus gives rise to motley events, decisions, and complex causal chains. At the international level, too, we encounter the foibles of human beings as individuals and in the aggregate and come upon a mix of the rational and irrational in human motivation. All that makes formal "modeling" of international politics a virtual impossibility—a fact which is itself a source of deep frustration to idealistic reformers and social scientists alike. On the other hand, precisely because international relations is so deeply humanistic a subject, it is a rich realm for the exercise of broad political and moral judgment. It is a natural arena for serious ethical reflection by and about those who frame foreign policies and practice statecraft. It is proper for scholars and informed citizens to praise or censure leadership decisions and actions. In short, as in all realms of human endeavor, moral judgment is not only implicit in every decision or action (or inaction) taken in international relations, it is a core duty of leadership, an apt function of scholarship, and a basic requirement for any educated citizenry.

These facts are clear and even self-evident. At its classical best, political science understood them and, therefore, drew its questions from the conversation across time of the great political thinkers, as well as from current policy debtes, to examine both in a rich discourse which was historically and philosophically aware, even as it was rigorous and well-grounded empirically. In contrast, much contemporary political science purports to describe and explain international relations through elaboration of objective "laws" of politics or economics, which entirely overlook its humanistic character. At its modern and "postmodern" worst, the discipline is prone to mere methodological preoccupations, striking elaborate poses about arcane topics, and impenetrable prose. For instance, positivism's search for a "rational choice" model of human conduct assumes that individuals are "rational actors" who purposively seek to maximize their interests. In seeking a universal, deductive theory (broadly modeled on academic economics, where similar methodologies are employed with little explanatory success), too many political scientists eschew historical or philosophically informed case study in favor of a crude reduction of all politics to formal models. These usually engage extreme simplifications, couched in an obscurantist terminology, which model what was already known, or is obvious, or are so generalized that they account for nothing specific. Over that thin substance is then spread a thick veneer of false rigor, packaged in mathematical formulae which are and are intended to be intimidating to the uninitiated. Left out is the fact that most things of lasting importance in human affairs may be explained not by "rational choices," but by ideology and ignorance, blundering and stupidity, courage and self-sacrifice, enlightened vision, fanaticism, or blind chance (what Machiavelli called *fortuna*).

Alternately, the "critical theory" school in political science rejects any epistemology holding that reality exists separately from the academic observer and is therefore objectively knowable to any real degree. All knowledge about international relations merely reflects the biases and power interests of the observer (the usual suspects are racial, class, or economic elites). Scholars are warned against the attempt to achieve objective knowledge of the reality of international relations, which traditionally was the moral and intellectual *raison d'être* of their profession. Rather than seek to impartially map out, explore, and explain the international society of states and its complex subsystems and mores, a feat said to be impossible, scholars are to directly engage and change the world (even though that, too, ought to be impossible, if they are unable to understand it in the first place). Too often, this leads to polemical studies which purport to unmask elites whose pervasive and corrupt power is said to sustain and operate a fatally unjust international system. There is much intolerance and angry posturing here as well, in calls for "exposure" of fellow-traveling academic approaches identified as legitimizing and reinforcing irredeemably illicit power structures. In sum, in its epistemological assertion that all knowledge is radically subjective or merely political, critical theory denies the possibility of objective knowledge or the value of other scholarly traditions.

This series does not support the contention that all significant political action is reducible to rational choice or that it is impossible to acquire objective knowledge about world affairs. Instead, it promotes a classical, humanistic approach to international relations scholarship. It is dedicated to reviving and furthering the contribution to understanding made by classical studies—by knowledge of history, diplomacy, international law, and philosophy—but it is agnostic regarding the narrow ideology or specific policy conclusions of any given work. It supports scholarly inquiry which is grounded in the historical antecedents of contemporary controversies and well-versed in the great traditions of philosophical inquiry and discourse. The series recognizes that, at its most incisive, international relations is a field of inquiry which cannot be fully understood outside its historical context. The keenest insights into the meaning of economic, legal, cultural, and political facts and issues in contemporary world affairs are always rooted in appreciation that international society is a historical phenomenon, not a theoretical abstraction or a radical departure from prior experience. Hence, the series welcomes interdisiciplinary scholarship dealing with the evolution of the governing ideas, norms, and practices of international society. It encourages a dialectic rooted in abiding intellectual, ethical, and practical interests which have concerned and engaged intelligent men and women for centuries, as they tried to reconcile the historical emergence of modern states with wider or older notions of political community.

This series is especially interested in scholarly research on the varied effects of differences in power—whether economic, political, or military—on relations among nations and states. The causes of war and the supports of peace, both in general and concerning specific conflicts, remain a core interest of all serious inquiry into international relations. Similarly, there is an enduring need for studies of the core requirements of international order and security and of international political economy, whether regionally or globally. Scholarship is also welcome which is concerned with the development of international society, both in the formal relations maintained by states and in broader demands for political, economic, social, and cultural justice on the subnational and even individual level. Finally, the series promotes scholarly investigation of the history and changing character and status of international law, into international organization, and any and all other means of decentralized governance which the states have invented to moderate their conflicts and introduce a measure of restraint and equity to the affairs of international society.

Cathal J. Nolan

Preface

Like so many Americans, I grew up with the Cold War and accepted it as the central political fact of my life. I was born in 1960 and spent my childhood practically within sight of the Strategic Air Command bomber base in my hometown. I knew from an early age that this meant our quiet New England city was an obvious target for a Soviet nuclear weapon. (This was something I probably realized around the time, during a "fire drill," that I impertinently asked a teacher exactly what kind of "fire" was best avoided by hiding under my desk instead of leaving the building.) Growing up under this constant threat of war was no small influence on my decision, in later years, to study the Soviet Union in hopes of better understanding the nature of the enemy.

When the Kremlin surrendered and struck the Soviet colors for the last time on Christmas Day 1991, I was astonished, but I was also (again, like so many Americans) relieved and grateful. I was also proud to be a citizen of a country that had waged a half-century of conflict with a dedicated and dangerous opponent and had not only survived but even prospered—and more important, had also largely managed to stay true to its own principles during the fight. At the time the Soviet Union fell, I was busy finishing the writing of a study of Soviet military politics, but I hoped at some point in the future to think more about just how the West had achieved such a stunning and relatively bloodless victory. I assumed that I might one day join a discussion about the end of the Cold War that would already be in progress. After all, it only stood to reason that the most momentous event in international life since the defeat of the Axis in 1945 would generate excited and wide-ranging investigations into its causes.

In this, I was to be disappointed. The Cold War, only ten years after its final chapter, is fading from scholarship and the public consciousness more quickly than anyone would have imagined. The lack of interest among ordinary Americans, in fairness, is more than understandable. A generation of Americans is now coming of age with no real memory of that conflict, for whom stories of schoolchildren engaging in nuclear air raid drills or of people stocking homemade fallout shelters are about as relevant as World War II scrap metal drives and war bonds. What matters to them, mostly, is only that it is over.

But among the scholarly community, too, there has a been a curious and unexpected silence about the Cold War, a reluctance to think about the nature of the Western victory—or even to think of it as "victory" at all. (To speak in those terms is to invite huffy cautions from offended intellectuals about "triumphalism," as though giving the events of 1989–1991 their proper name is somehow impolite.) There have been some attempts to think through the end of the Cold War, but these have been arid academic forays, typically self-referential, into questions about why practitioners of social science disciplines obsessed by high theory were unable to cope with events right in front of their eyes—as though the answer to that were not already obvious. To be fair, historians and archivists have been struggling to mine ever larger sources of information as they come available, but as some observers have pointed out, there seems to be little tension or anticipation in the academy and almost no curiosity among policymakers about what those sources reveal.

Instead of producing a new appraisal of the Cold War and of the Soviet Union as the dangerous and paranoid power that it was, these revelations have instead been largely ignored by academic revisionists who, like the last barricaded Japanese soldiers of World War II, refuse to accept the undeniable. Unfortunately, there is no longer much point to joining those partisans in debate; the world, dangerous as it is and getting more so by the day, is moving on, and so must we. As Vojtech Mastny has wisely written: "If the empire Stalin created was in fact every bit as evil as suspected, and much more, then those who waged the Cold War against it need not apologize for the effort. The pertinent question, rather, is whether they did the best they could."

I have titled this book *Winning the World* out of a conviction that the Cold War was a battle for the future of humanity, in which there was no second prize and no second chance—a situation I am certain we will face again from any number of enemies who seek nothing less than the West's extinction as a civilization. Before we leave the

Cold War behind in too much haste, there are things to be learned about how America conducted it, about which of our strategies against our Soviet enemy were effective, which were counterproductive or dangerous, and which of them might be useful again as we enter an era where the threat to engage in nuclear holocaust is no longer the sole privilege of the original five victors of World War II. Nuclear technology cannot be abolished, and nuclear arms will be sought—and gained—by the adherents of demented ideologies who want to use them in the service of their aggressive plans. At the dawn of the twenty-first century, it should be evident, however chilling it is to say it, that the Cold War of 1945-1991 was only the first of its kind, and we had best think about the sources of our previous victory before another such conflict is upon us.

The Cold War might seem particularly irrelevant after September 11, 2001. Suddenly, the threat to Western security is no longer a hypothetical one based on some science fiction scenario of global nuclear war. Instead, thousands of Americans lay dead in New York, Pennsylvania, and Virginia, as anthrax and heaven knows what scourges made their way through the postal system. What possible relevance could the long struggle with the Soviet Union—and for many people, the Cold War was never much more than an abstraction anyway—have at a time when the United States is actually at war with Islamic fanatics half a world away? But the war with terrorism, like the war against communism, is a war of ideas, against people who will one day seek again to hold us hostage with nuclear weapons. The Western ideal of liberty has always had enemies who despise it as a matter of first principles; this is something that Americans and their allies have always understood, but for a time, in the relief of victory and the absence of any visible threats, it might have seemed somehow less important. After the outrages of September 11, it is a realization that I suspect is now seared irrevocably in our minds.

Of course, no previous war can serve as a perfect template for the next. "Fighting the last war" is rightly an expression of derision, and any strategy that seeks to replicate in detail a victory from the past is not only uncreative but dangerous. Certainly, states that have tried to use previous conflicts as road maps for the next have suffered grievously for it. But the "lessons" of the Cold War are less a map for battle or a recipe for victory as much as they are propositions about fighting against nuclear-armed, ideologically driven, totalitarian regimes like the Soviet Union, about their relative strengths and vulnerabilities, and about how best to exploit their weaknesses without inciting a general war. While the Cold War claimed thousands of lives, the two central participants never directly attacked each other, and in the end, civilization was spared a Third World War. The lessons of the Cold War are, accordingly, lessons in the art of indirect warfare, of conflict by means other than direct combat between the primary contestants.

The USSR was a state founded (like the United States) on explicitly ideological propositions and was committed to the furtherance of those propositions, even if that at times meant risking Soviet national interests as realists might understand that concept. What this means in terms of lessons that are of importance to policymakers in the twenty-first century is that, first, understanding an enemy's ideological commitments promises predictive as well as explanatory rewards and can freshen Western thinking about various strategies that respond to such commitments. Second, it suggests areas in which such an enemy is vulnerable. (Attacking the state-society relationship in a repressive regime, for example, can reap great rewards against states that are obsessively concerned with social control.) Finally, we must remain cognizant of the immutability of the enemy: a struggle with an ideological opponent always promises to be a long and cruel one because when beliefs are at issue rather than territory or resources, there is by definition no compromise to be found. The conflict, by its nature, can only end in victory or defeat for one set of principles or the other, something that cannot be wished away no matter how many treaties, agreements, and truces there might be along the way, and this is a special challenge for leaders of democracy trying to guide their inherently impatient societies through a protracted conflict.

This book is not intended as a comprehensive history of the Cold War; that struggle is too large and too mulitifaceted to embrace in a single volume. It is instead an attempt to look to specific instances in the history of the Soviet-American conflict and to try to draw from them propositions and considerations for the future. Nor is this study meant to define a set of iron rules of engagement with a cold war opponent. Every war has its own character, its own idiom; strategy is not a one-size-fits-all solution. Situations, as every student of war knows, can change. Even the most fanatical regimes can at times find a sudden reserve of sobriety under the right conditions and be coerced into defying their own ideological code; undermining state control of a captive population can backfire and produce so much repression and misery among innocent people that humanitarian concerns demand that such measures be foresworn; and there are times when a relaxation of tensions and the encouragement of negotiations is more in Western interests than confrontation.

Nonetheless, policies that ignore the important role played in the life of the West's opponents by ideology (and thus underestimate the consequent pathological need of such regimes to impose their beliefs and their political systems as widely as possible), have little hope of succeeding. Those who would argue that time is on the side of the democracies are probably right, but any number of odious entities, especially once they are armed with nuclear weapons, can do a great deal of damage before they are finally swallowed in history's tar pits. The Western goal in the next cold wars, as it was in the last one, should be to escort them to oblivion, as safely and quickly as possible.

This study began as an article in *International Journal* called "Lessons from the New History of the Cold War," written at the invitation of *International Journal's* coeditor Margaret MacMillan for the autumn 1998 issue. Margaret was curious, as I was, about why so little was being said about the avalanche of shocking revelations coming from the Soviet archives, and her invitation was the spark not only for that article (excerpts of which appear here and are used with permission), but also for the book itself. Shortly thereafter, I had the good fortune to meet Cathal Nolan, the editor of Praeger's series in Humanistic Perspectives on International Relations, who encouraged me to pursue the idea at greater length. I am pleased to be a part of that series, and I appreciate the steady and sensible comments Cathal has provided throughout the development of the project.

I wish to acknowledge with gratitude the grant I received from the Smith-Richardson Foundation and the subsequent administrative assistance I received from the Naval War College Foundation. Without the aid of these two institutions, this book would not have been written. (I first came to Newport many years ago as a Fellow of the Naval War College Foundation, and it was gratifying to be able to return and work with the Naval War College Foundation again.) I would like to thank the anonymous reviewer engaged by the Smith-Richardson Foundation for his or her very useful and thoughtful comments on the original design of the work. I would also like to thank the Davis Center for Russian Studies at Harvard University for granting me Associate status during the term of this project.

The support of the Smith-Richardson Foundation not only helped to speed the research and writing of this study, but also enabled me to find and work with scholars in Russia who are similarly interested in Cold War issues and their current relevance. I wish to thank the many Russian scholars from the Institute of the USA and Canada, the Russian Academy of Sciences, the Institute of Military History, and the Diplomatic Academy of the Russian Federation who took the time to speak with me and share their insights, including Vladimir Batiuk, Natalia Egorova, Ilya Gaiduk, Karen Khachaturov, Ivan Kuzmin, Viktor Laptev, Vladimir Matiash, and Aleksandr Orlov. I want to extend special thanks to my friend and colleague Sergei Baburkin of Yaroslavl University for his ongoing help and advice.

Several students and friends provided assistance and encouragement during the writing of this book. My students in the graduate international relations seminar program at Salve Regina University in 1999 cheerfully undertook to challenge many of my propositions during the course and forced me to think harder about some of the main points in several chapters. Dirk Vandewalle and Tom Hengeveld reviewed both early and late drafts with an eye toward readability and common sense. My father, Nick James Nichols, was not only a source of support, but also a refreshing reminder to see the Cold War through the eyes of one of its older veterans. My mother, Joan Gavin Nichols (herself a military veteran of the Korean War era) also encouraged me to take up this project; while she is no longer with us to see its completion, her influence can be found in these pages.

As ever, my wife, Dr. Linda Titlar, provided more encouragement, advice, comment, and substantive contributions than I could ever reasonably expect. Her academic expertise and unerring editorial eye have led me at times to impose on her to the point of turning *my* projects into *our* projects, and I thank her, with love and gratitude.

I have had the great privilege to write this study as a member of the faculty at the United States Naval War College, and I owe a great debt to my friends and colleagues in Newport. This project benefited greatly from the ongoing support for such endeavors from the college's administration, and I wish to thank the President, Vice Admiral Arthur K. Cebrowski, USN, and the Provost, Rear Admiral Barbara McGann, USN, for encouraging such a supportive and energizing intellectual environment during the writing of this book. I wish to thank my colleagues in the Department of Strategy and Policy for their many conversations with me on the Cold War and on so many other subjects, and particularly David Kaiser for his thoughtful comments on draft chapters, although I should point out that the conclusions (and flaws) of this study are mine alone. I wish to thank as well my teaching partners over the past two years, Colonel Paul Aswell, USA, and Colonel Neil Hartenstein, USMC, for their patience and for many lively and helpful discussions. Finally, I wish to offer my thanks to my predecessor as chairman of the Department of Strategy and Policy, George Baer, who made great efforts to ensure that there was time to travel, to write, and to reflect. Without his uncompromising support for faculty research, this study could never have been completed in a timely fashion.

Over the years I have had the privilege to know three men whose wise advice, good sense, and continuing friendship have always been reminders to me of why I joined the scholarly community in the first place. Stephen Sternheimer, William C. Fuller, Jr., and Thane Gustafson have been inspirations as teachers and again as colleagues, and in my own career as an educator and scholar I have tried to follow their collective example. I know that many of the conclusions of this book would not be theirs, but without them I would not be here to write it, and so it is dedicated to them, with gratitude.

From the Cold War to "Cold Wars": Can It Happen Again?

Nothing ever lasts forever
Everybody wants to rule the world.

—Tears for Fears, 1985

IF WE HAD POSSESSED MISSILES THAT COULD REACH NEW YORK...

The world of the early twenty-first century seems a better place than the violent century that preceded it, for all the horror of the efforts of international terrorists to make it otherwise. The Soviet Union is now just another fallen empire, and successive administrations in the United States and the Russian Federation have maintained that the two states do not regard each other as an enemy. Russians and Americans, as well as so many millions in other nations, no longer live under the nuclear hair-trigger and the threat of planetary annihilation that dominated international life during the Cold War, and the immense Soviet and American arsenals are soon to be reduced to a fraction of their former sizes.

Unfortunately, America and its allies have not been irrevocably freed either from nuclear nightmares or the ambitions of ruthless states who would inflict them, as events around the world since the Soviet collapse attest.

In 1990, Libyan dictator Moammar Quadhafi looked back at the U.S. bombing of his country four years earlier, an act of retaliation for his role in terrorist acts against American military personnel in Europe that helped to take Libya out of the business of state-sponsored terrorism. Quadhafi chafed at American military superiority and saw a simple solution to gaining a more equal footing with the United States: "If we had possessed a deterrent—missiles that could reach New York—we would have hit it at the same moment. Consequently, we should build this force so that they and others will no longer think about an attack."[1]

A year after Quadhafi's comments, the chief of staff of India's armed forces was asked what lessons smaller powers might take from the 1991 Gulf War. "Never fight the U.S. without nuclear weapons," he answered.[2]

Five years later, in 1996, the People's Republic of China engaged in a direct campaign of intimidation during Taiwan's national elections, including missile tests off the island's shores. The movement of U.S. naval assets into the area did not seem to concern Beijing; the United States would not act to save Taiwan, a Chinese official told a U.S. Defense Department representative, because Americans "care more about Los Angeles than they do about Taiwan," and that China, unlike America, would sacrifice "millions of men" and "entire cities" to secure the unity of communist China.[3]

In 1998, North Korea launched a long-range, three-stage missile that overflew Japan before landing in the Pacific Ocean. Despite a 1994 agreement to freeze its nuclear weapons program, U.S. defense analysts believe North Korea is within reach both of nuclear weapons and the means to deliver them to Alaska, Hawaii, and the western United States.[4] By 2010, Iran will have an intercontinental missile capable of delivering a nuclear payload to the continental United States (and a medium-range missile capable of reaching Europe even earlier, perhaps by 2006).[5]

The first major attack of the first war of the new millennium took place over the skies of New York, Virginia, and Pennsylvania on the morning of September 11, 2001. The terrorists are, as President George W. Bush reminded Americans in the wake of the horrors, heirs to the fascists and totalitarians of the previous century, and their abiding hatred of Western values means that the United States and its allies face a long and grinding battle against them. The men who rammed the World Trade Center twin towers and the Pentagon with airliners were mere agents of a larger coalition including several nations, many of whom are actively seeking to acquire nuclear weapons. While the president has made clear the determination of the United States to confront any state found to be supporting the networks of international terror, it was a promise made easier by the fact that none of the state sponsors of such acts as yet can counter the American threat with a nuclear trump card of their own. That situation will end, and soon.

The great conflict between the Western democracies and the Soviet totalitarians will never be seen again, at least not in the form it took between 1945 and 1991. But the end of the Cold War does not mean the end of "cold wars"—confrontations with ambitious, ideologically hostile, nuclear-armed nations in which the costs either of direct combat or of outright capitulation are both too high. Although history is ever an imperfect guide, the most dangerous war of the twentieth century has much to tell us in the twenty-first century about fighting and prevailing in these new conflicts. The Western victory over the Soviet empire was neither an accident nor inevitable and offers lessons that are worth heeding in what promises to be a period no less perilous than the one that closed at the end of the 1980s. Those lessons are the subject of this book.

THE END OF THE COLD WAR: PUBLIC OPTIMISM AND INTELLECTUAL DENIAL

When the Soviet flag was lowered for the last time over the Kremlin on Christmas Day 1991, it signified the defeat and imperial dismemberment of America's greatest enemy since Nazi Germany (and in military terms, arguably the second most powerful state in the world at the time). The event was not marked by any of the usual trappings of victory: there were no triumphal parades in the streets of Moscow, trials of enemy leaders, or even a formal tendering of surrender. Instead, the hammer and sickle merely vanished, the Russian tricolor appeared, and the last Soviet leader was allowed to give a speech on national television and then vacate his office.

It was, in its way, a quiet victory appropriate to the struggle. Soviet communism and the Cold War it fostered had taken a terrible toll on all sides, including on the peoples of the Soviet Union, and few in the West were of a mind to punish or humiliate ordinary citizens of the former Soviet empire who had little to do with the conflict waged by their masters in Moscow. It was hard to imagine the end of the Cold War as anything but a common victory for mankind: for the first time since the 1950s, the threat of a planet-killing war finally seemed to recede and perhaps even vanish. In the wake of the Soviet collapse, the victorious Western powers heaved a sigh of relief and then went about their affairs secure in the belief that there could never again be a threat to rival the one that once emanated from the Soviet empire.

This optimism, as well as the exhaustion, that followed this sudden release of global tension was understandable. The coalitions led by

the United States and the Soviet Union had been at war for at least
forty-five years—nearly twice as long as the epic contest between
ancient Athens and Sparta, over ten times as long as the carnage of
World War I, and seven times longer than its immediate predecessor,
World War II. In the end, the Soviet Union disappeared with a
whimper rather than a bang, and in 1991, it seemed almost impossible
to imagine another period of prolonged, tense conflict between two
such powerful adversaries.

After all, whatever other sources of conflict there may yet be between
the world's major powers, the circumstances of the Cold War and, in
particular, the historically unusual condition of rigid bipolarity appear
almost impossible to reproduce in the twenty-first century. The chaos
caused by the collapse of the international order after World War II was
the central event that allowed two superpowers to compete for control
over weakened states in Europe, Asia, and Africa. Without the trauma
of a similar global catastrophe, it is difficult to see how bipolarity could
reemerge at all, raising the question of how the world could somehow
be refrozen into two opposing camps the way it was until 1991. (In any
case, if there ever is another such planetwide war, there will be far
bigger problems to deal with than wondering which two powers will
emerge to fight a cold war when all the dust settles.) The impact of
globalization and the emergence of multiple centers of power in international life are too broad a topic for this study, but multipolarity, even
in a world dominated by the United States, is a fact and will remain so
in the coming decades.

In any case, even if the world could be ideologically or culturally
divided in anything like the way it was during the Cold War, no nations
currently possess the former Soviet Union's nuclear capacity and the
consequent ability to keep future conflicts prolonged and "cold" by
deterring the United States from defending its interests or those of its
allies. The Soviet and American nuclear arsenals, even when aimed at
purely military targets, were nonetheless poised to inflict a combined
total of over 200 million casualties in the first hours of a Soviet-American war, a reality that reinforced the unwillingness of the superpowers
to risk complete destruction of their homelands—indeed, of the entire
Northern Hemisphere—for political gains. The world in the twenty-
first century has more nuclear armed states than it did during the height
of the East-West confrontation, but these budding nuclear powers seem
more interested in gaining relatively smaller forces and menacing their
neighbors rather than engaging in some sort of ongoing global contest
with the United States or NATO.

Why, then, consider "lessons" of the Cold War at all? If the epic
contest with Soviet communism was, like biological evolution, the
contingent result of a chain of unique circumstances that would be

almost impossible to duplicate, why not just record its major events for posterity and be done with it?

This is actually the approach that many observers have suggested, much to the dismay of others who still believe there is much to learn from the Cold War. As Vojtech Mastny recently lamented,

> Rarely has the present receded into the past more quickly than in the years that followed the end of the Cold War. Normally, people sense a continuity; even after great wars that break it do they feel an urge to come to grips with their recent experience by relating it to their new condition. No such urge has grown out of the sudden and unexpected denouement of the East-West conflict.[6]

There are many reasons for this flight from recent history, not least a kind of intellectual denial that has set in among many who believed that the United States and the Soviet Union were equally culpable for the Cold War, the Soviet Union was actually a more stable and productive society than it was (and even, to some, a role model for the West), and in any case the conflict could not be "won" in any meaningful sense. When it turned out that the Soviet Union was in fact responsible for driving much of the East-West competition, Soviet political and economic organization was in fact a barely hidden disaster, and by any reasonable standard—including the opinions of Russians themselves—the end of the Cold War was in fact a clear Western victory, a great many scholars and pundits were simply unprepared to assimilate or accept it.

Sovietologists and theorists of international relations in particular should have had the most to say about the conduct of the Cold War and its stunning end. Both communities were caught flat-footed, however, insulated by years of sterile theorizing even as the Soviet avalanche could be heard rumbling not so distantly. As Walter Laqueur wryly put it,

> thus it came to pass that ordinary Soviet citizens, total strangers to theory building and conceptualization, were feeling in their bones in what direction their society was moving, whereas many Western scholars, fortified by what they thought to be trustworthy theoretical models, had no such misgivings.[7]

It is to some degree unfair to ask anyone to predict the end of the Soviet Union—even if there were actually a few thinkers who did—but with the Cold War over, few academics are now inclined to try to explain the events leading up to 1991, even in retrospect.[8]

Scholarly reticence on the subject is understandable: revisionist historians who claimed that the USSR could not have been guilty of so many of the crimes with which it had been charged, as well as social scientists who had constructed elaborate but utterly unreal models of Soviet political and economic life, cannot now be expected to perform autopsies of their own work.[9] This is not to say there was a complete lack of self-awareness about these shortcomings. Sovietology, in an unfortunate case of tossing out the baby with the bathwater, has nearly collapsed as a field, in part due to attacks overall on regional specialists by scholars from other disciplines, but equally because of the startling poverty of so much previous work on the Soviet Union. International relations theorists have also been taken to task, as Richard Ned Lebow and Thomas Risse Kappen did in 1995:

> Measured by its own standards, the profession's performance was embarrassing. There was little or no debate about the underlying causes of systemic change, the possibility that the Cold War could be peacefully resolved, or the likely consequences of the Soviet Union's visible decline. None of the existing theories of international relations recognized the possibility that the kind of change that did occur could occur.[10]

Yet, while rightly deploring this manifest failure, Lebow himself coauthored a volume a year earlier whose title charged that "we all lost the Cold War," a nihilistic posture that can hardly be described as encouraging novel interpretations of the Soviet-American conflict.

By and large, the majority of academics studying either Soviet politics or international relations (very few studied both) did not believe a Soviet collapse to be possible and now reject the idea of a Western "victory," choosing instead to ascribe the end of the Cold War variously to nebulous, long-term economic trends, the visionary policies of Soviet leader Mikhail Gorbachev, or just plain luck. None of these are particularly conducive to further research, but then, they are not meant to be: they are meant to avert further debate about the Cold War and to forestall what many irate scholars see as an unseemly "triumphalism" in the United States. That word itself makes little sense and more reflects the discomfort of so many scholars with the failure of the Soviet experiment than with any intemperate celebrations in the academic community. (Were those who applauded the defeat of the Axis accused of "triumphalism?" The implication that scholars cannot maintain fidelity to standards of inquiry while still recognizing the difference between good and evil is itself disturbing.)

One important result of this intellectual retreat from the academy's poor record, when combined with the public's general optimism about foreign affairs, is that the term "cold war" itself has become something of a pejorative in twenty-first-century America. "Cold war thinking" is routinely used (by Americans, as well as by America's adversaries) to indicate a mindset that is ostensibly rigid and bellicose, one that is unwilling to accept that the fall of the Soviet empire has produced a new, more flexible, multipolar world in which strategies developed over the previous four decades are worse than useless. "Cold warriors" are now atavists who are presumably more comfortable with the simplicities of the Soviet-American struggle than with the complexities of a world riven by ethnic, cultural, and regional conflicts, where often the good guys and the bad guys are difficult to distinguish. (A similar charge is that American "cold warriors" cannot accept America's lessened dominance in a post–cold war world and are therefore hoping to ignite another one as a means of securing American hegemony for another generation.) By this reasoning, preparing for any kind of protracted conflict is not only politically provocative, but a foolish waste of resources. At the least—with the notable exception of national missile defenses, which many Americans mistakenly assume already exist—such measures are politically unpopular.[11]

Central to the whole issue of learning from the Cold War, then, is the question of what actually constitutes a "cold war" and whether it can happen again. If the conflict of 1945–1991 was sui generis and ended for natural, even mechanical reasons (or because Mikhail Gorbachev ended it), then the failures of the academy and the understandable wishes of the public are pretty much irrelevant to the future. Revisionist scholars could well argue that they should be spared further embarrassment and with a clear conscience press to close the books on five decades of confrontation and move on. Politicians, for their part, can reassure their constituents that despite the occasional miscreants like the late Timothy McVeigh or Theodore Kaczynski, or even the imported psychopaths of September 2001, America is still relatively safe from ultimate destruction.

But what if the Cold War was only the first—even if the biggest—of its kind?

THE COLD WAR AND "COLD WARS"

The Cold War of 1945–1991, like all wars, was the contingent result of a sequence of historical events and accidents. Great interstate conflicts usually have abiding causes, of course, but the actual eruption of war is often only a product of circumstance. The ancient Hellenic world expected that Athens and Sparta sooner or later would settle scores with each other, but it took a squabble between two smaller cities in a far-off corner of northwestern Greece to bring the two major players into direct conflict. Germany was set on a collision course with the rest of Europe before 1914, even if it took an event primarily of importance to Austrians and Serbians to ignite war between the Kaiser and his neighbors. Even wars of outright aggression, like those of Napoleon and Hitler, often take place in environments ripe for conflict. The historical competition between England and France long predated Napoleon, who campaigned in the disarray of post-Westphalian Europe; Hitler led a German state that was already chafing under—and in violation of—the Versailles Treaty.

In similar fashion, the series of events needed to produce the Cold War as we knew it until 1991 seem in retrospect to be one improbable accident after another. Without World War I and without Nicholas II's incompetence in leading Russia through it, the Tsarist regime might not have collapsed so quickly. Without Lenin in Petrograd (courtesy of the Germans, of course), the Bolsheviks might never have gained ascendancy over the other, larger elements of the Russian revolutionary movement or struck at the right moment against Alexander Kerensky's Provisional Government, a move that was resisted by the non-Bolshevik revolutionaries. Without the fatal error made by the leading Bolsheviks after Lenin's death of underestimating the importance of the post of General Secretary, Stalin might never have become supreme dictator of the Soviet Union. Soviet victory over the Germans in World War II was by no means assured. If the scientists at the Trinity nuclear test site had been less diligent and the first atomic explosion had been a magnificent failure, the world might have stayed at war for another year or longer, with Soviet and American soldiers fighting side-by-side in the Pacific instead of eyeing each other warily in divided Germany. By 1945, with Europe in ruins and the colonial world on the verge of liberty, the events of the previous quarter century—the averting of any one of which might have been enough to completely alter the later outcome—left the United States and the Soviet Union facing each other as enemies.

It is this sequence of events, seemingly impossible to reproduce, that has led to the widespread conviction that another cold war with any state is impossible and the term itself is useless. Indeed, there is some argument about whether the term is useful even in reference to the Soviet-American situation in the late twentieth century. The Cold War, the argument goes, was not a "war" at all, in that it could not be "fought" or "won" in a military sense. There was no central conflict between the major combatants; human movement and trade between them was limited but existed; ambassadors were exchanged and respected; and treaties and agreements were signed and mostly observed. In classical terms, Clausewitz might have understood the Soviet-American conflict as, at most, "armed observation" rather than an actual war. (Indeed, Clausewitz would find the Cold War something of a paradox since he writes of "wars of observation" as ones in which the two sides are *not* engaged in "a struggle of life or death—a struggle, that is, in which at least one of the parties is determined to gain a decision.")[12]

But to concentrate on the lack of a direct and decisive military engagement between the two superpowers is to miss the point about the Cold War: both sides *thought* themselves to be at war and *acted* as if they were, despite the fact that the relationship between them was usually conducted with an eye toward diplomatic norms of civility. Even at the height of détente, Moscow never abandoned the idea that the great task facing the USSR was to weaken and eventually to eradicate competing systems. "While pressing for the assertion of the principle of peaceful coexistence," Leonid Brezhnev said at a dinner in Cuba in 1972,

> we realize that successes in this important matter in no way signify the possibility of weakening our ideological struggle. On the contrary, we should be prepared for an intensification of this struggle and for its becoming an increasingly acute form of struggle between the two social systems.[13]

Americans, particularly those like Henry Kissinger who were stubborn partisans of *realpolitik* in dealing with the USSR, were more averse to such stark depictions of the superpower relationship. But as Kissinger was later to admit, even realists understood that "there had been a dominant ideological challenge rendering universal maxims, however oversimplified, applicable to most of the world's problems. And there had been a clear and present military threat, and its source had been unambiguous."[14]

The American and Soviet coalitions remained on a war footing for over four decades. (Even during the Grand Alliance of World War II, the Soviet Union engaged in "unrestrained espionage" that was, as two researchers have noted, "of the type that a nation directs at an enemy state.")[15] The economies of both superpowers were dedicated to maintaining not only national defenses, but also a capacity to fight and prevail should World War III break out. Although propaganda was more obvious and intrusive in the Soviet Union, popular culture and mass education in both nations reflected a conscious belief that East and West were at war. While there was no direct combat, this should not obscure the fact that Soviet, American, and Allied soldiers fought and died for the stated goals of the Cold War—on the American side, to contain communism, and on the Soviet side, to further Marxist-Leninist revolutionary processes around the world. In Berlin, Korea, and Vietnam, Soviets and Americans at times actually did shoot at and kill each other. In sum, to say that the Cold War was not a "war" defies common sense as well as the evident nature of the daily experiences of both Soviets and Americans.

What kept the Cold War "cold" was the presence of nuclear weapons, which promised that direct military action against either superpower could not yield much more than massive destruction and suffering. (Some Soviet leaders clung to the idea of "victory" in nuclear war even into the 1980s, but this does not mean they were willfully obtuse about what a nuclear exchange would look like or that they were eager to have one.) The idea that nuclear weapons prolonged the Cold War, that it "exchanged destructiveness for duration," is now almost universally accepted because it is (1) intuitively reasonable and (2) the major participants of the Cold War have since told us that it is so.[16] Although some Russian foreign policy thinkers have argued that the term "cold war" is itself little more than an invention of American political scientists who wanted to provide a label for their government's policies regarding the Soviet Union, they agree that insofar as the Soviet-American situation could be described as a "cold war" it is because of the unique effects (discussed following) of ballistic nuclear weapons.[17]

It is these two conditions—the explicit declaration of an enemy relationship between powers armed with nuclear weapons—that define a "cold war." The other aspects of the Soviet-American conflict, such as global bipolarity and the great distance between the primary antagonists, are important characteristics of that particular war, but they are not essential to a cold war. Two hostile powers without nuclear arms can retain outright war as an option; this is also true when a nuclear power faces a nonnuclear state. (China did not hesitate to attack Vietnam in 1979, Argentina was undeterred by British nuclear arms in 1981, and neither Iraq nor the U.S.-led coalition shrank from war in 1991.) But any two powers with the ability to eradicate each other will find themselves, much as Washington and Moscow did, in a struggle that is to all intents and purposes "war," but deprived of the large-scale violence that the logic of war demands. The world, to take a recent example, may already be seeing its first new "cold war" in India and Pakistan: after a round of nuclear saber-rattling in the late 1990s, both nations seem to have settled into a kind of stasis in which there is no lack of seething hostility but also no evident enthusiasm for attacking the enemy and in turn suffering a devastating nuclear response.

Thus, to maintain that a "cold war" is only understandable as one that replicates the contingent nature of the East-West struggle, in which two large international coalitions are nominally at peace but contest global supremacy while holding each other at bay with large inventories of nuclear missiles, is to miss the simplicity of the situation in which the Soviets and the Americans found themselves after 1945. Worse, it underestimates the relative ease with which that situation can be replicated. There is no shortage either of ideologically driven hatred (particularly directed against the West) or of nuclear weapons in the twenty-first century, and another "cold war," in which the United States will be forced to contend with an actively hostile nuclear-armed nation or coalition, is not only possible, but nearly certain.

A WORD FROM OUR SPONSOR, NUCLEAR MISSILES

The Bolsheviks had a formulation to render the abstract goal of communism in concrete terms: "Communism equals Soviet power plus electrification of the entire country." A similar formulation could define the abstraction of a "cold war": a cold war equals mutually hostile ideologies plus ballistic nuclear weapons. Without nuclear missiles, intense ideological hostilities are unlikely to smolder very long; they are the single technological innovation that have linked making war to the immediate risk of self-destruction for the first time in history. (Soviet thinkers in the 1960s argued that the uniting of nuclear charges to long-distance missiles was the only true "revolution in military affairs" in the postwar world, an attractively clear formulation given how much that term has become overused in recent years.) No other weapons system and no other munitions can match this ability to link war and suicide in the minds of policymakers. In an era where the term "weapons of mass destruction" is now commonplace, it is worth reflecting on the specific capabilities of nuclear missiles that will make them central to a future cold war.

First, whatever their qualities, Western policymakers have to cope with the fact that the relative simplicity of the concept (if not the construction) of missiles armed with nuclear weapons means that eventually, there will be more states capable of building them. It is startling to recall that nuclear weapons are based on technology that dates from the 1940s, created when airplanes still had propellers, radios had vacuum tubes, and television was a curiosity. Ballistic missiles, too, are now a familiar technology; the Scuds used by Iraq in the Gulf War of 1991 were of 1960s vintage, and other states have long since improved on such outdated technology. While proliferators and rogue states like China, North Korea, Iran, and Libya have so far been caged as much by their own backwardness as by international efforts, it is not a matter of whether other states will attain the ability to create a ballistic nuclear missile force, but rather only a matter of when.

But why focus on nuclear bombs delivered by long-range missiles, when states and organizations hostile to the United States could deliver the "poor man's bombs" of chemical or biological weapons by a variety of means? Why scan the skies for incoming nuclear missiles at the risk of missing the secret agent with a briefcase full of poison skulking in the streets of New York or Los Angeles?

The answer is that nuclear missiles are swift, sure, public, and permanent. That is, they are speedy (which brings them into play during a crisis as a means of deterrence rather than an eventual weapon of revenge), they are reliable (there is no defense against them, and even an inaccurate nuclear missile strike gives new meaning to the term "close enough"), they can be identified and independently verified as existing (as opposed to notional threats like a suitcase bomb), and the damage they do is, compared to the largely reversible effects of other munitions, unrecoverable.

Certainly, chemical and biological weapons are awful, and it is difficult to imagine an American president or British prime minister possessed of such *sangfroid* that they could view the dousing of Washington or London with nerve gas or some biological pestilence with equanimity. But biological and chemical agents are notoriously unreliable and produce largely transient effects: the use of deadly sarin gas in the 1995 terrorist attack against the Tokyo subway sickened 5,000 people but killed only a dozen or so, and within a short time, the city's underground was again up and running. Biological agents are more persistent and would no doubt induce a great many more fatalities, but like chemical arms are difficult to localize because of things as variable as wind conditions: the 2001 anthrax attacks against the United States produced much panic but few deaths. A chemical or biological attack on a major city might, on a good day, kill thousands of people; millions more, however, could take immediate measures (particularly in a chemical attack or against a biological agent like anthrax with a known cure) that would allow them to survive. While the death and contamination would require a massive national effort to repair the damage and could, depending on the target, cripple the American commercial and social infrastructure for months, the targeted cities would survive and return to something like normal at some point.

All of this pales next to the destructive force of nuclear weapons, a point so obvious as to risk belaboring it. Anthrax, cholera, sarin, and all the other ghastly biological and chemical agents are weapons of mass *death*, perhaps, but they are not weapons of mass *destruction*. The effects of a nuclear weapon are never in doubt; the prevailing winds and the time of day of the attack will affect only the schedule on which the victims will inevitably die and their final location when they do. Moreover, a nuclear strike in the heart of Washington or New York would not only kill millions of Americans, but would irretrievably destroy vital economic, cultural, and political institutions. Reconstruction would be measured in decades and only in the areas left (if any) that would still be habitable. Entire populations and industries, perhaps even the instruments of government, would have to be permanently relocated. While the east coast of the United States contains a disproportionate amount of national economic and political infrastructure, even a limited strike by an Asian power with a small handful of weapons against population centers along the west coast would easily kill tens of millions of people, eradicate a huge sector of the U.S. economy, and poison most of the immediate area to the east, thereby killing millions more with fallout and food shortages after the contamination of huge areas of prime agricultural areas. Contemplation of a chemical or biological attack is indeed horrible, but there is a finality to the destructiveness of nuclear weapons that creates the kind of caution, even paralysis, so characteristic of the confrontations between East and West during the Cold War.

The key to inducing this kind of paralysis, however, is the undeniable ability to deliver a nuclear weapon, and it is here that missiles play their crucial role. Missiles, as the U.S. national intelligence officer for strategic and nuclear programs told Congress in early 2000, "provide a level of prestige, coercive diplomacy, and deterrence that nonmissile means do not."[18] Only a missile can promise the certainty and speed of destruction that is essential to the kind of deterrent standoff seen during the Cold War. While terrorism is a real and continuing problem that can lay dubious claim to killing more people during the Cold War than nuclear weapons, it is an uncertain threat in the midst of a crisis or confrontation.

Consider, for example, the "terrorist-with-a-briefcase" scenario. During a confrontation, an enemy leader threatens the United States, saying that an American city will be destroyed if Washington persists in a particular course. In other words, the threat is that *at some future point*, a *relatively small* nuclear weapon *which may or may not have been compromised in transport*, will destroy some part of an *unidentified* American city if an agent *who may or may not have been captured or discovered* manages to make his way to his target and *plant his weapon correctly*. None of this will likely happen in time to affect the present crisis, if any of it happens at all, and the lack of credibility—to say nothing of the loss of face—that would ensue if Western intelligence measures were to thwart the enemy agent make such a threat risky almost to the point of criminal stupidity. (During the attacks on Afghanistan in 2001, for example, Osama bin Laden claimed to possess nuclear bombs that he would use in retaliation for any American use of chemical or biological weapons; this brash threat only made him seem delusional while at the same time providing a pretext for striking his organization harder and more thoroughly. All in all, a poor bluff.)

Contrast this with a state that controls a field of perhaps no more than five or ten intercontinental weapons, with silos placed in plain sight and, if the enemy is clever and ruthless enough, located close to population centers. The threat is now no longer a putative threat to one day, maybe, destroy some city with a weapon if all goes well; rather, it is a concrete and credible threat to destroy New York City, Philadelphia, Washington, and Miami and render the most densely populated part of the United States uninhabitable for years, in thirty minutes. America will then face two terrible alternatives: striking first and risking catastrophic damage if U.S. missiles do not arrive in time (and killing millions of innocent people in any case) or acquiescing to the enemy's demands. As Richard Betts rightly points out, "a threat to destroy the downtown of one or two American cities would be puny, indeed infinitesimal, by comparison to the old standard of Soviet capabilities. It could, however, more than offset whatever is at stake in a confrontation with some Third World troublemaker or non-state actor."[19]

Nuclear weapons and the attendant problems of deterring small missile forces are here to stay. "Nuclear deterrence will remain at the core of the security policies of the world's great powers," Avery Goldstein notes,

> and will remain an attractive option for many other less powerful states worried about adversaries whose capabilities they cannot match. The importance of this strategy for ensuring vital interests will endure as long as (1) the international system remains an anarchic realm, (2) states place their national interests above supranational interests, and (3) no fully effective counter to the destructiveness of nuclear weapons is devised.[20]

None of these conditions are likely to change even in the distant future. While critics might argue that to accept anarchy, self-interest, and the ubiquity of nuclear missiles shows a certain pessimism and lack of vision, to plan for any other environment in the near term would be unsupportable, to say nothing of foolish or even dangerous.

OLD THREATS, NEW ENEMIES

How likely is it, even with the proliferation of nuclear missile technology, that the United States will again find itself in a cold war, opposed by a regime or coalition (or some other entity, perhaps) that is willing to run the risk of nuclear confrontation with a superpower? Who, exactly, is likely to contend for power against the Western alliance in a new cold war?

Threats to the security of the United States and its allies like that posed by the Soviet Union are still embryonic, but they exist and are growing. Aside from the Russian Federation, no single state possesses the capability to hold the entire United States or all of NATO at risk in the way the Soviets did, although the Chinese arsenal is already capable of destroying several major American cities, including Washington. And while there is no single ideology contesting the world's loyalties, there are others that are as implacably hostile, if not more so, to liberal democratic capitalism than was Soviet communism, championed by leaders far less rational than Moscow's communist bureaucrats.

These kinds of states, committed to aggressive, ideologically driven goals and willing to run high military risks heedless of international opprobrium, were dubbed "crazy states" almost thirty years ago by Yehezkel Dror, and as Dror was later to point out, their numbers seem to be growing rather than shrinking.[21] At the dawn of the twenty-first century, the greatest hostility to Western beliefs and values comes not from sclerotic Marxist-Leninists in the Kremlin, but rather from more dynamic regimes and movements in Asia and the Middle East. The melding of Chinese nationalism and communism, to take the most obvious case, has produced a more robust mutation that is potentially more dangerous than either of its constituent parts. Would-be regional bullies like Iraq as well as Islamic fundamentalist states such as Iran— the latter are bitter enemies of the West as a matter of first principles— continue their quest for nuclear weapons and the means to deliver them at intercontinental range. Even if these states are not completely "crazy," they are angry, ambitious, and share not only a common hatred of the Western powers, but a belief as well that nuclear weapons offer the best of hope of prevailing against them.

Confrontations with China in particular are already beginning to resemble the previous Cold War, as the thinly-veiled nuclear threat during the 1996 Taiwan Straits crisis indicates. The rhetoric about sacrificing "millions of men" and "entire cities" was of a kind that Americans had not heard since the fulminations of Nikita Khrushchev in the early 1960s, and had a Soviet official made similar comments— even if a Russian official were to say it now—it would have been a major international crisis. (Right or wrong, it was only the Clinton administration's dedication to a policy of appeasement that prevented it from becoming a more serious incident at the time.) Four years later, an internal Chinese analysis "made clear that [the PRC] views the United States as potential enemy No. 1"; when asked if the Chinese military is preparing for action against the United States in the Pacific, a Chinese scholar at Beijing's Tsinghua University said, "My answer is very clear: Yes."[22]

This has led to concerns like those voiced by Colin Gray, who has suggested that the current "nuclear age," dominated primarily by concerns about nonproliferation, "will be succeeded [by 2020] by a bipolar security architecture that pits American against Chinese power and influence."[23] (Gray is especially worried that Americans have fallen into a comforting assumption that other nations share our belief that nuclear arms are the weapons of last resort, and he argues that "the postulate of a nuclear taboo is an ethnocentric delusion on the part of Western theorists.")[24] In late 2000, the outgoing chairman of the U.S. Joint Chiefs of Staff put it bluntly: "I am firmly convinced that we need to focus all elements of U.S. power and diplomacy on ensuring that China does not become the twenty-first-century version of the Soviet bear."[25]

Whether China will or wants to become this century's new menace to international peace and order is hotly debated among Westerners, but it is hard to imagine that the United States and the People's Republic will not clash at least over regional issues in the Pacific in the near future. When they do, it will be the first time since the Soviet collapse that America will be militarily confronting a hostile power able to reach the entire territory of the United States with nuclear weapons.[26] In any event, it is difficult to disagree with Paul Bracken's assertion that the world "is in a second nuclear age, an Asian nuclear age," in which "Asian states have learned from the West. They have learned how to use nuclear weapons without actually detonating them in an attack, for political maneuvers, implicit threats, deterrence, signaling, drawing lines in the sand, and other forms of psychological advantage."[27]

Other states seeking a ballistic nuclear capability include North Korea and Iran, who at this point are actually working with one another (and with China) to that end. While there are hopes that the regime in Pyongyang will fall before it finally achieves a nuclear missile, those hopes so far are unfounded, as is optimism that North Korea's leaders can be induced to act reasonably with the equivalent of bribes from the international community.

But if the Korean peninsula is the source of a small, immediate threat, Iran is a better candidate for a long-term conflict with the United States. Iran identifies America as its greatest enemy, and while most observers of Iranian politics do not see the mullahs as likely to engage in risky nuclear challenges to America or its allies, the Middle East is laden with areas of potential conflict between Tehran and Washington. (Iranian President Mohammed Khatami has, in the wake of the "9/11" attacks, reached out to the Americans, but this probably reflects an ongoing internal struggle among the Iranian leaders whose outcome is not likely to be clear for some time.) If a future crisis should go badly for a nuclear-armed Iran, according to one analysis, the message to the world might well be "if you attempt to destroy us, we may go down, but we will take as many Americans, Europeans, and Israelis with us as we possibly can."[28]

Another ominous possibility arises from the increasingly parasitical relationship between weak or even "failed" states and terrorists. The conventional wisdom has always been that terrorists, at best, might be able to set off a small nuclear device in an urban area, but that anything beyond such a hit-and-run attack (as hideously destructive as it would be) is beyond them. A standing nuclear arsenal of any kind requires maintenance and a certain amount of complicated infrastructure, none of which terrorists could get or would want, since a fixed address would open them to retaliation or even preemption.

In any case, the whole point of terrorism is terror; it is not to engage in an ongoing confrontation with the major powers in the formal setting of the international arena, as Kenneth Waltz argues.

> Terrorists do not play their deadly games to win in the near term. Their horizons are distant. . . . [they] live precarious lives. Nobody trusts them, not even those who finance, train and hide them. . . . Nuclear weapons would thrust them into a world fraught with new dangers. Terrorists work in small groups. Secrecy is safety, yet to obtain and maintain nuclear weapons would require enlarging the terrorist band through multiplication of suppliers, transporters, technicians, and guardians. . . . Moreover, as the demands of terrorists increase, compliance with their demands becomes harder to secure. . . . However they may be armed, terrorists are not capable of maintaining pressure while lengthy efforts toward compliance are made.[29]

Waltz and others argue that these are among the many reasons terrorists would not want to acquire a large, fixed arsenal of nuclear weapons, and they are quite right. Given the Al Qaeda organization's attack on New York and Washington in 2001, the idea that terrorists will not challenge state actors directly at length seems less supportable now, but in any case, what this argument misses is that these are the very reasons a terrorist organization might well avoid their own nuclear *capability*, but nonetheless seek to acquire their own nuclear *state*.

The logistical problems that plague terrorists, including the constant need for movement and the consequent high financial costs of doing business, are more severe now that the Soviet bloc is no longer a reliable terrorist haven or source of funding. (It is even more of a problem in the post–September 11 crackdown against terrorist finance networks.) Control of an actual state, through subtle or even violent manipulation of a weak government, would provide them with a sanctuary, in turn creating an entity that may be little better than a terrorist camp with a flag. This could create a variety of unforeseeable situations, including one in which the nominal government may not have full control over weapons on its own soil.

Some analysts believe that this is at least part of what terrorist leader Osama bin Laden hoped to achieve with the September 2001 airliner attacks in America: the object, ostensibly, was to bait the United States and its allies into massive strikes which would in turn destabilize the Middle East to the point of "turning the world's most wanted terrorist into a regional powerbroker with control over a nuclear arsenal and much of the world's oil, not to mention the West's biggest source of opium:"

> This is Osama bin Laden's "golden domino" blueprint for regional domination, in which fundamentalist rule in Afghanistan is cemented, radical generals take over in Pakistan, and the Saudi royal family fractures as its kingdom disintegrates in a civil war.... Bin Laden has alluded to Pakistan's nuclear weapons in interviews in recent years. A "Talibanized" Pakistan could give him access to as many as 30 tactical warheads, each with a power roughly 2½ times that of the Hiroshima bomb.[30]

Thus a "weak" state could become a "rogue" state, a menace both to a region and to international peace. ("Rogue state" is a term the U.S. State Department tried to remove from common usage in 1999, but with little success, since the phenomenon exists regardless of what it is called.)

Still, the natural question remains of why states or organizations engaged in terrorism would ever want to be identified, implicitly or explicitly, as possessing nuclear weapons. Entities that oppose the international status quo should have the least interest in gaining a nuclear arsenal, since it strips them of all the advantages they could accrue from terrorism or from the support of terrorism: deniability for their actions, a reputation for unpredictability, the creation of subsequent fear, anxiety, and hesitance among their targets, and aloofness from a system they are openly dedicated to changing by any means available.

One answer to this is that terrorism, whether state-sponsored or independently organized, has produced little in the way of results for its practitioners, and it should be no surprise that opponents of the international status quo would look to more dramatic or immediate means to press their demands. Terrorism is an uncertain weapon over the long term, and speculative threats are even less useful than demands made in the wake of actual attacks. Terrorist acts can also be less effective because they are often difficult to trace—sometimes, the real culprits have to clamor to claim the credit they actually desire in the midst of a great deal of confusion.

The poor track record of terrorism—what major terrorist goals have been achieved anywhere in the past thirty years?—combined with a craving for recognition and leadership like that shown by terrorist bosses such as bin Laden make the takeover of a weak state a tempting alternative.[31] Even as spectacular an attack as the outrages in New York and Washington in 2001, while inflicting human misery and undeniable financial costs on the United States, seems destined to produce little in the way of a reduced American presence in the Middle East or to fulfill any of the other supposed hopes of the attackers. (Indeed, it could be argued that the terrorists, by arousing the West to focus united attention on their extermination, have only sparked a self-defeating chain of events.) Also, there is a constant danger to the terrorists from their acts of violence and blackmail: because they take place outside of the framework of accepted international norms, they free the targets of such threats to engage in preemption or to undertake revenge, with relative impunity in the eyes of the international community, as the United States did in Afghanistan in the wake of the 2001 attacks. But a terrorist organization hiding behind a national flag would put the United States and its allies in the position of having to deal with an existing state whose ownership of ballistic weapons will force the international community to take its demands much more seriously.

Optimists might point to the number of states that seem to have abandoned their nuclear pretensions or, in the case of South Africa after 1991, actually dismantled what small arsenal they had. Again, why would smaller states, even those under the influence of terrorist organizations, ever want to risk creating a standing nuclear force? Waltz speaks for many when he argues that the world's dictators are a wily bunch who are not nearly stupid enough to court the intervention of the major powers by unveiling a nuclear arsenal that would do little more than place a huge bull's-eye over their nation (and on their own foreheads). "Are hardy political survivors in the Third World," he asks, "likely to run the greatest of all risks by drawing the wrath of the world down on them by accidentally or in anger exploding nuclear weapons they may have? At least some of the rulers of the new and prospective nuclear states are thought to be ruthless, reckless, and war-prone. Ruthless, yes; war-prone, seldom; reckless, hardly."[32]

But the credibility of a nuclear threat from an inferior power lies, ironically, in the sheer imbalance of power between America and its potential enemies. (*Pace* Waltz, the leaders of China, Iraq, and North Korea, to say nothing of the Taliban, seem in any case to be good candidates for description as "ruthless" and "reckless." How "war-prone" they are remains to be seen.) Nations confronting Washington and its allies, even a state as large as China, would stand little chance against Western military power and thus would have ample reason to threaten the use of nuclear weapons if war with the United States or a U.S.-led coalition were perceived as inevitable. Indeed, they might rationally conclude that their only hope of escaping destruction would be to attempt to deter the Americans at the strategic level by pointing out that they are in fact so weak that they will be left with no option but to use nuclear arms at some point. (Americans can hardly claim to be shocked by such a strategy, since it is the one NATO employed against the Soviet Union in Europe for much of the Cold War.) "Confronting a weaker, but nuclear-armed state," Goldstein points out, "even the most capable adversary's options—ranging from compellent threat, through limited military assaults, to full scale war—all carry an unknowable risk of escalation to disastrous consequences."[33]

Dramatic nuclear threats from a small state or group might be credible if only because there would not be much else that could be done with so small an arsenal. Betts argues that large-scale strategic deterrence is logically forced by the small number of the weapons involved—that is, that it makes no sense for a state with a limited inventory to waste its time threatening military targets when its only hope of survival lies in shocking the United States into a cease-fire. (A similar dynamic currently governs the standoff between India and Pakistan, apparently: Indian military officials admit that they have made no provision for attacking Pakistani nuclear weapons, but rather have adopted a "pure minimum deterrent" in which Pakistan will be completely destroyed in retaliation for an attack.)[34] "Thinking of a small enemy nuclear force," Betts adds,

> as a tactical problem—or as a threat to civilian society only in allied countries closer to the scene, such as Japan—is too comforting. . . . Whatever the reason for a small rogue regime to confront the United States, the stakes could not plausibly outweigh the loss of one or two American cities.[35]

Here, the very disparity of power between such states and a giant like the United States works to their advantage, increasing the credibility of their own threats while undermining any made by the West.

This is a new wrinkle on deterrence that neither the Soviets nor the Americans had to consider in the twentieth century. During the Cold War, the NATO allies and the Soviet Union were clear in their intentions that in the end, if war came, only one coalition or the other would eventually control the planet, and this made the American promise (backed by the additional British strategic arsenal as well) to engage in a nuclear *Götterdämmerung* rather than to choose slavery to be at least somewhat credible. This, again, was driven by the scale of the forces involved, only in the other direction: the huge size of the inventories meant that even a "limited" Soviet strike on U.S. land-based nuclear forces would easily have killed upward of at least 40 million people instantly, and it took no great feat of imagination for the Soviets to envision an American president utterly destroying the USSR in retaliation.[36] The idea of either superpower launching five or ten nuclear weapons could not be taken seriously; even the tactical use of nuclear arms against Soviet forces invading West Germany would have required (given the size of the probable Soviet offensive) the release of dozens, if not hundreds, of nuclear weapons and would have turned most of Central Europe into a wasteland.

But what price would the United States or Great Britain exact for a relatively small strike from a lesser power, perhaps located in the midst of several innocent noncombatants? Would the Western allies eradicate an entire nation and radioactively poison an entire region, killing friends and enemies alike, indiscriminately—an act, perhaps, of genocidal proportions in a country the size of Iraq and perhaps even a "crime against humanity"—over anything less than the complete destruction of North America or the enslavement of the American people? In such a confrontation, it is David's desperate threat to act in self-preservation that is far more credible than Goliath's promise to exact a savage and ruthless revenge.

ONE, TWO, THREE, MANY COLD WARS

Under such circumstances, the United States and its allies will find themselves trying to manage relations with these hostile, nuclear-armed regimes, rather than continually forcing them into actual combat (as we have with Iraq for over ten years). Where once Washington had to worry whether Che Guevara's threat of "one, two, three, many Vietnams" would come to pass, the proliferation of nuclear weaponry and ballistic missile technology promises a more arduous future of many "cold wars." Whether the opponents are China, a Middle Eastern power or group of powers, a terrorist-controlled state, or some combination of these threats in addition to others still unforeseeable, the results will be the same: tense standoffs, in which the Western powers attempt to contain expansionist, aggressive states whose beliefs and values are antithetical to our own. All the while, the presence of nuclear weapons will make both sides careful to avoid a conflict that could result in unacceptable damage or even outright annihilation. Such a situation should be instantly recognizable in form, if not in scale, for what it is: a cold war. One will be difficult enough; several will be a challenge greater even than that of containing the Soviet empire.

The spread of nuclear arms and the capacity to deliver them with ballistic missiles are inevitable. The question, then, is not how to choose among horrible alternatives in war, but rather to consider ways during peacetime to manage or even win a long-term conflict with an ideologically hostile, nuclear-armed opponent. The inability to wage strategic nuclear war with even a small opponent will not only replicate the basic dilemma of the Soviet-American cold war, but will require, in general, strategies based on the same kind of indirect warfare engaged in by both

Moscow and Washington during that conflict. The next cold war cannot be avoided, but it can be managed. In this endeavor the Soviet-American experience may have things yet to teach us. In the following chapters, we will investigate that experience and ask not only how the Western allies were able to prevail once, but how they might be able to prevail again.

OVERVIEW

The Soviet Union was, to use a recent term, an "ideological state," and the Cold War an ideological conflict. Chapter Two explores the importance of ideology and its role as the motivation of a likely enemy in a cold war. Chapter Three considers the Stalinist ideological origins of the Cold War and how the Soviet declaration of a world divided into "two camps" found its expression in the communist aggression against South Korea. The Korean War, of course, was not the last time the West would have to respond to a communist attack, and Chapter Four considers the question of fighting on the periphery in a cold war, including in Vietnam. After the defeat in Vietnam, the United States withdrew from the global competition, engaging instead in "détente," a period—and a strategy—discussed in Chapter 5.

Few opinions about the Cold War are as divided as those about Ronald Reagan's confrontational approach in the 1980s, and accordingly, Chapters Six and Seven seek to trace the origins of that approach both under Reagan and his predecessor Jimmy Carter and to consider its value. The concluding chapter offers thoughts both on the Cold War past and the cold wars yet to come.

NOTES

1. Quoted in Thomas Mahnken, "America's Next War," *The Washington Quarterly*, Summer 1995, p. 177.
2. Quoted in Mahnken, p. 177.
3. Patrick Tyler, "As China Threatens Taiwan, It Makes Sure U.S. Listens," *The New York Times*, January 24, 1996, p. A3.
4. North Korea, according to the Defense Department, has "demonstrated several of the key technologies required to develop an ICBM." See "Proliferation: Threat and Response," U.S. Department of Defense, Office of the Secretary of Defense, available at http://www.defenselink.mil/pubs/prolif97/.
5. See Robert D. Walpole, "The Iranian Ballistic Missile and WMD Threat to the U.S. Through 2015: Statement for the Record to the International Security, Proliferation and Federal Services Subcommittee of the Senate Governmental Affairs Committee," September 21, 2000.
6. Vojtech Mastny, *The Cold War and Soviet Insecurity* (New York: Oxford University Press, 1996), p. 3.

7. Walter Laqueur, *The Dream That Failed* (New York: Oxford University Press, 1994), p. 114.

8. One such example is Bernard Levin. See "One Who Got It Right," *The National Interest* 31, Spring 1993, pp. 64–65.

9. As Walter Laqueur points out, even as late as 1988, when the Soviet situation was clearly in violent flux, "a report by a committee drawn from the leading scholarly institutions in the field on 'bridging the methods gap' in Soviet foreign policy studies was wholly preoccupied with operational definitions of variables, deductive theory, the interaction of multiple factors, predictive underdetermination, and other issues bothering the theoreticians of international politics." Laqueur, p. 114.

10. Richard Ned Lebow and Thomas Risse Kappen, "Introduction," in Richard Ned Lebow and Thomas Risse Kappen, eds., *International Relations Theory and the End of the Cold War* (New York: Columbia University Press, 1995), p. 2.

11. A 1998 Claremont Institute poll found that 54 percent of registered voters believed the United States could destroy an enemy missile in flight, the same number who reported themselves from "surprised" to "shocked and angry" to find out no such capability exists. "1998 Missile Defense Poll," http://www.claremont.org/ballmiss/ bmd_poll.cfm.

12. Clausewitz was drawing a distinction between the limited wars of the nineteenth century and the immense scale of the Napoleonic wars. "Armed observation" was meant to convey a situation in which the political goals at hand were not pressing enough to fight over or where each side was exhausted and both remained idle in their current positions rather than seeking further battle. Carl von Clausewitz, *On War*, Michael Howard and Peter Paret, eds. and trans. (Princeton: Princeton University Press, 1976), pp. 81 and 488. My thanks to Jack English for his helpful comments on this subject.

13. Quoted in Robert Conquest, *Reflections on a Ravaged Century* (New York: Norton, 2000), p. 169.

14. Henry Kissinger, *Diplomacy* (New York: Simon and Schuster, 1994), p. 802.

15. "The massive size," they continue, "and the intense hostility of Soviet intelligence operations caused both American counterintelligence professionals and high-level policy-makers to conclude that Stalin had already launched a covert attack on the United States." John Earl Haynes and Harvey Klehr, *Venona: Decoding Soviet Espionage in America* (New Haven, CT: Yale University Press, 1999), p. 22.

16. John Gaddis, *We Now Know* (Oxford, UK: Clarendon Press, 1997), p. 291. John Mueller is the notable exception here; he claims that the Cold War ended primarily because of a change of ideas and that nuclear weaponry had little to do with it. See John Mueller, "The Escalating Irrelevance of Nuclear Weapons," in T. V. Paul et al., eds., *The Absolute Weapon Revisited* (Ann Arbor: The University of Michigan Press), p. 78.

17. Interview with Karen Khachaturov, Moscow, February 3, 2000.

18. Robert D. Walpole, "Statement for the Record to the Senate Subcommittee on International Security, Proliferation, and Federal Services on the Ballistic Missile Threat to the United States," February 9, 2000.

19. Richard K. Betts, "What Will It Take to Deter the United States?," *Parameters* 25, no. 4, Winter 1995–1996, p. 72.

20. Avery Goldstein, *Deterrence and Security in the 21st Century* (Stanford, CA: Stanford University Press, 2000), p. 1.

21. Yehezkel Dror, *Crazy States: A Counterconventional Strategic Problem* (Millwood, NY: Kraus Reprint, 1980), pp. xiii–xix.

22. The scholar interviewed was Yan Xuetong. John Leicester, "Chinese Prepare for War with U.S.," *The Washington Times*, October 23, 2000, p. 1.

23. Colin Gray, *Modern Strategy* (Oxford: Oxford University Press, 1999), p. 326.

24. Colin Gray, "Nuclear Weapons and the Revolution in Military Affairs," in Paul et al., eds., p. 119.

25. The remarks were made by Gen. Henry H. Shelton during a speech to the National Press Club. See *The Washington Times*, December 15, 2000, p. 1.

26. A 2001 U.S. Defense Department report places the range of China's 20 CSS-4 missiles at 13,000 kilometers, putting Washington well within China's reach. See "Proliferation: Threat and Response."

27. Paul Bracken, *Fire in the East: The Rise of Asian Military Power and the Second Nuclear Age* (New York: Perennial, 2000), p. 97.

28. Caroline Ziemke, "The National Myth and Strategic Personality of Iran: A Counterproliferation Perspective," in Victor A. Utgoff, ed., *The Coming Crisis: Nuclear Proliferation, U.S. Interests, and World Order* (Cambridge, MA: MIT Press, 2000), p. 115.

29. Scott Sagan and Kenneth Waltz, *The Spread of Nuclear Weapons: A Debate* (New York: W. W. Norton, 1994), p. 95.

30. Tom Walker, "Deadly Dominoes," *The Sunday Times*, October 7, 2001, p. 9.

31. It could be argued that the 1983 bombing of the U.S. Marine barracks in Beirut succeeded in removing the United States from Lebanon, but this, at best, was a tactical victory, especially given that the long-term goal of Middle Eastern terrorist organizations has always been, among other things, to force the United States to disengage from the region overall.

32. Sagan and Waltz, p. 97.

33. Goldstein, p. 53.

34. As one Indian defense official put it, "If New Delhi goes up in a mushroom cloud, a certain theater commander will go to his safe, open his book, and start reading at page one, paragraph one..." See Stephen Peter Rosen, "Nuclear Proliferation and Alliance Relations," in Utgoff, ed., p. 126.

35. Betts, p. 78.

36. Indeed, it is hard to imagine the President waiting for a casualty count. During the Cold War, America had roughly 1,000 ballistic missile silos. Any credible attack would have to assign at least two warheads to each silo. While this would mean something on the order of several hundred megatons reaching the United States, it also means—assuming the Soviets accompanied those warheads with dummy projectiles and other decoy measures—that the very first word the President would have would be of an attack by literally *thousands* of Soviet warheads.

2

The Centrality of Ideology

The importance of ideology for the Soviet leadership—*any* Soviet leadership—is seldom understood in the West. . . . Their rule is anchored in ideology, as the divine right of kings was in Christianity; and therefore their imperialism, too, has to be ideological or else it commands no legitimacy. This is why the men in the Kremlin can lose no territory once acquired, why they cannot abandon friends and allies no matter how burdensome they may have become to them . . . or admit alternative interpretations of the true faith.

—Milovan Djilas, 1979

LENINISTS IN THE JUNGLES

In 1998, several former Soviet officials and their American counterparts met at Brown University to discuss the end of the Cold War. Among the puzzles the Americans were most interested in was why, despite the enormous costs involved, the Soviet Union had for so long remained intent on making mischief so far from its own borders, in Africa and Latin America. It was an understandable line of questioning; looking back, the superpower competition in corners of the Third World that have since fallen into obscurity now seems fairly ludicrous to Russians and Americans alike. There was no major geopolitical prize at stake in this competition, and certainly nothing of value to a continental power like the Soviet Union. Two decades later, American policymakers were still scratching their heads in confusion at Soviet moves that made little sense from a strictly strategic point of view.

In response to the question, former Gorbachev aide Anatolii Cherniaev said, "You mentioned Cuba and Angola. Those were ideological issues. We had to maintain our image as an ideological superpower. This was important to us."[1] It hardly mattered if these and other nations in the less developed world were led by actual socialists: as Aleksander Yakovlev, former Soviet ambassador and advisor to Mikhail Gorbachev, noted some years earlier,

> It seems to me that the Soviet leadership of that time acted somewhat blindly. It was sufficient, for example, for any African dictator to declare his "socialist orientation," and then to add to this some complimentary words about a star-wearing Soviet leader who's keen to be flattered, for assistance to be practically guaranteed.[2]

The star-wearing leader, of course, was Leonid Brezhnev, who despite his condescension and vanity, nonetheless saw in the Third World (as did other Soviet leaders and not a few Western intellectuals) a new wave of Marxist-Leninist revolution. Brezhnev's racism and revolutionary ardor coexisted quite easily, as is evident in an exclamation he made to his inner circle about socialist movements in the Third World: "Why look, even in the jungles they want to live like Lenin!"[3]

Brezhnev's odd enthusiasm for jungle Leninists is only intelligible in an ideological context, as are many seemingly irrational or counterintuitive Soviet policies. While former Soviet officials admit this candidly now, the disrepute surrounding the word "ideology" leads them to do so a bit sheepishly: Cherniaev, for one, coupled his admission of the ideological nature of Soviet foreign policy with his claim that the Kremlin leadership was not without a good grasp of *realpolitik*. The ideological motivation to support regimes in the Third World, he reassured the audience, "did not mean that we were planning to organize or begin a nuclear war."[4] While few people in Moscow or Washington probably worried very much about an African Armageddon, Cherniaev's comment is nonetheless revealing as an illustration of how "ideology" and "realism" are still juxtaposed as causes of the Cold War and especially of how "realism" has been boiled down to mean little more than that neither superpower was willing to incinerate humanity over peripheral issues. (It is also telling in that it indicates how even the most avowedly ideological regimes regarded "realist" as a compliment.) The avoidance of a global nuclear war during the Cold War is often taken as evidence in itself that, no matter what sort of pap the Soviets and Americans might have manufactured to feed to their own populations and their allies, in the end these attempts at ideological bravado were no match for the irresistible logic of realism.

If by "realism" we mean a healthy respect for the implications of exchanging six or seven thousand megatons across three continents in the course of a few hours, then there can be little question that the United States and the Soviet Union were governed by "realists." But to say that the superpowers were not outright suicidal is not to say very much, and provides little explanation for why Washington and Moscow undertook actions that risked the very war they both feared most. In order to understand some of the more bizarre and tragic incidents of the Cold War—and more important, to understand the Soviet vulnerabilities revealed by those incidents—it is imperative to consider the role of ideology in the Soviet-American conflict.

IDEOLOGY AND THE REALIST DELUSION

What is surprising is not the realization that the Cold War was an ideological conflict, but rather the reluctance of Westerners to see it as such for so long. Even during the 1980s, a period of severely heightened Cold War tensions, there was a stubborn reluctance among some leading Americans to take ideology seriously. "We shouldn't [assume] that if someone happens to be a Marxist," Senator Christopher Dodd said while discussing events in Central America in 1983, "that immediately they're going to be antagonistic to our interests or going to threaten our security."[5] Given that Marxism is explicitly dedicated to the revolutionary destruction of regimes like the United States, one would think that such antagonism is exactly what should be expected from self-identified Marxists, but Senator Dodd's comment was typical in reflecting a skepticism about whether declared ideologies and actual *interests* are ever the same. Russian scholars and memoirists, for their part, are often baffled by the inability of their American counterparts to grasp the essentially ideological nature of Soviet foreign policy or the role that the collapse of ideological coherence played in the demise of the USSR.[6] The Western belief that the Soviet Union was motivated by realist conceptions of "national interest" is a fundamental misapprehension of the nature of the enemy and consequently a dire misunderstanding of what was at issue in the Cold War itself.

That ideology was the mainspring of the Cold War might seem plain, even obvious, in the twenty-first century, but it remains an explanation that does not sit well with many Americans, and American scholars in particular. During the latter years of the Cold War and particularly during the period of détente, simple explanations prevailed over accurate ones. It was fashionable to describe the Cold War in realist terms, as the mechanical result of two large powers seeking geostrategic advantage on the global chessboard. Why these powers were contending was supposedly self-evident: big states have overlapping interests (primarily regarding things like energy, food, trade, and military reach), and occasionally, those interests would conflict. When they did, the resulting tensions needed to be "managed," especially among antagonists armed with nuclear technology. This view of the superpowers had great staying power not just among policymakers and scholars, but even in Western popular culture, which often portrayed Soviet-American wrangling as some sort of tiresome, macho dispute between men in Moscow and Washington that had little to do with the lives or interests of ordinary people.[7]

This is puzzling not only in light of what we know about the Cold War, but in view of the problem, as one observer succinctly put it, of how little realist considerations ever actually manage to explain about anything.[8] During the Cold War, as will be seen, the Soviets and the Americans were willing to engage in dangerous or even plainly foolish policies that simply cannot be explained with reference to traditional realist propositions, unless they are submitted to a reductio ad absurdum that says, in effect, any state action that is not plainly self-destructive is therefore an attempt to seek power and security. Clearly, the superpowers sought strategic advantage over one another, but their battles were fought in ways and in areas that cannot be explained in anything but ideological terms. To take but one example on the Soviet side: anyone in Moscow who thought that giving Gus Hall and the American Communist Party millions of dollars from the precious Soviet hard currency reserve would have any effect on American politics or foreign policy cannot possibly be described as a "realist."[9]

Another reason why it has often been so tempting to dismiss ideology is that it is an intellectually and politically inconvenient concept. Social science strives for universalism, and a peculiar or unique set of beliefs inherent in a particular regime is an obstacle to generalization and comparison. Besides, to grant any definitive importance to ideology would undermine the kind of cynicism about international politics that was pervasive during the Cold War, and thus would disrupt a neat symmetry in which both the Soviet Union and the United States were seeking wealth and power in the world and only incidentally thinking to drag a fig leaf of principle over their avarice. Even less critical views of the superpowers assumed that institutions and bureaucracies were basically alike everywhere and that the major powers lumbered through international life on a realist autopilot.

A well-regarded and widely used international relations text from the early 1970s, for example, asserted that ideologies in general "establish foreign policy goals, evaluative criteria, and *justifications for action*,

[and] have important effects on perceptual processes as well" [emphasis added].[10] In other words, ideology is important to the choice of a regime's ultimate goals, but not much else, especially in the Soviet Union: "Its relevance to day-to-day problem solving and to the development of specific actions in concrete situations may be only very slight. In these realms a Communist government operates like any other."[11]

> No Communist state has been willing to commit resources to "world revolution" if by doing so it would seriously endanger its own security or other more specific interests. It is one of the advantages of the flexibility of Marxism-Leninism that when such situations arise—and they do frequently—some ideological principle can be put forth to justify the choice of national over doctrinal imperatives.[12]

Notice that "national" and "doctrinal" interests are necessarily not the same, since national interests are rational and therefore dominant, and everything else is, presumably, just so much baggage. Likewise, it is noteworthy that "specific interests" are by definition almost never revolutionary or ideological interests.

If this approach was understandable during a time when the USSR was being run by Brezhnev and Aleksei Kosygin in what was seen as a "managerial" style, its persistence throughout the Cold War is not: after a particularly sharp period of ideologically driven conflict in the 1980s, a 1986 comparative work on Soviet and American foreign policies would only be able to get as far as admitting that "it is a basic tendency of great powers to attempt to forward a worldview."[13] But even this throwaway observation—one of many that is obvious to ordinary people, but less so to scholars—represented little change in the American intellectual tendency to discount ideology.

The origins of this realist delusion are a complicated story. To some extent, the lure of realism was probably a reaction to the depressing implications of ideology. Realism promises a world in which problems can be managed, wars averted (or at least kept within some sort of boundaries), and opponents manipulated, all through the common language of power and interest. Vojtech Mastny, discussing Soviet war plans in the 1960s that were based on an "assumption that the war would start with a Western surprise attack [that] was mainly justified in Marxist-Leninist terms by the implacable hostility of an inherently 'imperialistic' capitalist system," noted that this was "but one illustration of the sway ideology continued to hold over leaders whom many Westerners wishfully came to regard as 'normal' practitioners of power politics, presiding over a state like any other."[14] If the Soviets were "realists," any comparison of the Warsaw Pact and NATO would have to lead to the realization that NATO could only attack first if it were already committed to turning Europe into a nuclear war zone immediately. If they were "ideologues," with all the irrational intractability the word connotes, no amount of reasoning with them would sway them, a pessimistic conclusion that ever-hopeful Western statesmen wanted to avoid.

But there is a deeper problem as well. Americans (more so than Europeans) have never been comfortable with the concept of "ideology" itself. For most Americans, the word "ideology" conjures up images of dour old men poring over the texts of Marx and Lenin as though they were the Dead Sea scrolls. Ideology was not something to be taken seriously, since it could only be mere justification for pragmatic action or the underpinnings of an irrational set of beliefs, and therefore mainly the province of charlatans or fanatics. "Realism," by contrast, was ostensibly the mark of sober statesmanship. Certainly, ideology was not seen as relevant to the United States, even if it was accepted to be important to America's chief opponent. "The belief that ideology is a schematic, inflexible way of seeing the world," one leftist scholar correctly noted in 1991, "as against some more modest, piecemeal, pragmatic wisdom, was elevated in the postwar period from a piece of popular wisdom to an elaborate sociological theory," particularly in America.[15]

Indeed, in the early days of the Cold War, conventional wisdom held that America was a reasonable and realistic nation engaged in a struggle with hardened ideologues. This image of ideology as the secular religion of Marxist mullahs held such sway that one of the seminal works on Soviet politics, Nathan Leites' 1956 *The Operational Code of the Politburo*, offered quotations from Lenin and Stalin as actual guides to future Soviet policy.[16] Leites' book is still a milestone, if for no other reason that it is an attempt to take Soviet ideology seriously rather than to brush words aside as so much Orwellian duckspeak. This respect for ideology, however, was short-lived. By the 1970s—a period of cynicism about ideology and much more—American policymakers could be heard talking about the need to sway Soviet marshals from their "primitive" notions (particularly their belief that the inherent superiority of socialist economic organization would allow the USSR to win a nuclear war).[17]

The scholarly community was particularly eager to embrace the hard data of realist analysis, not least because such data is relatively easy to work with and understand and because it is all in English. For many reasons, including the collapse of language requirements in American colleges, scholars of international affairs by the 1980s were more likely to be conversant in statistics rather than in foreign languages, ideologies, or cultures, while regional specialists gravitated away from the increasingly convoluted, pseudoscientific models of international relations theory. (This disconnect between theory and empirical knowledge became so severe with regard to the study of the Soviet Union that in the early 1980s a major fellowship program was instituted for a time to try and remedy it, with little evident success.) Entire books were written about Soviet-American relations by people who had no background in Soviet affairs and spoke no Russian, while microscopically detailed works on the Soviet Union were written by people who had not studied foreign affairs and made no reference to the influence of the Cold War on their primary subject of study. By the end of the Cold War, the rift was nearly complete, and integrated debate over Soviet intentions had been replaced with a tired dialogue over the relationship between culture and ideas on one side and economic and military realities on the other, an artificial distinction that real leaders and policymakers need not make and in general do not bother to think about.[18]

The situation remains much the same today, with regional specialists careful to steer clear of the models, formulas, and abstractions that dominate the study of international relations, and international relations specialists resolute in their determination to avoid being bogged down in what they see as empirical trivia. There have been recent pleas for both intellectual communities to set aside this artificial division, particularly where study of the Cold War is concerned, but so far they have gone largely unheeded.[19]

Although there have since been acknowledgments—some of them only grudging—that ideology was at the core of the Cold War, a faith in *realpolitik* continues to dominate Western thinking about international affairs. Recent challenges to realism have had little effect on the fundamental views of policymakers, not least because these challenges have so far resulted in a series of debates that have grown increasingly unintelligible and arcane and therefore of interest only to the scholarly community. Tragically, the murder of thousands of Americans by Islamic extremists may yet prove to be the catalyst for once again thinking about ideas, but it is a pity that it would take such a dramatic reinforcement to get Americans to take ideology seriously again.

This reluctance to accept the importance of ideology was dangerous during the Cold War, and it is dangerous now. As Yehezkel Dror complained over two decades ago, in a warning that remains applicable today:

Falling on the fertile ground of economic thinking (including rationality-espousing cost-benefit calculations) and nurtured by domestic hopes for détente, peace and prosperity—a tendency to downgrade the importance of ideologies constitutes one of the most dangerous fallacies in United States strategic thinking. Despite intensified ethnic politics, reassertions of ideology in major Communist countries and very visible fanatic-crazy behavior by terrorist groups and by some countries, a belief that these are temporary features sure to disappear with more enlightenment and economic growth and after redress of some "historic injustices" still survives and even dominates.[20]

In the coming years, the West must learn to accept the central role ideology plays in the life of other states and organizations. This will become especially pressing as the United States and its allies find themselves in conflict with more diverse and more foreign ideologies; however bizarre Marxism-Leninism was, it was still in fact a European phenomenon and thus more easily accessible to Westerners who took the time to study it. In the future, ideological challenges to the status quo will more likely come from non-Western sources, and while it may take time to fully comprehend these new belief systems, American and allied policymakers should at least proceed from the initial assumption that beliefs matter in a fundamental way. They are not just important to a cold war: they are the motive force of such a conflict.

THE SOVIET UNION AS AN IDEOLOGICAL STATE

States are born, broadly speaking, in one of three ways. The most common way, of course, is by historical chance. Groups of people following food or trade routes settle in a particular area, form bonds of language, ethnicity, and religion, and lay claim to that area as a homeland. The second is by force, either malevolent or benign. The former case, the creation or expansion of a state by conquest, is common enough. The latter case is a bit rarer, but the states created by the Soviet collapse in Central Asia (some of which were hardly enthusiastic about independence) would be good examples, as they were summarily pushed into the world as nations whether they wanted to be or not.

It is the third way that states come into the world—that is, by design—that is most relevant to the Cold War. In this, the United States and the Soviet Union share a common heritage. Both were the results of revolutions (although the Americans did not obliterate the society in which they lived, but rather only its political arrangements), and both were founded on explicitly universalist principles. The terms "Soviet" and "American" themselves have no proper ethnic or territorial denotation, but instead refer to citizens of a particular kind of regime.[21] This means that ideas were not just important to Americans and Soviets, but central to their national identity. Contrast this with a more "traditional" nation-state: if the fundamental organizing principles of government in Korea or France were to change overnight—and at times, they have—

the inhabitants of those nations would likely feel no less "Korean" or "French" the next morning, even if they found their new political system to be uncongenial or even evil. But what would it mean to be an "American" in a country without a public commitment to the ideals of the Declaration of Independence, the U.S. Constitution, or the other founding documents of the American Republic? What could it mean to be "Soviet" if Moscow were to abjure its faith in the works of Marx and Lenin? While we have no answer to that first question, the answer to the second question became clear in 1991.

That nation-states, as communities of human beings, believe in *something* should not come as a revelation, even if there are a strange few that seem as if they do not. (Artist and singer Laurie Anderson once made the cutting and funny observation that the lyrics of virtually all national anthems can be translated and rephrased as "We're Number One, this is the best place to live," but it is rare that nations limit their self-image and belief about their role in the world to such a simple sentiment.) Some nations find it more of a challenge than others to build or defend a coherent identity, particularly those artificial creations that struggle to survive or prosper outside of the political hothouses in which they were created. This is particularly true of stitched-together federations such as Yugoslavia, Czechoslovakia, Nigeria, and other amalgams (even Canada might be an example here) for whom national purpose and national identity are often bound up in the immediate task of making sure the state does not literally come apart at the seams. Still, few nations exist only for their own sake; even small states or subnational entities often profess commitment to universal principles.

The circumstances of its birth made the USSR, in terms of such commitments, necessarily different from most other nations and even from the United States in three respects.

First, the Soviet Union was brought into being on the foundation of a preexisting set of beliefs, which in short order became an official, promulgated ideology. Although nations most often incorporate their founding myths, principles, and values in a written constitution (Great Britain is a major exception), fewer maintain a library of works that are the official touchstone for all political and social life. From the moment of its inception, however, the fundamental doctrinal framework on the which the USSR was to rest was already in place in an existing body of thought and literature.

In this, the Bolsheviks created a communist state not unlike an Islamic theocracy, in which the Koran and subsequent works are not just expressions of religious belief but also a detailed guide to the organization and daily conduct of social and political life. (Indeed, in keeping with this comparison, Dmitrii Volkogonov has written that the "intellectual diet of Leninism was as compulsory for every Soviet citizen as the

Koran is for an observing Muslim.")[22] Article Six of the Soviet Constitution declared that the Communist Party was "the leading and guiding
force of the Soviet society and the nucleus of its political system, of all
state organizations and public organizations," and that "armed with
Marxism-Leninism," the Party

> determines the general perspectives of the development of society and the
> course of the domestic and foreign policy of the USSR, directs the great
> constructive work of the Soviet people, and imparts a planned, systematic
> and theoretically substantiated character to their struggle for the victory
> of communism.[23]

Article Four of the Iranian Constitution similarly states that "all civil,
penal, financial, economic, administrative, cultural, military, political,
and other laws and regulations must be based on Islamic criteria. This
principle applies absolutely and generally to all articles of the Constitution as well as to all other laws and regulations," and that "the wise
persons of the Guardian Council are judges in this matter."[24] This
metaphor of a theocracy is one that many Soviets themselves accepted,
with the top Soviet leader of the day a kind of Pope whose ex cathedra
pronouncements could not be challenged without undermining the
authority of the entire church. The theocratic nature of Communist
Party rule in the Soviet Union was in fact so strong that, in later years,
Aleksandr Yakovlev would refer to Gorbachev's famed policy of perestroika as "the Reformation."[25]

   This has several implications, not the least of which is that a promulgated ideology creates standards for the regime as well as for the
ordinary citizen, setting standards by which the governing elite's behavior and ideological rectitude can be measured and judged by friends
and foes alike. This might be less important if the regime were cynical
or hypocritical enough to design ideology merely as a means of social
control, with no real commitment to it other than as a public justification for keeping power. But communism was not the empty civil religion of the Soviet Union; the Kremlin actually believed most of what it
was saying and conducted the business of the Soviet state accordingly.
As Mastny has put it, there was no "double-bookkeeping" in Moscow,
with Soviet leaders saying one thing atop Lenin's tomb or before a Party
congress and then privately saying another. Indeed, some of the most
secret Soviet documents were phrased in such formal ideological terms
that they "could have been published in *Pravda* without anybody's
noticing."[26] Even into the late 1980s, major decisions on both foreign
and domestic policy were taken on an ideological basis, in which "all
public phenomena were judged in terms of benefit to one side or the
other in a worldwide unappeasable conflict."[27] Soviet ideology was not

merely a general orientation toward, say, socialism or social justice, but an explicit set of guidelines which Soviet leaders themselves could only ignore at the risk of their own sense of identity and rectitude.

Also, because the Communist Party was the sole source and sole interpreter of ideology, the legitimacy of both the Party and the official ideology were closely bound together. Obedience to one was obedience to the other, and to challenge the tenets of Soviet ideology was, by extension, to challenge the revolution that was carried out in its name and thence the Party itself. The Kremlin, unsurprisingly, put down such challenges with almost theocratic zeal. This was an important difference between the Soviet Union and the democracies, in which there is no single ideological fountainhead of government. "The democracies," Jean Francois Revel has written, "do not have an ideology, they have a thousand, a hundred thousand. Democracy is revealed by the mutual criticism of the groups that compose its political and cultural pluralism."[28] No single administration in the United States is the arbiter, for all time, of the constitution or the law, nor does the legitimacy of the American system rest on a perfectly shared understanding of the fundamental principles of the system. This makes clearer why communist regimes were so keenly sensitive to dissent over intellectual points that Westerners might see as trivial or tangential: the principle of Party supremacy lurked behind even the most minor of debates. "Soviet power," writer Isaak Babel (himself liquidated under Stalin) once said, "is only sustained by ideology. Without that it would be over in ten years."[29] To admit other sources of truth or knowledge would be the first step to admitting that there may be other sources of political legitimacy as well. As Yakovlev has put it: "Ideological monopolism guarantees universal control over each and every person."[30]

This inherent inability to tolerate ideological diversity is why religion was an object of special hatred and the cause of a unique kind of paranoia among communist regimes. Organized religions are nothing less than communism's competitors, with similar claims to being the arbiters of justice, morality, and the right order of society. Religion turns the individual from earth to heaven, just as communist ideology seeks to do the exact opposite, and it demands loyalties higher than the Party or the state that must be obeyed even at the risk of death. This is not to say that the struggle between the Kremlin and the churches, synagogues, and mosques of the Soviet Union was one of ongoing martyrdom—although there was plenty of that—but rather that religion was seen as especially deadly because it was inaccessible either to proof or propaganda. It was far easier to attack "rightists" or "bourgeois elements" or "falsifiers" with lengthy explanations of their heresy than to confront popes and patriarchs, whose crimes amounted to nothing less than contesting the spiritual allegiances of the citizenry.

This was an especially touchy subject where the young were concerned. The regime cared less about the old women crowding Soviet churches than they did about their grandchildren, whom they saw as targets of an anticommunist war led by clerics—which itself was an admission of how many young people were regularly turning away from the state ideology and toward various faiths.[31] The sheer clumsiness and vitriol with which religion and religious leaders were attacked is itself evidence of the degree to which the threat of the most powerful alternate ideologies of all reduced Soviet propagandists to near incoherence.[32]

Finally, and from the point of view of the Cold War, most important, Soviet ideology was explicitly committed to external revolution. To be the "Soviet Union" meant by definition to be committed to a reordering of the international system. Even the state motto—"proletarians of all nations, unite!"—spoke to this transnational goal. While it is true that Stalin allowed manifestations of a kind of ethnic solidarity and "Soviet nationalism" during World War II, the Soviet regime never escaped the burden, present at the moment of the state's founding, of its own self-proclaimed destiny. Indeed, "Soviet nationalism" is a contradiction in terms, since by definition to be a Soviet patriot meant to be a Marxist-Leninist—which in turn meant being an internationalist. None of this foreclosed Soviet chauvinism or imperial ambition—Moscow was, after all, the center of the first revolutionary state and made special claims of loyalty from both Soviet citizens and revolutionary movements based on that—but it was indicative of how seriously the Kremlin took the transnational dictates of Marxism-Leninism that it tried to wed narrow patriotism and internationalism in the minds of its subjects. Soviet international goals, however much they may at times have served the direct material interests of the Soviet Union, were not really traditional great power goals and could not be accommodated within the traditional international system. To abandon the struggle to transform the system would mean accepting that the ideological foundations of the Soviet state itself were either a lie or unattainable and that the USSR had no reason to exist. In the end, this is very close to what happened, but the restless dynamism inherent in Soviet ideology was the primary reason the Soviets were in perpetual conflict with so much of the rest of the world in the first place.

What all of this describes is a USSR that was, to use Nigel Gould-Davies' expression, an "ideological state," a regime that defies realist assumptions about power and interest and seeks to replicate itself abroad for reasons of belief, rather than raw power or resources.

Ideological states seek power to spread their domestic system rather than to enhance their own security ... they define *security* in terms of the expansion of their domestic system and *threat* in terms of the expansion of their adversary's domestic system . . . such states see the basic dynamic in international relations not as a competitive interaction between discrete sovereign entities, but as a conflict between two camps defined in terms of their domestic systems. Alliance relations are based not on temporary convergence of state interest, but on long-term solidarity of regimes, and international change takes the form not of a shifting balance of power that responds to common threats, but of a stable "balance of faith" affected only by conversion or defection between camps [emphases original].[33]

Even a state with so strong an exceptionalist and universalist streak as the United States falls short of this kind of messianism. Although the American ideological foundations of the Declaration of Independence or the Constitution are revolutionary and universal—claiming, after all, that all men, not just those in North America, are endowed with inalienable rights—the American revolution was fought to secure those rights for *Americans*, not for the people of the planet. As John Quincy Adams wrote in 1821, America "goes not abroad in search of monsters to destroy"; she is "the well-wisher to the freedom and independence of all," but "the champion and vindicator only of her own." This is a sentiment that would make no sense to a Soviet, even one committed to the Stalinist line of "socialism in one country" (which only argued for the protection of socialism in the USSR *first*, not exclusively). The idea that there could be any eventual safety for the USSR without the revolutionary spread of the Soviet system of government is something that even a more flexible Marxist-Leninist thinker would have to reject as a matter of first principles.[34]

One objection that might be raised here is to ask whether Soviet citizens really understood or cared about Marxism-Leninism. Indeed, given the rather limited intellectual abilities of men like Brezhnev and Chernenko, it is fair to ask if the leadership understood it, either. It is doubtful that most top Soviet leaders, much less ordinary Soviet citizens, had a deep acquaintance with every line of *State and Revolution* or *Civil War in France*—although there is actually evidence now that Stalin attentively read Marx's *Critique of the Gotha Program* and even derived some of his policies from it toward the end of his life.[35] But does the level of public literacy with the communist canon speak to the power of the basic ideological tenets of the Soviet state?

Again, a comparison with religion might be helpful. Very few believing Christians could probably explain in any detail the Book of Habakkuk or the letter of St. Paul to Philemon. Does this make them less Christian or render an understanding of Christianity useless in explaining their beliefs and actions? Early Christians only understood the basic fact of the Resurrection and the basic doctrine of the Redemption, and those are still the beliefs that essentially define "a Christian." Likewise, the Soviet regime was committed at its inception to the single Marxist dogma of class-based international revolution and organized around the single Leninist principle of the leading role of the Communist Party. While much would be written after the fact about both Jesus and Lenin, Christianity and communism kept simple assertions at their core as institutions. The average Soviet citizen, like the average Christian, may not have been a professional ideologist or theologian, but he or she knew what the state expected them to believe. The faithful Christian has the duty to await the Second Coming; the faithful Marxist-Leninist was not to await but to help bring about the next revolution. It could not be otherwise for either of them, or the very words they use to identify themselves as part of a particular community would be meaningless.

None of this means that ideological states must always act as if they were led by wild-eyed fanatics, or conversely that any state that adopts reasonable or prudent strategies has somehow lost its faith in its underlying goals. "There is no necessary connection," Gould-Davies rightly argues, "between the radicalism of ultimate objectives and the choice of means to achieve them."[36] Robert Tucker, describing the entwined strands of ideological fervor and naked Machiavellian cunning in Stalin's personality, has put it more elegantly: "To treat opportunism as incompatible with deeply held beliefs is to take a simplistic view of political man."[37]

IMPLICATIONS OF THE IDEOLOGICAL STATE

Although a promulgated ideology provides a foundation for government that is more compact and in theory more stable than anything so messy and difficult as the consent of the governed, it carries a price. Because the leaders and peoples of such states judge themselves and, in fact, must judge themselves by the degree of success they achieve in the stated goal of altering the world around them, ideological states face the ongoing dilemma of dynamism or decay, as the U.S. authors of the famous 1950 report on the Soviet threat, *NSC-68*, presciently saw:

> In a very real sense, the Kremlin is a victim of its own dynamism. This dynamism can become a weakness if it is frustrated, if in its forward thrusts it encounters a superior force which halts the expansion and exerts a superior counterpressure. Yet the Kremlin cannot relax the condition of crisis and mobilization, for to do so would be to lose its dynamism, whereas the seeds of decay within the Soviet system would begin to flourish and fructify.[38]

Such regimes cannot simply say that they are muddling along and protecting the average citizen's life, liberty, and pursuit of happiness. Rather, they must show progress in the struggle to realize whatever totem has been erected at the center of the state's life, be it communism, Islam, racial supremacy, vegetarianism, spelling reform, or any other concrete goal. If that struggle is advanced, the state can lay greater claim to loyalty from its citizens and allies; if it is thwarted or abandoned, the very existence of the state itself is threatened—first and foremost from within. The need to maintain at least the façade of internal rectitude, along with the drive to expand and reproduce the state abroad, means that ideology, whatever its usefulness as the powerful, binding force at the center of the regime, is also a considerable strategic vulnerability.

This vulnerability is primarily a function of the constant cost of thwarting challenges to the state's ideological monopoly. This is, in effect, a problem of maintaining control over the population in general: all repressive states have to commit a great deal of human and material resources to internal policing, to make sure that citizens do not act in proscribed ways. (China currently earmarks ten divisions—the size of the entire U.S. Army in 2001—for keeping internal order.)[39] But ideological states have the added, self-imposed burden of making sure citizens do not *think* in proscribed ways as well.

Examples of this mania for rigid ideological conformity in the Soviet Union abound. The Soviets, like C. S. Lewis' fictional demon Screwtape, were suspicious of anything enjoyed outside of state control for its own sake, even as a hobby. (As Screwtape complained, "there is an innocence and self-forgetfulness about them I distrust.") The true depths of the Kremlin's insecurity about its ideological hold over its citizens was best reflected not in its gravest crimes, such as torture, psychiatric imprisonment of dissidents, and even murder, but in its most petty policies. The Soviet regime went to absurd, even comical, lengths to interfere with the smallest activities in the lives of ordinary Soviets, to squash any independent centers of social activity lest they provide views and loyalties to compete with those of the state.[40]

An internal 1980 KGB memorandum to the Central Committee, for example, promised to find the "instigators" of a meeting at Moscow State University in memory of slain Beatle John Lennon and to prevent "all participation" in "this unauthorized meeting," as though vigils for a dead rock star were on a par with outright demonstrations against Soviet power.[41] In addition to Lennon's fans, recent documents now show that the Soviets remained absurdly vigilant in suppressing, controlling, and arresting members of other such dangerous groups as yoga devotees and karate enthusiasts well into the 1980s. Even something so trivial as stamp collecting fell under the government's control; one historian has described an "elaborate process" dating from the 1960s that "socially reconstructed the hobby of stamp collecting," undertaken mostly by mid-level Soviet bureaucrats who could not tolerate the idea of a hobby as "an autonomous realm of social activity."[42]

By comparison with attempts to maintain ideological purity, discipline, and commitment at home, similar efforts abroad are even more complicated and expensive. The effort to show the legitimacy, to say nothing of the superiority of the state's particular crusade, can be excessively time-consuming and expensive because it requires more than military or economic conquest. It requires the political cloning of the system in areas that come under the ideological state's control; unlike authoritarian systems that seek only obedience and material tribute from their imperial possessions, the ideological state seeks social and political transformation. These states "take the considerable trouble of reordering the domestic structures" in their sphere of hegemony, something that realists would not do and cannot explain.[43] The net effect is to alter the international system by altering its units, one state at a time. This, to use Gould-Davies' words, is not geopolitical "but geoideological" expansion, aimed more at spreading the faith than acquiring territory per se.[44]

This is not as novel as it may seem. The ancient world was no stranger to ideological competition: Athens and Sparta were rarely content to defeat each other's allies, choosing instead to follow victory with the imposition of their own forms of government. Eventually, the strains of war turned Athens from an ideological power intent on replicating its democratic practices throughout the Aegean to a rampaging empire that promised genocide to any that opposed it. But even at the end, despite the utter and complete military defeat of Athens, Athenian democracy was so threatening to Spartan oligarchs that dismantling it was one of the conditions for accepting Athens' humiliating surrender.

The need to spread the state's domestic system abroad consequently leads to the costly need to maintain those newly seeded regimes. Messianism is not amenable to reversal; if these cloned regimes fail to prosper, their failure will cast a long shadow of doubt all the way back to the heartland of the ideological state itself. Again, the contrast between the United States and the Soviet Union is telling in this regard. Because the United States never set the transformation of the world system at the core of its identity as a nation, democracy could rise and fall in other nations—and even those allied with the United States— without much effect on the legitimacy of the American project itself. But counterrevolution in a Soviet ally carried a dual danger: it suggested that the spread of the Soviet system was not inevitable or irresistible and that a revolutionary regime, perhaps even including the one in Moscow, can be opposed and even defeated. The need to transform other states and gain converts is so strong that nothing can ever be allowed to threaten the relationship between the ideological state and its imperial holdings. This is why, as Milovan Djilas once wrote, "the men in the Kremlin can lose no territory once acquired, why they cannot abandon friends and allies no matter how burdensome they may have become to them . . . or admit alternative interpretations of the true faith"[45]

The Prague Spring of 1968 is a good example of the unique costs imposed by the need to maintain a "geoideological" empire. Unlike Hungary twelve years earlier, Czechoslovakia did not throw off Communist Party rule or descend into internecine violence; in fact, the Czechoslovaks had pledged loyalty to the USSR and the Warsaw Pact in the hopes of avoiding Hungary's fate. The ideological damage being done to the concept of Communist Party rule, however—ironically, damage Gorbachev would emulate in the late 1980s in the Soviet Union—was as intolerable as any actual threat to Soviet security, perhaps even more so. Moscow could not allow Prague to remain part of the Soviet imperial system while it was openly rebelling against the Soviet ideological model. "If we let Czechoslovakia go," Foreign Minister Andrei Grechko warned, "others might be tempted, too," even though it was hardly clear that Prague could "go" anywhere.[46]

The issue was not of a sudden bolt to NATO's side—Gromyko was quite right in his evaluation that NATO would not risk a fight over this—but rather the contaminating effect of Prague's heresy on the rest of the empire. Soviet leaders were disgusted by Czechoslovak leader Alexander Dubcek's inability to keep the situation under control. "Liberalization and democratization," Defense Minister Andrei Grechko said of the situation, "are in essence counterrevolution."[47] Leonid Brezhnev, upon reading a plea for help from the hard-line communists fecklessly opposing Dubcek, leveled this simple judgment against them: "What lousy Marxists."[48] There could be no negotiation or parting of the ways, as there was between Washington and Paris when France left NATO in 1966; a threat to the legitimacy of one communist government was a threat to the legitimacy of all of them. Eventually, Moscow invaded not only because of its own distress at the events in Prague, but because of the panicked pleas of the other leaders of the Soviet empire who feared the Czechoslovak disease would strike them, too. (They were right, but about a decade too early.)

Nor was this costly ideological vigilance limited to the Eastern European states. The use of outright force to maintain a communist government in power—the "Brezhnev Doctrine"—was mistakenly thought to apply only to the Warsaw Pact nations until the 1979 invasion of Afghanistan. But even in lesser theaters, the added burden of the ideological state was evident. The Soviets seemed genuinely to care, for example, about creating an ideological extension of itself in places like

Grenada or Ethiopia. In retrospect, this seems almost comic: while investments in a Grenadian runway or an Ethiopian port might make sense, warehouses full of materials for ideological indoctrination do not, especially since the Soviet presence in these nations was already more than welcome. The Soviet presence around the world was more costly and cumbersome than it needed to be, and Soviet prestige ended up strongly tied to regimes that Moscow supported out of a fundamental belief that it was obligated to so in order to maintain a self-conscious fidelity to its own mission in the world as well as to enforce its claim to international revolutionary leadership.

This last point is especially important because it illustrates the rigidity and myopia that ideological regimes place upon themselves. They are slow to react in both the domestic and international arenas because their leaders need time to categorize everything around them in ideological terms. This is to some extent a truism; all leaders interpret the world through a cognitive prism. But Soviet thinking was smothered by a formal, complicated, and highly articulated ideology that provided a collective set of cognitive rules that could take a petty military dictator like Mengistu and turn him into a "Marxist." Yakovlev has described the reflexive support of even the most questionable Third World regimes as driven by "the dogma that imperialism was doomed," while noting the leadership's "inability and unwillingness to see and evaluate immense changes in the world, to understand the interdependence of those events, and to realistically evaluate themselves and others."[49]

All of human existence is political in the eyes of the ideological state, and everything needs to pass through that ideological filter before it is even intelligible. Foreign events were never just occurrences that may or may not be of interest; they either furthered Soviet ideological goals or they did not. Likewise, at home, the activities of ordinary Soviet citizens were never without political content. Rock music, for example, was never just music: it was an attack on the nation's youth, and people who listened to it were victims of propaganda warfare. There can be no better illustration of this kind of bizarre warping of the official Soviet cognitive map than the Party ideologist who in 1986 accused the U.S. group Village People of having "written several songs with pseudopatriotic lyrics, [and] propagandizing militarism with the words 'Join the U.S. Navy.'"[50] While it is true that the Village People—better known in the 1970s for their flamboyant wardrobes and disco hits featuring barely veiled homoerotic lyrics like "Macho Man" and "YMCA"—did land a song called "In the Navy" on the charts seven years earlier in 1979, only someone completely steeped in Soviet dogma could think that it was an ode to militarism rather than a barely disguised reference to behavior that today's U.S. Navy would almost certainly classify under "don't ask, don't tell."

Ironically, the lumbering sluggishness and indiscriminate paranoia of the ideological guardians sometimes meant that real threats were countered too late or confused with more harmless events. For example, the Kremlin saw things like cultural exchanges, radio broadcasts, and even ordinary tourism as weapons of ideological warfare—and rightly so. But because it saw almost *every* exposure to the West as a breach in the regime's wall around the citizen, and every piece of information from the West as a direct challenge to the Kremlin's official view of the world, the system often overwhelmed itself trying to discriminate among threats. The reaction against these intrusions was not only slow and ineffective but expensive: in the case of broadcasting, Soviet electronic jamming of foreign broadcasts in the late 1950s was so intense that it ended up jamming official *Soviet* broadcasting, too, and by the mid-1980s, the annual cost of keeping Radio Free Europe out of the Soviet Union, insofar as it could be done, was running upward of three billion dollars.[51]

The inability to discriminate among threats meant that on occasion the Soviets actually sanctioned highly damaging events. The 1959 U.S. exhibit at Sokolniki, an important moment in the post-Stalin "thaw," was an obvious blow to the regime's credibility, giving "residents of the Soviet empire . . . ever increasing exposure to an alternative way of life" even as "their own social systems delivered stagnation instead of progress"; eventually it was closed, but not before it was visited by over two million Soviets.[52] Travel, even to nearby Europe, was fraught with risk, and here again, the Kremlin's policies showed the slowness of its ideological reflexes: citizens were told horror stories about the West, but the regime hoped that proper political conditioning could protect Soviet citizens who traveled abroad from the inevitable moment of massive cognitive dissonance. As a Soviet cabdriver recalled of his visit to West Germany in the 1980s: "There were dozens of types of bread. I never in my life saw such abundance and I felt pain for my country. I began to think that only fools live in Russia."[53] Even spies were at risk: rather than tell them the truth about life in the West before they left, the regime stubbornly stuck instead to rigid political indoctrination, only to find later, as in the case of one defector, that their agents were reading up on Russian dissident literature in the very universities they had been sent abroad to penetrate.[54]

These wounds, however small or large, were self-inflicted. The Communist Party could not simply claim that it was working for a better future for the cabdriver; the uncompromising nature of the regime's ideological foundations meant that the Kremlin leadership was irresistibly driven to claim as well that life in the West was exploitative and impoverishing, even if it meant risking that a single trip to West Berlin could detonate years of carefully constructed propaganda and plant the very thoughts the regime was trying to prevent in the first place. The fear of unsanctioned information—indeed, even the fear of the seductive power of American jazz music (or those infamous disco militarists mentioned earlier)—led to vilification of Western broadcasts that only made Eastern Europeans *more* eager to listen to the forbidden fruit of foreign radio. "The whole propaganda against listening just made us more curious to listen to Western stations," a Romanian woman was later to recall.[55] Few Westerners, by comparison, huddled around their radios to listen to Radio Moscow's openly available English-language service. The restrictions on travel into the USSR likewise made Westerners themselves objects of intense curiosity, especially outside of Moscow and Leningrad, but even in the largest cities, Soviets would defy laws prohibiting them from consorting with Americans, if for no other reason just to find out why they were not supposed to talk to Americans.

The USSR was not the only ideological state to exhibit this kind of systemic rigidity and exaggerated allergy to foreign influences. In modern Iran, for example, leading government clerics worry, as the late Ayatollah Khomeini did, about what Khomeini called "Westoxification," the poisoning of Iranian youth by Western culture, even though the mania for that culture is evident and probably only strengthened by the sheer hatred with which Iran's aging clerics revile it.[56] (One could argue that the French worry about this kind of American cultural contamination too, but the Fifth Republic was not founded in a revolution against it and therefore does not have the same stake in it Teheran does.) As a 1998 report put it, "Iran was supposed to be impervious to the corrupting power of "Baywatch" and Barbie. Resistance to Western, and especially American, cultural influence was a pillar of the 1979 Islamic revolution."[57]

North Korea, too, has a long tradition of outright paranoia about foreign influences and remains one of the most closed regimes left on earth. A Western doctor who worked there for a time before finally leaving in 2000 described the nightmarish measures taken to keep North Koreans in isolation and the effect of those measures on ordinary people:

> In North Korea, a repressive apparatus uncoils whenever there is criticism. The suffocation, by surveillance, shadowing, wiretapping, and mail interception, is total. Most patients in hospitals suffer from psychosomatic illnesses, worn out by compulsory drills, innumerable parades, "patriotic" assemblies at six in the morning and droning propaganda.[58]

The North Korean regime is in fact so paranoid that it actually goes abroad in search of enemies to kill, and is suspected of bizarre schemes like kidnapping Japanese women and forcing them to train spies and terrorists (presumably by acculturating the Korean agents to foreigners).[59]

China faces the greatest challenge in this regard because Beijing has tried to have it both ways. Chinese citizens have access, even if limited, to Western culture, to travel, and to seek education in the West, and they live among outposts of Western consumerism (like the inevitable McDonald's restaurants). But this policy of tolerance is aimed at gaining the financial and technological benefits of trade and intercourse with the West while avoiding the spread of Western ideas and influence. The Chinese regime has been vigilant to the point of ruthlessness in seeing to it that China's citizens do not confuse the ability to buy a Big Mac with the ability to speak their minds or worship as they please. Like the détente-era Soviets before them, they are determined to counter the increased interaction with the West by stepping up the cost of dissent at home; unlike the Soviets, however, the Chinese seem willing to impose the most brutal measures with little care for what the West says or thinks about it, if it means avoiding the Soviet Union's eventual fate.

Ideological states are prone to do themselves a great deal of needless damage, but this does not mean that their opponents cannot help steady their aim while they are shooting themselves in the foot. The costs of policing an ideological empire are immense, and increasing those costs by bombarding the regime with a series of challenges great and small can be done with relatively modest means. At times, struggle with an ideological state will entail either a resort to military action or the rejection of combat and the acceptance of a reversal, and at such times, struggle with an ideological regime might be little different than any other kind of interstate conflict. But the susceptibility to being paralyzed by a direct attack on the ideological and political foundations of the regime is unique to ideological states and is a strategy that can produce great rewards.

Whether by propaganda, travel, media broadcasts, emigration, or any of a number of other measures (including new media like the Internet in the twenty-first century), the West can force ideological regimes to account for the kind of doublethink it expects from its citizens. The object should be to encumber such regimes with increased costs of internal policing, imposing upon them the need to divide their attentions and energies between foreign and domestic policy as often as possible. Whether used against the regime itself or its imperial holdings, a strategy that remains determined to present the opponent's population with alternatives to the official ideology, that demands the state explain the rift between words and deeds before the international community, and baits the enemy into trying either to emulate the West or to be truer to its own ideological formulations—that is, an approach that will not let an ideological state pick and choose which parts of its canon it will emphasize—is a strategy that runs little risk of war abroad or bankruptcy at home, but can inflict heavy costs on an opponent for whom response is not an option but a duty. This is a strategy that is relatively useless when contending with an open society, but can be devastating when used against an enemy whose control over its own society is heavily dependent on strict control of the official "truth."

CONCLUSIONS: IDEOLOGICAL STATES AND COLD WARS

To know what a state will fight to defend, it is important to know what it believes. Most states at most times will fight for territory, for the lives of their citizens, and for access to vital resources. But it is in situations where the threat is less immediate that the peculiarities and the attendant vulnerabilities of the ideological state become clear. The most important conclusion to draw from this discussion of ideological states is that any policy based strictly on realist assumptions is not only unlikely to strike at the most exposed vulnerabilities of such states, but also will be limited in its ability to predict and explain a wide range of its opponent's moves.

From a realist perspective, the Soviet Union probably should not have showed much interest in distant African revolutions, any more than they should have worried about whether their own factory workers were covertly being introduced to Duke Ellington in the privacy of their homes, but they did (on both counts) and understanding why is central to grasping the meaning of Soviet actions.

Understanding an opponent's ideological disposition will not provide a magic key to its actions. There was no master plan in the Kremlin, no schedule to which the Soviets were adhering as part of a grand plan of conquest. But successful strategy is based in part on understanding what the enemy wants, what price it will pay (or can be goaded into paying) and contending with what it is likely to do and capable of doing, not what seems logical or prudent to others. It goes almost without saying that it is most certainly not based on planning for what we find sensible, what we would prefer, or what we would find most advantageous, even if that has been the practical effect of the realist delusion about ideological states. To grasp what the Soviet Union wanted, and to predict, as much possible, what it would do to fulfill those goals, required a firm understanding of what was transcendentally valuable to the Soviets. Ideology cannot explain everything about any state, even one so ideologically bound as the USSR, but it does far better than competing explanations at revealing those aspects of Soviet behavior and vulnerabilities of the Soviet state that were central to containing and defeating it in the Cold War.

In the next chapter, we will see how ideology drove the origins of the Cold War itself. Any hope that the postwar world of 1945 could be managed and divided among the great powers was shattered early and decisively by Stalin's proclamation that the socialist world and the West were now irrevocably divided into "two camps," and nowhere were the aggression and daring of the Soviet ideological state more of a tragic surprise than in Korea.

NOTES

1. Nina Tannenwald, ed., *Understanding the End of the Cold War, 1980–1987: An Oral History Conference* (Providence, RI: Watson Institute for International Studies, 1999).

2. A. N. Yakovlev, *Gor'kaia chasha: Bol'shevizm i Reformatsiia Rossii* (Yaroslavl': Verkhne-Volzhskoe, 1994), p. 190.

3. See Yakovlev, pp. 190–195.

4. Tannenwald, ed., p. 32.

5. Quoted in Mary Anastasia O'Grady, "Castro and Dodd Object to a Bush Nominee," *The Wall Street Journal*, June 22, 2001, p. A15.

6. Interview with Vladimir Batiuk, Moscow, Russia, February 4, 2000. See also N. I. Egorova, "Evropeiskaia bezopastnost' i 'ugroza' NATO v otsenkakh stalinskogo rukovodstva," in I. V. Gaiduk, N. I. Egorova, and A. O. Chubar'ian, eds., *Stalinskoie desiatiletie kholodnoi voiny: fakty i gypotezy* (Moscow: Nauka, 1999), p. 56.

7. As John Gaddis points out, it became conventional wisdom that a leader like Hitler was prone to emotionalism but that Stalin was brutally realistic, and so "the 'old' Cold War history failed to take ideology very seriously." John Gaddis, *We Now Know* (Oxford, UK: Clarendon Press, 1997), p. 290. In the pop culture, even an anti-Soviet movie like John Milius' 1984 *Red Dawn* fell prey to this realist simplification. When asked how World War III started, one of the characters describes the United States and the USSR as "the two biggest kids on the block" and adds that "sooner or later, they're gonna fight, I guess."

8. David A. Welch, "Remember the Falklands?," *International Journal* 52 (3), Summer 1997, pp. 483–507.

9. Dmitrii Volkogonov, *Sem' vozhdei*, vol. 2 (Moscow: Novosti, 1995), pp. 133-134.

10. K. J. Holsti, *International Politics*, 2nd ed. (Englewood Cliffs, NJ: Prentice Hall, 1972), p. 366.

11. Holsti, p. 366.

12. Holsti, p. 368.

13. Jeffrey Hughes, "On Bargaining," in Jan F. Triska, ed., *Dominant Powers and Subordinate States* (Durham, NC: Duke University Press, 1986), p. 185.

14. Vojtech Mastny, "Introduction: Planning for the Unplannable," in *Taking Lyon on the Ninth Day? The 1964 Warsaw Pact Plan for a Nuclear War in Europe and Related Documents*, http://www.isn.ethz.ch/php/documents/introvm.htm.

15. Terry Eagleton, *Ideology* (London: Verso, 1991), p. 4.

16. Nathan Leites, *The Operational Code of the Politburo* (New York: McGraw Hill, 1951).

17. "It seems to me," Paul Warnke said in 1977, "that instead of talking in those terms which would indulge what I regard as the primitive aspects of Soviet nuclear doctrine, we ought to be trying to educate them into the real world of strategic nuclear weapons, which is that nobody could possibly win." Quoted in Douglas Hart, "The Hermeneutics of Soviet Military Doctrine," *Washington Quarterly*, Spring 1984, p. 79.

18. See Michael C. Desch, "Culture Clash: Assessing the Importance of Ideas in Security Studies," *International Security* (23) 1, Summer, 1998.

19. William Wohlforth and Nigel Gould-Davies have made recent attempts in this regard. For a review of their arguments, see Thomas Nichols, "Brezhnev's Elephant: Why Can't International Relations Theory Integrate New Revelations About the Cold War and the Role of Ideology in It?" H-DIPLO (H-Net List for Diplomatic History), September 1999, http://www2.h-net.msu.edu/~diplo/.

20. Yehezkel Dror, *Crazy States: A Counterconventional Strategic Problem* (Millwood, NY: Kraus Reprint, 1980), p. xvi.

21. I am aware that native North American Indians might object that the term "American" does indeed have ethnic or racial meaning to indigenous peoples, but I am using the word as it is commonly understood in the modern era.

22. Dmitrii Volkogonov, *Lenin* (New York: Free Press, 1994), p. xxx.

23. The Soviet Constitution is available online at www.uni-wuerzburg.de/law/r100000_.html.

24. The Iranian Constitution is available online at www.uni-wuerzburg.de/law/ir00000_.html.

25. See Yakovlev, pp. 199–201.

26. Vojtech Mastny, *The Cold War and Soviet Insecurity* (New York: Oxford University Press, 1996), p. 9.

27. Robert Conquest, *Reflections on a Ravaged Century* (New York: Norton, 2000), p. 113.

28. Jean Francois Revel, *How Democracies Perish* (New York: Doubleday, 1984), p. 161.

29. Quoted in Conquest, p. 112.

30. Yakovlev, p. 150.

31. Soviet writers were explicit in this charge of targeting the young. See "Otchiznoi svoei gordost'," *Komsomol'skaia Pravda*, April 4, 1981, p. 2.

32. A typical example was the charge that church leaders in Poland were taking orders from Western spymasters via Radio Free Europe broadcasts. See V. Makhin, "Religiia v ideinom arsenale antikommunizma," *Politicheskoe Samoobrazovanie* 12, 1982.

33. Nigel Gould-Davies, "Rethinking the Role of Ideology in International Politics During the Cold War," *Journal of Cold War Studies* (1) 1, Winter 1999, pp. 102–103.

34. As Stephane Courtois and Jean-Louis Palme have written: "What had first been simply a need of the moment was transformed into a full-fledged political project: world socialist revolution." Stephane Courtois, et al., *The Black Book of Communism* (Cambridge, MA: Harvard University Press, 1999), p. 271.

35. Gould-Davies, p. 92.

36. Gould-Davies, p. 96.

37. Robert Tucker, "Stalinism as Revolution from Above," in Robert Tucker, ed., *Stalinism* (New York: Norton, 1977), p. 93.

38. Ernest R. May, ed., *American Cold War Strategy: Interpreting NSC 68* (Boston: Bedford/St. Martin's, 1993), p. 36.

39. Richard J. Newman and Kevin Whitelaw, "How Big a Threat?" *U.S. News and World Report*, July 23, 2001, p. 43.

40. For more on the destruction of Soviet society, see Thomas Nichols, "Russian Democracy and Social Capital," *Social Science Information* 35 (4), December 1996.

41. "Memorandum from the KGB Regarding the Planning of a Demonstration in Memory of John Lennon," *Cold War International History Project Bulletin* 10, March 1998, p. 219.

42. J. Grant, "The Social Construction of Philately in the Early Soviet Era," *Comparative Studies in Society and History* 37 (3), Spring 1995, p. 495.

43. Gould-Davies, p. 103.

44. Gould-Davies, p. 104.

45. Milovan Djilas, "Christ and the Commissar," in G. R. Urban, ed., *Stalinism: Its Impact on Russia and the World* (Cambridge, MA: Harvard University Press, 1986), p. 197.

46. Quoted in John McGinn, "The Politics of Collective Inaction," *Journal of Cold War Studies* 1, no. 3, Fall 1999, p. 136.

47. Volkogonov, p. 44.

48. Volkogonov, p. 46.

49. Yakovlev, p. 194.

50. I. Zaitsev, "Etot 'neitral'nyi rok'," *Sovetskaia Belorussiia*, December 24, 1986, p. 3, Subject File "Ideologicheskaia bor'ba," Soviet ("Red") Archives, Records of Radio Free Europe/Radio Liberty Research Institute, Open Society Archives, Budapest, Hungary.

51. See Michael Nelson, *War of the Black Heavens* (Syracuse, NY: Syracuse University Press, 1997), p. 92, and Alvin Snyder, *Warriors of Disinformation* (New York: Arcade, 1995), p. 166.

52. Walter L. Hixson, *Parting the Curtain: Propaganda, Culture, and the Cold War, 1945–1961* (New York: St. Martin's Press, 1998), p. xv.

53. Paul Hollander, *Political Will and Personal Belief: The Decline and Fall of Soviet Communism* (New Haven, CT: Yale University Press, 1999), p. 282.

54. "I came to realize," the defector said later, "that all my knowledge, all my ideology was based on a lie." Graham Brink, "Spy's Life One of Danger, Deceit," *St. Petersburg Times Online*, June 9, 2001.

55. Nelson, p. 64.

56. John Lancaster, "Embracing the Great Satan's Culture," *The Washington Post Weekly Edition*, December 14, 1998, p. 2.

57. Lancaster, p. 2.

58. Norbert Vollertsen, "A Prison Country," *The Wall Street Journal*, April 17, 2001, p. A20.

59. Courtois, et al., p. 561.

3

From the Two Camps to Korea: Soviet Ideology and the Origins of the Cold War

We will have to struggle with the Americans. But we are already reconciled to that.

—Stalin, 1950

TO HELL WITH YALTA

The dawn of the Cold War, that grim period between the end of World War II and Stalin's death eight years later, is a stark illustration of the impact of ideology in action and the necessity of understanding the motives of an ideologically driven opponent. Thinking about the nature of the Soviet enemy in this period has been obscured by Western introspection, as Westerners have become understandably self-referential in thinking about the costs of the struggle with the Soviet empire. Was the price, we wonder, worth it? Did we perhaps cause it or contribute to it? There is a growing literature that looks back to the origins of the Cold War and asks, with a certain tone of contrition and regret, whether the whole business might have been avoided. Central to this belief that the Cold War was all somehow a mistake is a rather wistful look back at what might have been, at roads not taken. The Marshall Plan, the Truman Doctrine, uniting the western zones of Germany, and even the atomic bombing of Japan all vie for pride of place in explanations of how the Cold War might have been averted.

But lost in the recriminations about the Cold War's origins is an appreciation for the kind of state that the future members of NATO faced after World War II. As one analyst has cautioned, "Western perceptions of Soviet Communism must not be seen in isolation . . . it seems as though U.S. revisionist historians were worrying about the mote in their own government's eye, while paying little attention to the beam in Stalin's."[1] This refusal to consider the ideological roots of the conflict is finally under attack by what might be called "antirevisionist" historians, including many in Russia, but ideology (as noted in the previous chapter) still finds few takers as an explanation for the emergence of the East-West conflict. Thus much of the early Cold War remains ostensibly inexplicable—or, more accurately, partially explicable only by recourse to weakly constituted economic and realist assertions that do not seem to correspond to what actually happened.

An emphasis on the intensely ideological nature of the Soviet Union's foreign policy in this period, however, provides a richer picture of the early days of the Cold War. The Soviet-American conflict was inevitable not because of the relative wealth of the West, or the distribution of power after the collapse of the Axis, or even because of some atavistic antagonism between East and West dating back to the days of the Teutonic knights. Rather, the Cold War was the direct result of the ideological worldview of the Soviet regime, an approach to international relations that could not but help to divide the world into "two camps." Any hopes in the West that the agreements reached at Yalta would prevent this rift between East and West were misplaced because Stalin, as a good Marxist-Leninist, did not share the fundamental precepts of international order on which the Yalta accords—or any other, for that matter—were based. In discussing the renegotiation of a new Sino-Soviet treaty with Mao Zedong in early 1950, Mao asked if such an act would not violate the Yalta agreements. "It does," Stalin answered, "and to hell with it! Once we have taken up the position that treaties must be changed, we must go all the way. It is true that for us this entails certain inconveniences, and we will have to struggle with the Americans. But we are already reconciled to that."[2]

Although the "two camps" formulation would not be explicit policy until 1947, the belief that the world was destined to fall into a confrontation between the forces of progress and reaction was inherent in Marxism, found expression in Bolshevism, and finally came into full flower in Stalinism. It made the ultimate transition to the outbreak of war in Korea in 1953.

BOLSHEVISM AND THE TWO CAMPS

Tempting though it is to blame Stalin personally for the East-West rift after 1945, the very idea of an inevitable confrontation in a divided world is inherent in the closed nature of Marxist thought. For Marx, of course, the modern world was simply expressed as the interaction between two groups of people, one exploiting the other. More than that, however, Marxism requires an enemy to make itself comprehensible, for the world it describes is one characterized by struggle. (The Bolsheviks would adapt this concept of eternal warfare to their own domestic needs as well, a phenomenon rendered perfectly in literary form in George Orwell's *1984*: Oceania alternates without hesitation between war with "Eastasia" and "Eurasia," with the presence of conflict obviously of more importance to the ruling party than the identity of the enemy itself.) The teleology of Marxism demands conflict and eventual victory; it is, in a way, structured as a conquering religion, in which revealed truth must inevitably face and overcome lies and oppression.

Although the Bolsheviks adopted a military style in organization and rhetoric—they were forever "storming" on "fronts" and the like—the idea of the world as one large no-man's-land punctuated by trenches of class did not originate with Bolshevism. As Leszek Kolakowski has put it:

> Marx really, consistently, believed that human society would not be "liberated" without achieving unity. And, except for despotism, there is no other technique known to produce a unity of society; no other way of suppressing the tension between civil and political society but the suppression of civil society; no other means to remove the conflicts between the individual and "the whole" but the destruction of the individual; no other road toward "higher," "positive" freedom—as opposed to "negative," "bourgeois" freedom—but the liquidation of the latter.[3]

This is war, a pure, ideological, and continual form of war, but war nonetheless, and it is instructive to recall that some of the most bitter schisms among the European left after the Second International occurred precisely over the issue of the degree to which one might find accommodation with the class enemy.

While there is plenty in Marx to reinforce this notion, the more important point is the degree to which Lenin and his heirs, especially Stalin, internalized this worldview of "permanent civil war" and incorporated it into the political DNA of the Soviet state.[4] Indeed, in the end the unviability of the Soviet state was probably foreordained in the very nature of the regime born from Lenin's romantic attachment to abstract theory. As Lenin biographer Dmitrii Volkogonov has written:

> Lenin's dream of turning the planet red was based on false thinking bred by years of sitting in isolation and making up schemes for Communist revolution, without taking account of ethnic, national, religious or geographical factors. He saw only class and economic motives, and the only

value he was prepared to defend was power. . . . Because his delusions to some extent reflected universal values of social justice, he succeeded in converting them into a program for millions of people, and imposing it by force. . . . The Party kept both the delusions and the image of Lenin alive as its most valuable asset.[5]

Thus, even to exist as a "Soviet" entity meant to be in conflict; other states were either allies or enemies on the road to a wider revolution. To be a Marxist-Leninist was to believe in revolution and in a world of conflict from which there could be but one escape: the overthrow of the old order.

In other words, the very nature of the Soviet state would forever force Lenin's heirs to adopt a commitment to conflict and revolution. It is true that later Soviet leaders would try to elide this question, but Stalin was not among them. As two Russian researchers have written, the dictates of revolution and the needs of Soviet security intersected forcefully under Stalin long before World War II:

Stalin was the first statesman to grasp the notion that promoting world revolution was not a goal in and of itself, but rather that it provided the rationale for building a strong Soviet Union. . . . The logic [enunciated in 1924 and 1925] was beyond criticism: if the world revolution was to happen, the Soviet Union must become invincible; in the meantime, ideology, winning souls and space, would strengthen the USSR as a state.[6]

Or, as Volkogonov once wrote, Stalin's "entire life was war: war with his own people, war with imperialism," and it was this attachment to an ideology of conflict, a worldview of confrontation, that created the Cold War into which NATO was born.[7]

Much has been made of Stalin's hopes for cooperation with his wartime allies after the victory over the Axis in 1945. But these analyses miss the point between tactical accommodation and a genuine acceptance of the fundamental nature of the international order—that is, of a system based on nation-states, the free movement of people and capital, and a rough but customary rule of international law.[8] Stalin never accepted these as essential principles of international life; in fact, no Soviet leader except Gorbachev ever accepted these principles because they are in effect Soviet heresy. (Even Gorbachev did not dare enunciate an understanding of international life as governed by state interaction rather than class conflict until 1987, and as will be seen later, this admission in itself represented an abandonment of the Soviet global mission that helped to accelerate the collapse of the USSR.) When Averell Harriman asked Maxim Litvinov, then the deputy foreign minister, in 1945 what the West could do to satisfy Stalin, Litvinov said:

"Nothing." In 1946, when Litvinov was asked by a journalist what would happen if the West suddenly gave in and granted all of Moscow's demands, he answered that it would "lead to the West being faced, after a more or less short time, with the next series of demands."[9]

Even before the Grand Alliance (or the Axis) had collapsed, Stalin understood that the end of the war would simply mean the resumption of the previous, grand historical struggle with the West. Diplomacy was part of that struggle, a complimentary strategy rather than a competing one. Stalin, as Vladislav Zubok and Konstantin Pleshakov have put it, "believed that skillful manipulation of the rules of the old world would someday allow him to sweep that world completely away—with its capitalist states and bourgeois civilization."[10] There could be no doubt, at least in Stalin's mind, that bourgeois civilization would someday put up a fight: in 1944, standing before a map that showed Soviet gains in Eastern Europe, he exclaimed to his colleagues: "They will never accept that so great a space should be red, never, never!"[11] While there is some evidence that others (particularly the ambassador to London, Ivan Maisky) felt that Soviet gains could be consolidated without risking an utter collapse of Allied cooperation, these voices were a minority and in any case were about to be warned of a new line.

PRELUDE TO THE TWO CAMPS

In 1946, the new line was previewed in Stalin's so-called election speech at the Bolshoi Theater. Historians still disagree about the degree to which Stalin was actually signaling a new policy; some argue that it was boilerplate, while others see in it a more sinister turn against the West. Whatever Stalin's intentions at that moment, it represented a change in official Soviet expression about the Grand Alliance, and William Wohlforth is right to point out that the practical impact of the speech, "with its reassertion of Lenin's theory of imperialism," was that it "had the effect of silencing arguments that further Big Three cooperation in anything like its wartime intimacy was possible. The relationship would [now] be some form of cooperation and competition with the other great powers."[12]

Discussion behind the scenes was as important as Stalin's public declarations. In September 1946, Ambassador to the U.S. Nikolai Novikov sent a report to the Foreign Ministry that provided a rationale for Moscow's abandonment of cooperation with the West. In retrospect, it is clear that President Franklin D. Roosevelt's death had jolted both Stalin and the Soviet foreign policy bureaucracy. Harry Truman's America was now, in the eyes of the Soviet leadership, in the hands of a "politically unstable person," in effect a bumpkin who, led along by his sinister Secretary of State, James Byrnes, believed that "the United States has the right to lead the world."[13] The United States, Novikov wrote, was striving for "world supremacy"—Foreign Minister Viacheslav Molotov took care to underline those words in the text—and "all the forces of American diplomacy," including "the army, the air force, the navy, industry, and science" were being "enlisted in the service of this foreign policy." Nor was there any hope of dividing the Americans from within: Novikov warned that "the constantly increasing reactionary nature of the foreign policy course of the United States, which consequently approached the policy advocated by the Republican party, laid the groundwork for close cooperation in this field between the far right wing of the Democratic party and the Republican party." Novikov was hardly out of step with his masters in Moscow; this "harsher, more pessimistic treatment of the United States" was only some six months ahead of eventual public Soviet declarations.[14]

None of this meant that Stalin or anyone else had given up their cherished belief that contradictions between the capitalist powers might yet prove, in the near term, more important than disputes between East and West. Even Novikov, in a stunning, ideologically driven failure of intuition, dismissed relations between Great Britain and the United States, "despite the temporary attainment of agreements on very important questions," as "plagued with great internal contradictions and cannot be lasting." But the eventual emergence of such contradictions did not necessarily forestall the emergence of bipolarity in the interim; even if "judging from what he wrote and how he acted, he definitely did not believe that this bipolarity would last long . . . from 1947 on Stalin regarded the consolidation of the two blocs and the relative growth of the U.S. influence in Europe as a foregone conclusion."[15] What seemed to surprise Stalin and the other Soviet leaders was not the emergence of bipolarity between 1945 and 1947, but that it seemed to be strengthening rather than weakening. By 1950, Stalin's faith that the capitalist camp would fall into internal squabbling would weaken, and later, the united and forceful reaction of the West to communist aggression in Korea would dispirit him deeply.[16]

As Molotov would later explain, Stalin had built a strict logical chain: "The First World War pulled one country out of capitalist slavery. The Second World War created a socialist system, the third will put an end to imperialism once and for all."[17] This, according to Zubok and Pleshakov, represented "the theoretical fatalism of an aging potentate who sought in the Laws of History the ultimate revenge on his former imperialist allies . . . by the late 1940s Joseph Stalin was again turning to ideology to explain a hostile and uncertain world."[18] Rather than wait any longer for the Allies to collapse in upon themselves, Stalin reasserted the ideological line of demarcation between East and West that had always been present in Soviet thinking. The Third World War and the consequent end of capitalism would come one day, but if it were to be delayed in arriving, then there was no alternative but to put the Soviet house in order (which meant bringing to heel upstarts like Yugoslavia's Tito in the process) and to settle in for a protracted struggle.

THE TWO CAMPS DECLARED

The enunciation of the new line came in a 1947 speech by ideologist Andrei Zhdanov, given in secret before an audience of European communist leaders at the creation of the Cominform (the successor to the Comintern) and made public shortly thereafter. It was a rejection not only of the memory of the Grand Alliance, but a call to arms coupled with a warning that there was about to be a period of imperial consolidation in the communist world.

America was no longer the firm ally of the war years, but now was disparaged as having "entered the war only in its concluding phase"— that is, in 1944—"when the issue was already decided."[19] This was clearly a return to the bitterness over the Second Front and a back-handed dismissal of the achievement at Normandy, and it is testimony to the depth of Stalin's feelings on the matter that Zhdanov was allowed to make the incredible claim that U.S. participation came only in 1944, when "the issue was already decided," and not, as actually happened, in December 1941, as the Nazis were rolling their tanks through the rubble of Moscow's suburbs and blowing Leningrad's pedestrians to bits with artillery fire. Echoing Novikov, Zhdanov described America as an arrogant nation untouched by the real costs of the war, "alarmed by the achievements of socialism in the USSR, by the achievements of the new democracies, and by the postwar growth of the labor and democratic movement in all countries," and taking upon itself "the mission of saviors of the capitalist system from communism." (Despite the many distortions in the speech, this description of America in the wake of the Marshall Plan and the Truman Doctrine at least had the virtue of being relatively accurate.)

The key moment in the speech came when Zhdanov declared the postwar period to be over and described the new world that had taken its place.

A new alignment of political forces has arisen. The more the war recedes into the past, the more distinct become two major trends in postwar international policy, corresponding to the division of the political forces operating on the international arena into two major camps: the imperialist and antidemocratic camp, on the one hand, and the anti-imperialist and

democratic camp, on the other. The principal driving force of the imperialist camp is the United States of America. Allied with it are Great Britain
and France.

In one sense, this was unremarkable, a summary, as one writer has
put it, of "stock-in-trade Leninist cliches."[20] The Bolsheviks (before
Stalin liquidated most of them, anyway) had always accepted the
basic Marxist-Leninist teaching that international, state to state relations were ephemera, a mere overlay on a more permanent problem
of class warfare.

But what is striking is the pessimism about the foreseeable future: so
much for the hope that Britain and the United States (much less France)
would fall upon each other after a temporary comity. Gone as well was
any toying with Roosevelt's belief that the planet needed to be administered and safeguarded by the coalition that had vanquished Hitler.
For some in the audience, the speech was a welcome relief, an antidote
to the distasteful (if necessary) alliance and popular front policies of the
war, while for others it was a tangible and depressing acknowledgment
that Churchill's "Iron Curtain" actually existed.[21] But whether received
with joy or sorrow, it heralded a new world, "a failure," as Zubok and
Pleshakov rightly note, "to abandon the revolutionary-imperial para-
digm and switch to a purer *realpolitik* mode. Stalin [provided] the Soviet
satellites and the whole Communist world with a clear-cut ideological
perspective on global confrontation with the United States."[22]

There could no longer be any doubt about where the USSR stood on
the matter of confrontation with the United States, and thus by extension, there could no longer be any doubt where the states of Eastern
Europe stood—or more to the point, where they had to stand. Although
the Warsaw Pact would not come into being as a military force for
another eight years, the Soviet "bloc" and the division of Europe were
now a reality.

It is important to acknowledge that the dominant interpretation of
Zhdanov's speech that has emerged among Western historians is that it
was a reaction to the Marshall Plan, an ideological inoculation of the
People's Democracies against the siren song of American money.[23]
Certainly, the Marshall Plan was a proximate contribution to Soviet-
American tensions, a clear threat to Soviet encroachments in Europe
that helped encourage Stalin to circle the wagons at the time he did.[24]
But part of what drove Stalin was the sense that Soviet control and
communist indoctrination in Europe were incomplete and that programs like the Marshall Plan were a risk precisely because they would
be so appealing. There was a concern in the Kremlin that ideological
laxity had crept into Soviet life during the war, and it is unsurprising
that Stalin would think that ideological rigor had to be reintroduced

both at home and abroad. At the least, Zhdanov's speech was as much a declaration against the West as it was yet another article of indictment in Stalin's death warrants for the many Eastern European communists who would face the gallows and firing squads of the 1948–1952 purges. Other interpretations, including some Russian versions, suggest that the threat of the Marshall Plan was less pressing than the need to maintain Soviet steadfastness in the face of the U.S. nuclear monopoly, but again, these probably affected only the immediate timing but not the inevitability of the "two camps" pronouncements.[25]

Moreover, while it would be irresponsible to ignore the domestic and intraparty origins of the speech, there was still more to it than mere political housekeeping.[26] To say that the declaration of "two camps" in 1947 had many causes or was a solution to many different Soviet needs does not alter the fact that it declared that there were now two Europes, two *worlds*, and that those worlds were in conflict. Vojtech Mastny has emphasized, rightly, that "the policy implications followed less from what Zhdanov declared in his published speech than from what was said and done during the confidential meetings afterward."

> He and Stalin's other current favorite, [Georgii Malenkov], explained to the assembled communist dignitaries that the purpose of their gathering was not merely the exchange of information and experiences mentioned in the original invitations but also the establishment of the Cominform as a coordinating center to ensure that they would fight the capitalist enemy together rather than separately.[27]

The belief that the enemy needed to be fought at all in 1947 reveals not only Soviet concerns about the commitment of American power and wealth to the defense and reconstruction of Europe, but also about Marxist faith in the certainty of conflict between oppressors and the oppressed. The Zhdanov speech reads almost like a call to battle, likening any concessions to the United States and "the imperialist camp" to the Munich crisis of 1938, and demanding that communist parties "head the resistance to the plans of imperialist expansion and aggression along every line."

Stalin, inadvertently perhaps, had created the situation he feared most. Certainly, it was seen as a direct challenge by many American observers; the U.S. chargé d'affaires in Moscow wrote to Secretary of State George Marshall that the speech and the establishment of the Cominform were "patently a declaration of political and economic war against the U.S. and everything the U.S. stands for in world affairs."[28] Even Craig Nation, who suggests that Stalin's goals were primarily defensive after 1945, admits that

Stalin's foreign policy was at the least insensitive to the special demands of maintaining a climate of cooperation in the difficult postwar environment. Despite his repeated pleas for accommodation, Stalin refused to surrender an "enemy image" of the leading capitalist powers, useful as a tool of internal mobilization as well as means for reinforcing ideological orthodoxy.[29]

As U.S. Ambassador to Moscow Walter Bedell Smith wrote at the time: "That the perceived threat was more in the eyes of the beholder and was in any case very much of his own making did not make it any less of a threat."[30] Stalin may not have wanted to engage the Americans in direct conflict at that particular time, but he believed that the Soviet view of history took little account of the desires of men: conflict would follow as surely as any other course of nature, and any Soviet leader would be, by that reckoning, a fool not to apprehend that natural reality. Thus, it is difficult to disagree with Mastny that by 1947 Stalin's actions and beliefs meant that "the forthcoming Cold War was both unintended and unexpected" but also that "it was predetermined all the same."[31]

The dawn of the Cold War can only be seen as a tragedy or a mistake if it is assumed that the Soviet Union could somehow have been accommodated within the structure of the international system and swayed from its aggressive aims. To believe that this was possible is to believe that Soviet goals were almost entirely opportunistic, little more than a territorial imperative devoid of any other objective but to satisfy a lust for ever larger chunks of real estate. But the desire to spread the reach of the Soviet Union was inherent in the very nature of the Soviet state. This desire may have found a special virulence in the way it was expressed by Stalin, but it was nonetheless a defining characteristic of the Soviet system that both predated and outlived him. As Robert Conquest later put it: "The Soviet assumption that all other political life-forms and beliefs were inherently and immutably hostile was the simple and central cause of [the] Cold War."[32]

This early period in the Soviet-American relationship should serve as a reminder even in the twenty-first century that a state that takes revolutionary ideology seriously, as Stalin did, will not and, indeed, *cannot* adopt the norms and values of the international system. In the end, the ideological state must either maintain its commitment to its founding mythology—the destruction of the status quo—and participate in international life solely as a tactical maneuver for short-term goals or accept the basic framework of the international state system and compromise its own ideological rectitude. Thirty-five years after Stalin's death, Mikhail Gorbachev would attempt to square this circle and fail. But the experience with Stalinism after World War II makes clear that it is dangerous to assume that a revolutionary state values peace in any sense that status quo powers do, as the West was soon to learn in a place that was of no conceivable value to the Kremlin but where Stalin chose to fight anyway: Korea.

"WE STARTED THE WAR. EVERYONE KNOWS THIS."

No emphasis on ideology or any other mode of analysis could have led to the prediction that war would break out on the Korean peninsula. What an emphasis on ideology provides, however, is a coherent explanation for why the Soviet Union and its allies would attack an American ally in an area that could hardly be considered strategically important.

In 1990, historian Bruce Cumings plaintively argued that the question of "who started the Korean War" was a pointless one that "should not be asked."[33] Fortunately, later historians rejected this helpless relativism and established a clear answer: responsibility for the war itself rests in Moscow, where Stalin gave Korean leader Kim Il Sung his blessing (and Soviet air support) for the June 1950 invasion of the South. The Soviets themselves knew who started the war, as the newly available account of a tense 1955 meeting of the Central Committee reveals. Nikita Khrushchev, in typically direct fashion, blurted out the truth in a confrontation with Foreign Minister Molotov over Stalin's policies.

> Viacheslav Mikhailovich, if you, as minister of foreign affairs, analyzed a whole series of our steps, [you would see that] we mobilized people against us. We started the Korean War. And what does this mean? Everyone knows this. . . . We started the war. Now we cannot in any way disentangle ourselves. For two years there has been no war. Who needed the war?[34]

As it turns out, Kim needed the war, or thought he did, to consolidate his hold on his own satrapy, first in the north and eventually over the entire peninsula. The more important question is why Stalin acquiesced in a minor gauleiter's dreams of grandeur and agreed to a plan that carried the risk of a world war.

The answer lies in Stalin's ideological ambitions and the frustration of those ambitions in Europe. Stalin, like other Soviet leaders of his generation, believed that the next wave of revolution would take place in the industrial nations of Europe, a firmly ideological view from which even the formation of NATO did not sway him. Nor was Stalin alone, as Mastny points out.

> Moscow was long in recognizing the Western alliance as a force in its own right rather than an American tool. Victims of their Marxist preconcep-

tions, Soviet leaders could not disentangle their thinking from their caricature of NATO as a Wall Street creature rent by contradictions between competing capitalist interests. Presiding over an empire held together by force, they could hardly be expected to grasp the Europeans' readiness to rally voluntarily behind American leadership and cooperate in their own interest rather than on command from Washington.[35]

But by 1950, Soviet momentum in Europe had been blunted. From the rearming of Germany to the failure of the Berlin blockade and the creation of NATO, Soviet attempts to increase Moscow's influence and to erode Washington's position had been frustrated. The major capitalist powers, far from falling into squabbling among themselves, had formed a united front against the Soviet Union. Commenting on Austria, where capitalism had made gains despite the presence of the Red Army, Stalin concluded: "Europe is still not ready for socialism."[36]

There is little evidence that Stalin thought much about Asia or anywhere else in the Third World after the one disastrous Soviet foray into Chinese affairs in the 1920s.[37] (He had no interest in Ho Chi Minh, for example, and by Khrushchev's account treated him dismissively and even rudely when Ho was in Moscow in 1949.)[38] Initially, Korea hardly seemed the most promising place for the Soviet Union to recapture the revolutionary initiative that was dwindling away in Europe. Indeed, it is important to note just how pessimistic and hardheaded Stalin was about the situation in Korea before 1950, if only to illustrate the distance his ideological preconceptions eventually carried him. Kim had made earlier requests to invade and had been rebuffed by Stalin, whose best advice in the late 1940s was to let South Korea's Syngman Rhee attack *first*, after which, he assured Kim, "your move will be supported and understood by everyone."[39] Kim assured Stalin repeatedly that he could win quickly in Korea and, more incredibly, that Koreans in the south were eagerly awaiting his liberating war: "I can't sleep at night because I am thinking about the unification of the whole country," he told the Soviet ambassador, but "if the cause is postponed, then I may lose the confidence of the Korean people."[40] Why Kim thought he had that confidence is another matter, but his Soviet patrons were unmoved: both the Soviet embassy in North Korea and Stalin's advisors in Moscow treated Kim's sunny scenarios with evident skepticism and even disdain.

But Soviet reluctance would fade after the West's *annis horribilis* of 1949, in which several nightmares came true, including the two most relevant to Korea: Mao Zedong's communists took control of the most populous nation on earth, and the Soviets detonated their own atomic bomb far earlier than anyone had expected. The sudden appearance of a Chinese communist regime, coupled with the breaking of the American nuclear monopoly, put Asia in play as a new theater in the Cold War. Soviet strategy in the far East until 1949 had recognized the USSR's relative weakness in the region and sought to keep the West placated in Asia by supporting a weak, pro-Western China while Moscow concentrated on the more important contest in Europe.

> On Stalin's side, what mattered most was the coming confrontation between communism and capitalism, the inevitable Third World War that would deliver the death blow to world imperialism. He wanted to enter this war with maximum military readiness and reliable allies. His central priority was to create the conditions under which only Moscow could determine the time and place of the showdown. As a result, during the immediate postwar years, he did everything possible to avert a direct clash with the US over China. For him, the time and place were wrong. . . . Stalin regarded Europe as the main battleground.[41]

Mao's victory, however, changed all that. Whatever the strategic value of an alliance with the new People's Republic of China, how could Stalin possibly refuse an alliance with a new communist power on his own doorstep? (Besides, better to control events than to be surprised by them: Stalin had already learned a painful lesson in Yugoslavia about losing control of a communist ally, and he was no doubt determined that there would be no Asian Tito complicating his plans elsewhere.) With the Sino-Soviet alliance in place by early 1950, the Soviets would now actively limit Western power in Asia by bolstering a strong, unified, and harshly anti-American regime in China.

Asia, in the wake of the Chinese communist victory, now seemed to be the more promising arena in the fight against imperialism. John Gaddis, noting Stalin's "geriatric romanticism," rightly describes Stalin as overtaken in this period by an "ideological euphoria" that "allowed Kim Il-Sung to talk him into something he had earlier refused to do," namely, allowing Kim to attack South Korea.[42] It is true that there were numerous developments in the international situation that made the use of force in Asia tempting, regardless of ideology. But as propitious as these developments were, they were not the cause of the Korean War; Stalin was no more prone than any other world leader to wake up, check the prevailing winds, and decide it was a good day for war. Besides, from a strategic viewpoint, Korea was not a gem worth the price of war. The USSR already had a Pacific presence on its own and a new (and huge) Asian ally in China to boot. Something more important than real estate was at stake; this would be Stalin's last crusade, a final plunge into combat with imperialism. The geopolitical situation in 1950 may have made the Korean attack more tempting, but only an understanding of Stalin's ideological precepts and their relationship to his restless need to counter the standoff in Europe can explain why the attack took place at all.

If Stalin's motives were highly ideological, his methods were pragmatic to the point of cynical. The key, for Stalin, was to support the Korean attack without involving the USSR in an ill-timed war with the United States. (That would come one day, of course, but more likely in the wake of a world war begun among the imperialists themselves.) Several things contributed to Stalin's sense that war with America, particularly over a region in Asia, was increasingly unlikely, including the obvious effect of the Soviet bomb. Secretary of State Dean Acheson did not help matters in early 1950 when he gave a speech delineating America's concerns in the Pacific but left out reference to Korea. Kim was absolutely certain that the United States would not fight to protect South Korea, but Stalin rightly refused to place his faith in Kim Il Sung's strategic acumen, and this meant finding an insurance policy in case Kim failed. Kim could expect no direct help from the Soviet Union if things went sour, Stalin warned. "If you should get kicked in the teeth," he told Kim in April 1950, "I shall not lift a finger to help you."[43]

The answer was to obligate Moscow's new Chinese ally to the Korean affair. From Stalin's point of view, a situation in which three communist allies went to war but only the frontline Asian states would fight had to be considered nearly perfect: if Kim succeeded, the entire continent of Asia, from the Soviet Far East to Indochina, would be Red, and both China and Korea would owe their continued security to the USSR. A communist victory in Korea would also pile one more defeat on the West, coming so soon after the Chinese revolution. If Kim failed, then the Chinese would have to stand and deliver, and show just what kind of communists they really were. In any case, the Chinese guarantee would occupy Beijing and at least forestall the much hairier possibility of war over Taiwan; while no one thought the Americans would return to save Korea, there was considerably less confidence that Washington would sacrifice Chiang Kai-shek so easily. The mystery, then, is not why Stalin in 1950 saw so much promise in the Korean adventure, but rather why the Chinese were willing to risk their own considerable gains at Stalin's behest.

The Chinese reaction to Kim's plans reveals that the new People's Republic was itself a budding "ideological state." Even if we not did have the actual pronouncements and telegrams of the Chinese leaders of the time to help reach the conclusion that this was an ideological issue, there is little else save sheer stupidity that could explain Beijing's willingness to be the Soviet ace in the hole under such questionable circumstances. Mao and his fellow leaders were not yet fully in control of China itself in 1950, and Mao himself had been in Moscow asking for help in conquering Taiwan at the same time Kim was there seeking the green light for the Korean invasion. Now, Kim's plans would trump Mao's, and if he was wrong, China could find itself at war with the United States. In theory, a Chinese-American war could trigger the Sino-Soviet defense treaty and spark World War III, but Soviet reticence to provide direct assistance—the very reason Kim had to get a Chinese commitment in the first place—had to cast doubt on whether the USSR would save either of its Asian allies if general war broke out.

But in fairness to the Chinese leaders, the whole business probably seemed less risky than it turned out to be later. Beijing believed "the Americans will not enter a third world war for such a small territory." Moscow was somewhat less sure, but there was no serious expectation of a global war over Korea.[44] Even Syngman Rhee, after all, did not believe that the United States was willing to fight for South Korea.[45] Still, the possibility that the United States would intervene could not be ruled out, and there was always the risk that an American return to Asia would include rearming the Japanese. Also, Stalin had put Beijing in a bind, by shifting the burden of the final decision. "If the Chinese comrades disagree," Stalin insisted, "the decision must be postponed till a new discussion."[46] The Chinese were faced with either accepting a major obligation to the Koreans or looking like they had vetoed a plan for communist expansion that had already been approved by Stalin himself.

Still, it was ideological affinity rather than lead-pipe diplomacy that initially convinced the Chinese to sign on. (The arm-twisting and re-crimination between Moscow, Pyongyang, and Beijing would only come later, when the whole enterprise was in tatters.) There is no evidence that Mao in particular was anything but supportive of the widest possible spread of revolutionary activity in Asia; this is the same Mao, after all, who had already decided to send assistance to Ho Chi Minh in Vietnam only months before the invasion of South Korea.[47] All in all, China had little to gain from supporting the Korean attack, but much to lose if they opposed it. As Gaddis points out, intervention in Korea was for Mao "an investment in geopolitical, ideological, and personal credibility."[48]

When disaster struck, however, the Chinese leadership found its revolutionary zeal draining away as United Nations troops began to charge up the Korean peninsula toward China's borders. As Kim's military position collapsed, he cabled Stalin begging for Soviet help; Stalin, as good as his word, cashed in his Chinese insurance policy, cabling Beijing literally within minutes after reading Kim's plea. The initial Chinese response was to try to wriggle out of the Korean guarantee. Still, Mao himself was eager to fight. In an earlier draft of a response, he promised to send troops to fight for the sake of the Asian revolutions against the United States and its "running dog," Rhee.[49]

This telegram was not sent, however. "Having thought this situation over thoroughly," the Chinese leadership said in the eventual cable to Moscow, in a combination of obviousness and understatement, "we now consider that such actions may entail extremely serious consequences."[50] Apparently at the behest of other members of the Politburo, Mao argued that China was not quite ready to fight and that the civil war was unfinished—both true, and good reasons that Beijing should never have agreed to the whole escapade in the first place. There was even a veiled warning that Chinese intervention could lead to war with the United States, which would in turn obligate the Soviet Union to fulfill its treaty obligations to China and join the fray.

Stalin's response to this Chinese wavering was a combination of ideological goading and blustery military analysis. He attacked the argument about World War III head-on:

> Should we be afraid of this possibility? In my opinion we should not, because together, we will be stronger than the United States and Great Britain, whereas none of the other European capitalist states . . . possess any serious military forces at all. If war is inevitable, then let it be waged now, and not in a few years when Japanese militarism will be restored as an ally of the USA and when the USA and Japan will have a readymade bridgehead on the continent in the form of the entire Korea run by Syngman Rhee.[51]

Although the Chinese relented and offered to send even more men than they had originally promised, elements of the Beijing leadership clearly wanted to avoid getting mired in the Korean disaster, and a delegation was sent to Moscow. Stalin was in no mood to hear Chinese excuses and told his guests point-blank: "That you do not want to send troops to Korea is your decision, but socialism in Korea will collapse within a very short period of time."[52] According to one account, Zhou Enlai "actually gasped" at the realization that Stalin was "wash[ing] his hands of the war."[53] This was no bluff, either: as Stalin told the Politburo, "So what? Let the United States of America be our neighbors in the Far East. They will come there, but we shall not fight them now. We are not ready to fight. If Kim Il Sung fails, we are not going to participate with our troops. Let it be."[54]

The Chinese, of course, did intervene. (As an aside, it is now plain that the Yalu River, it turns out, was not the line in the sand that prompted Chinese intervention, which had been planned and discussed long before the United Nations ever reached it.) As part of the bargain, they were given Soviet air support, despite Stalin's considerable fear that any evidence of Soviet participation would spark a war with the United States. The measures Stalin tried to enforce to this end are nearly comical; at one point, he wanted to forbid Soviet pilots from speaking anything but Korean in the air, until it was pointed out to him that there were precious few Red Air Force pilots who spoke Korean.[55] Still, in November 1950, Soviet pilots had their first engagements, and for the first time in the Cold War American and Soviet military forces engaged in direct combat—although only one side knew it.

Stalin's willingness to give up so quickly on the Korean War reflected the contrast between his romanticized, overblown hopes and the more disappointing actual events on the ground. His euphoria about the Korean adventure faded once a grand and humiliating victory over the South was out of reach. The failure of the North Korean attack apprently depressed him and contradicted his beliefs and expectations at a deeper level than geopolitics. Even when the Chinese counterattacked in late 1950 with great success, Volkogonov tells us, "it was clear to him: he had already taken his shot and missed." Stalin was old and tired, worn down from a lifetime of struggle, and now he had lost his last great battle: once victory in this final crusade was out of reach, "he simply lost interest in it."[56] Not that he would allow his junior allies to negoti-ate their way out of the conflict, of course. As he told Mao in June 1951, "a drawn out war, in the first place, gives the possibility to the Chinese troops to study contemporary warfare on the field of battle and in the second place shakes up the Truman regime in America and harms the military prestige of the Anglo-American troops."[57]

KOREA AND THE MEANING OF "PEACE"

Criticizing American Cold War policy in 1950 is always somewhat unfair, since U.S. policymakers could see little more of the inner work-ings of the Kremlin than they could of the dark side of the moon. Perhaps if the Americans had taken more seriously the possibility that Stalin would not settle for stable spheres of influence in Europe and Asia, the Americans might never have invited Stalin to join in the occupation of Korea in 1945, nor promised to withdraw U.S. forces in 1949. Barring such signals of resolve (which assuredly would have led to President Truman being labeled the initiator of the Cold War in Asia), there is little to suggest that the Korean attack could have been pre-vented. In the wake of the Chinese communist victory in 1949 and the signing of the Sino-Soviet defense treaty, it could be argued that the Americans should have thought more seriously about the possibility that the Kremlin was no longer willing to accept the postwar arrange-ment in East Asia. This would be a labored criticism, given that Stalin's actions in the West—the Berlin blockade had only recently concluded—logically kept U.S. attention focused on Europe.

But there is one lesson that might be learned from the Korean attack that is as applicable to future cold wars as it was to the world of 1950: an opponent who takes revolutionary ideology seriously cannot be counted upon to value peace in the same way that status quo powers do. Although the sanctity of the Yalta accords would not be seriously questioned by American leaders until Ronald Reagan's presidency, it should have been clear early in the contest with the Soviet Union that such agreements are unsustainable because the two sides do not have a shared understanding of their meaning. It was logically impossible for a state like the USSR to fully accept an agreement that enshrines the existing international system, the nation-state, and even bourgeois concepts of law and justice other than as an expedient. The goal is to dismantle those structures, not to bless them. One cannot be committed to Marxism and to Yalta at the same time, and in the end, one or the other must, to use Stalin's words, go to hell.

Korea also serves as a cautionary tale about the dangers of "mirror imaging" an opponent's strategy, particularly by basing calculations of the enemy's likely moves on the raw logic of realism. That war in Korea was likely was not the question. Both Rhee and Kim were itching to attack each other, and the peninsula was hardly an outpost of stability in the Pacific region. Cumings has argued that by 1950 the logic for both Koreas was to see "who would be stupid enough to move first," but Kathryn Weathersby has rightly countered that "the end of the story is that the Soviet Union eventually decided to support its client's plan for military reunification while the United States did not."[58] The salient point is not that war broke out, but that it came as part of a communist coalition effort to expand the reach of their own social system. From a realist perspective, there was little to be gained in Korea, especially when coupled with the small, if finite, risk of a third world war. But geostrategic gain was not the goal of the June 1950 sneak attack. Rather, the gain of another ally, another addition to the communist camp of forced converts, was the impetus for war.

In this, the communists were to be disappointed. The "geoideological" temptation led the three partners into an adventure that took the lives of tens of thousands of Western soldiers (and hundreds of thousands of Chinese and North Koreans), but in the process showed little gain for all the bloodshed. Although Stalin could claim that his steady helming of the Korean events had, as the expression goes, turned "fish soup back into an aquarium," in the end the war was a defeat for Soviet foreign policy. Americans have long internalized the idea that Korea was, at best, a draw, but it was nothing of the sort. A group of historians put it this way in 1994:

From the short-term Soviet viewpoint, Stalin emerged as the net winner from the Korean War. A bloody line had been drawn between China and the United States, and the possibility of their reconciliation had all but disappeared. North Korea had survived as a socialist state within the Soviet security zone. In the final count, the USSR's casualties were low, and its forces, when introduced, had gained substantial experience in modern warfare. Over the long run however, the real interests of the Soviet state were badly served. The war provoked an unprecedented buildup of American nuclear forces and militarized the Cold War. Soviet security declined, and the USSR's economic and intellectual isolation in a hostile world was to shackle all its modernization efforts for decades to come.[59]

If Stalin had turned to Asia because communist momentum in Europe had been slowed, he was to find that in Asia it had been, however belatedly, stopped cold for the moment. South Korea remained intact and would never again be as weak as it was in the summer of 1950. The United States would return to the region and stay (American troops are stationed in Korea even now); more to the point, there could no longer be any illusions in the West about the lengths to which the communist bloc would go to expand its reach. Indeed, an equally interesting question about the outbreak of the Korean War is not whether U.S. policymakers should have been able to predict it, but why Eastern leaders were so blinded by ideological fervor that they could not anticipate the force of the Western response and the consequent long-term damage to communist goals it entailed.

Before leaving this early period of the Cold War, it is interesting to consider what the Soviet Union, too, should have learned from the Korean disaster. Despite Khrushchev's thundering at Molotov about the stupidity of Stalin's support for the Korean War, later Soviet leaders learned little from the war. (Khrushchev was more likely looking to take Molotov, a political enemy, down a notch for the war's outcome rather than expressing any guilt over its origins.) Nor did the war dissuade the bellicose Kim from his dreams of forceful reunification. In 1985, he came to the Soviets with a shopping list that included jets, artillery, communications equipment, and some 500 helicopters for special forces raids. Volkogonov, then a senior Soviet general, was present and remembers thinking: "Have the leaders in Pyongyang learned nothing from the awful war in 1950–1953, that cost the country tens of thousands of lives?"[60]

Stalin's successors in fact would outdo Stalin in their willingness to involve the USSR in adventures much farther from Soviet borders. It could not be otherwise; the pressure of ideological expansion was inherent in the Soviet system and was not, itself, a Stalinist phenomenon, even if Stalin gave it an especially violent character in Korea. "The imprint of Bolshevik radicalism," Volkogonov wrote, "[was] on all of Khrushchev's foreign policy activity, although there can be no doubt that he sincerely wanted peace and strove, in his own way, to attain it."[61] Brezhnev, too, would cast Soviet forces far from home in the ongoing attempt to enshrine the legitimacy of the Soviet system, vindicate the Revolution, and overawe the USSR's increasingly numerous enemies.

Moscow in later years was not seeking war in the Third World but, like Stalin in Korea, hoping for conquest on the cheap. As it would turn out, these efforts rarely resulted in a clear enhancement of Soviet security, and they were certainly not cheap. They were not even evident ideological conflicts, although the Kremlin was incapable of seeing them in other than those terms. After Korea, of course, the United States became increasingly vigilant—critics would say obsessively so—about Soviet moves around the globe, which in itself was a problem for the Soviet Union, given America's superior capacity to project and sustain force almost anywhere it chose. This constant dueling with the United States took a toll on the Soviets, not only in terms of material drain, but also psychologically, in that it convinced the Kremlin that there was almost nowhere that Washington would not go if it meant countering Soviet influence.

The "two camps" doctrine declared the Soviet Union's rhetorical commitment to the Cold War; the Korean War turned rhetoric to military reality. As the Soviet-American conflict wore on, soldiers from Eastern and Western coalitions would meet again on remote battlefields. Meanwhile, the growing and eventually overwhelming fear of nuclear war would lead the superpowers to try to isolate their own relationship from the struggles they were engaged in elsewhere. Soviet and American commitments began to multiply across the globe, an expensive and tiring contest that necessarily placed more of a burden on the weaker Soviet economy. Although American opposition to these Soviet moves could be (and often was) criticized as wasteful, it was the American presence that made the cost of many of these regional adventures an even greater strain on the USSR. Like Korea, these Third World outposts were of questionable strategic value. But the ideological compulsion was too strong, and the Soviets could not ignore "revolutionary" or "socialist" movements in Vietnam, Cuba, Nicaragua, Angola, Somalia, Ethiopia, Grenada, or anywhere else—even if, as we will see in the following chapters, they would have much preferred to set their own agendas and timetables rather than have events forced upon by their enemies and allies alike.

Stalin has emerged from the history books over the years as a cunning realist, a nationalist, an opportunist, a sly old man who supposedly would have avoided so many of the quixotic Third World quests embarked on by his supposedly less intelligent and more excitable successors. But as the unremittingly hostile "two camps" doctrine and the attack on South Korea show, the "geriatric romantic" was not so different from the generation of leaders who followed him. The gray mediocrities who one after another led the Soviet Union into the morass of foreign entanglements were not bumblers deviating from some sort of Stalinist realism; they were heirs to a system that would die if it were not kept in constant, outward motion.

NOTES

1. Beatrice Heuser, "Stalin as Hitler's Successor: Western Interpretations of the Soviet Threat," in Beatrice Heuser and Robert O'Neill, eds, *Securing Peace in Europe, 1945–62* (New York: St. Martin's Press, 1992), pp. 31–32.

2. "Stalin's Conversations with Chinese Leaders," *Cold War International History Bulletin* 6–7, Winter 1995/1996, p. 8.

3. Leszek Kolakowski, "Marxist Roots of Stalinism," in Robert Tucker, ed., *Stalinism* (New York: Norton, 1977), p. 296.

4. See Martin Malia, "Foreword," in Stephane Courtois, et al., *The Black Book of Communism* (Cambridge, MA: Harvard University Press, 1999), p. xix.

5. Dmitrii Volkogonov, *Lenin* (New York: The Free Press, 1994), pp. 473–474.

6. Vladimir Zubok and Constantine Pleshakov, *Inside the Kremlin's Cold War: From Stalin to Khrushchev* (Cambridge, MA: Harvard University Press, 1996), p. 13.

7. "Stalin and the Korean War," unpublished manuscript, The Dmitrii A. Volkogonov Papers, Library of Congress, Washington, box 12, folder 7, p. 3.

8. While some of these assertions about Stalin's "defensive" orientation are plainly partisan, there are also some reasonably well-argued works to this effect. R. Craig Nation, for example, makes a plausible case that the creation of the Cominform "had a narrowly defensive character" and that "its first purpose was to unify the European communist movement around a general line supportive of Moscow in view of the climate of hostility engendered by the Cold War." R. Craig Nation, *Black Earth, Red Star: A History of Soviet Security Policy, 1917–1991* (Ithaca, NY: Cornell University Press, 1993), p. 176. For a discussion of revisionism as it relates in particular to the Marshall Plan, see Scott Parrish, "The Turn Toward Confrontation: The Soviet Reaction to the Marshall Plan, 1947," Cold War International History Project Working Papers #9, available at the CWIHP Virtual Library at http://cwihp.si.edu/cwihplib.nsf.

9. Quoted in Robert Conquest, *Reflections on a Ravaged Century* (New York: Norton, 2000), p. 154.

10. Zubok and Pleshakov, p. 18.

11. Quoted in Milovan Djilas, *Conversations with Stalin* (New York: Harcourt Brace, 1962), p. 74.

12. William C. Wohlforth, *The Elusive Balance* (Ithaca, NY: Cornell University Press, 1993), p. 66.

13. These and other quotations from the Novikov report are from *Origins of the Cold War: The Novikov, Kennan and Roberts "Long Telegrams" of 1946* (Washington: U.S. Institute of Peace, 1991).

14. Wohlforth, p. 66.

15. Zubok and Pleshakov, p. 53.

16. See Volkogonov, "Stalin and the Korean War."

17. Zubok and Pleshakov, p. 53.

18. Zubok and Pleshakov, p. 53.

19. This and other quotes from the Zhdanov speech are from Gale Stokes, ed., *From Stalinism to Pluralism: A Documentary History of Eastern Europe Since 1945* (New York: Oxford University Press, 1991).

20. Nation, p. 174.

21. As Zubok and Pleshakov put it, "for many East European intellectuals, the report that Zhdanov gave on the new Soviet foreign policy at the meeting in Poland was a signal of doom; among the advocates of the Communist millennium it was received as a new gospel after years of ideological famine." Zubok and Pleshakov, p. 111.

22. Zubok and Pleshakov, p. 111.

23. Wohlforth, p. 71.

24. See N. I. Egorova, "Evropeiskaia bezopastnost' i 'ugroza' NATO v otsenkakh stalinskogo rukovodstva," in I. V. Gaiduk, N. I. Egorova, and A. O. Chubar'ian, eds., *Stalinskoie desiatiletie kholodnoi voiny: fakty i gypotezy* (Moscow: Nauka, 1999), p. 58.

25. Interview with Aleksandr Orlov, Moscow, February 4, 2000.

26. Adam Ulam, in his seminal work *Expansion and Coexistence*, wrote only that the creation of the Cominform "was caused primarily by certain internal needs of the Communist bloc, but the Soviet spokesmen Zhdanov and Malenkov utilized its initial meeting...to dramatize the division of the world into two camps...." Adam Ulam, *Expansion and Coexistence: Soviet Foreign Policy 1917–1973*, 2nd ed. (New York: Holt Rhinehart and Winston, 1974), p. 449.

27. Vojtech Mastny, *The Cold War and Soviet Insecurity: The Stalin Years* (New York: Oxford University Press, 1996), pp. 31–32.

28. Quoted in John L. Gaddis, *Russia, the Soviet Union and the United States: An Interpretive History* (New York: McGraw Hill, 1990), p. 194.

29. Nation, p. 168.

30. Quoted in Mastny, *The Cold War and Soviet Insecurity*, p. 29.

31. Mastny, pp. 23-29.

32. Conquest, p. 152.

33. Bruce Cumings, *The Origins of the Korean War: The Roaring of the Cataract, 1947-1950* (Princeton, NJ: Princeton University Press, 1990), p. 621.

34. Quoted in Vladislav Zubok, "CPSU Plenums, Leadership Struggles, and Soviet Cold War Politics," *Cold War International History Project Bulletin* 10, March 1998, p. 30.

35. Vojtech Mastny, "Did NATO Win the Cold War?" *Foreign Affairs*, May/June 1999, p. 180.

36. Quoted in Sergei Goncharov, John Lewis, and Xue Litai, *Uncertain Partners: Stalin, Mao and the Korean War* (Stanford, CA: Stanford University Press, 1993), p. 72.

37. Courtois, et al., p. 280.

38. "Stalin," Khrushchev later wrote, "didn't believe the Vietnamese could prevail, so he treated Ho insultingly." *Khrushchev Remembers: The Glasnost Tapes* (Boston: Little, Brown, 1990), p. 155.

39. Quoted in Evgueni Bajanov, "Assessing the Politics of the Korean War, 1949–1951," *Cold War International History Bulletin* 6-7, http://cwihp.si.edu/.

40. John Gaddis, *We Now Know* (New York: Oxford University Press, 1994), p. 73.

41. Goncharov, Lewis, and Xue Litai, p. 207.

42. Gaddis, *We Now Know*, p. 83.

43. Goncharov, et al., p. 145.

44. Kathryn Weathersby, "New Findings on the Korean War, Translation and Commentary," *Cold War International History Bulletin* 3, http://cwihp.si.edu/.

45. Gaddis, *We Now Know,* p. 73.

46. Quoted in Bajanov.

47. Gaddis, *We Now Know,* p. 161.

48. Gaddis, *We Now Know,* p. 160.

49. Chen Jian, *Mao's China and the Cold War* (Chapel Hill, NC: University of North Carolina Press, 2001), p. 56.

50. Alexandre Mansourov, "Stalin, Mao, Kim, and China's Decision to Enter the Korean War, Sept. 16–Oct. 15, 1950: New Evidence from Russian Archives," *Cold War International History Bulletin* 6–7, http://cwihp.si.edu/.

51. Quoted in Mansourov.

52. Quoted in Chen Jian, "The Sino-Soviet Alliance and China's Entry into the Korean War," *Cold War International Project Working Paper* no. 1, http://cwihp.si.edu/.

53. Goncharov, et al., p. 189.

54. Strobe Talbott, trans., *Khrushchev Remembers* (Boston: Little, Brown, 1970), p. 147.

55. Orlov, interview.

56. "Stalin and the Korean War," unpublished manuscript, The Dmitrii A. Volkogonov Papers, Library of Congress, Washington, box 12, folder 7, p. 3.

57. Cited in Kathryn Weathersby, "New Russian Documents on the Korean War," *Cold War International History Project Bulletin* 6–7, Winter 1995–1996, p. 59.

58. See "Bruce Cumings and Kathryn Weathersby: An Exchange on Korean War Origins," *Cold War International History Bulletin* 6–7, http://cwihp.si.edu/.

59. Goncharov, et al., p. 202.

60. Dmitrii Volkogonov, *Sem' vozhdei* (Moscow: Novosti, 1995), vol. II, p. 254.

61. Volkogonov, *Sem' vozhdei*, vol. I, p. 415.

4

Contesting the World

The future competition with the United States will take place not in Europe, and not in the Atlantic Ocean. It will take place in Africa, and in Latin America. We will compete for every piece of land, for every country.

—Yuri Andropov, 1965

DISTANT WARS, FROM ATHENS TO AMERICA

When Athens, flush with utter confidence in the superiority of its own system, embarked on its great conflict with Sparta in the fifth century B.C., the Athenian leader Pericles cautioned his fellow citizens that he was "more afraid of our own blunders than of the enemy's devices," and warned them not to engage in "schemes of fresh conquest," but instead to let Sparta exhaust itself in a fruitless war against their impregnable and prosperous city. Time was on the side of the Athenian Empire, he said: against its powerful economy and command of the seas, the Spartans could do nothing so long as Athens concentrated on keeping its imperial system in order rather than reaching beyond the safety of the Aegean and seeking new conflicts elsewhere. Years later, however, long after the war had settled into a stalemate, Athens strayed far from its home waters and tried to subdue Sicily, not only to gain Sicily's resources for itself but to preempt any possible alliances with the Spartans. Pericles' warnings should have been heeded: the result was a military and strategic disaster for Athens that eviscerated much of the Athenian navy and took the lives of some of its most prominent commanders.

The Sicilian Expedition has at times been presented as a cautionary tale for America, who during the Cold War also learned the painful limits of its ability to control events far from home. The attempted conquest of Sicily and the consequent military disaster that Athens suffered has stood as a lesson in great power hubris and the unpredictable tendency of democracies to go off on ill-considered crusades. Many Westerners have argued this was exactly what plagued the United States in its continual forays against Third World communist movements, nowhere more so than in Vietnam after 1965. Like the Athenians at Sicily, these critics saw a great power led to entanglement in a costly commitment by its own overblown rhetoric. There is an uncomfortable truth in that image: when John F. Kennedy said in 1961 that America would "bear any burden" and "pay any price" to assure the survival of liberty, it is hard to imagine that most Americans of the time saw that promise being kept in the jungles of Southeast Asia less than five years later. But to a generation of U.S. leaders who had seen, in the previous two decades, the rise and fall of Hitler, the loss of China, and the trauma of Korea, the issue was not Kennedy's rhetoric. It was, in the end, about standing and fighting against what seemed at the time to be the relentless expansion of communism.

What, then, is to be learned from the Soviet and American contests in the Third World? Is contesting peripheral areas a reasonable strategy in a cold war, or is it a diversion, a waste of resources better directed toward shoring up the domestic economy and strengthening defenses in the primary areas of conflict? Athens actually survived its terrible defeat at Sicily but eventually lost the war through arrogance and carelessness. America obviously fared better, but what effect did Soviet and American "Sicilian Expeditions" have on the Cold War?

INTERNATIONALISM IN THE BOLSHEVIK MANNER: IDEOLOGY AND EXPANSION

It is impossible (and pointless) to discuss the wisdom of confronting an enemy on the periphery without asking why the enemy is there in the first place. Certainly, during the Cold War both superpowers at times fell into a reflexive pattern that can be summed up as "whither thou goest, I will go." Aleksandr Yakovlev put it another way:

> The Cold War had a rather primitive logic: the worse for the USA, the better for the Soviet Union, and vice versa. Washington and Moscow rigorously

followed that logic. There are plenty of examples: Korea, Vietnam, the Cuban crisis, the Near East. . . . In the 1960s, and especially in the 1970s the Soviet Union found itself drawn into several expensive and senseless adventures. Almost every time, in one form or another, the United States was right there.[1]

Anatolii Dobrynin, meanwhile, says that some in the Kremlin "were flattered at our country's involvement in faraway conflicts because they believed it put the Soviet Union on an equal footing with the United States as a superpower," an idea he derides now as "hare-brained."[2] But there was also more, he adds, to the competition in the Third World than shadowing each other's steps. Underlying the burst of Soviet activity outside of Europe "was a simple but primitive idea of international solidarity, which meant doing our duty in the anti-imperialist struggle. It made no difference that often it had nothing to do with a genuine national liberation movement but amounted to interference on an ideological basis into the internal affairs of countries where domestic factions were struggling for power."[3]

Whatever the potential value of their acquisition—and it is almost impossible now to take seriously the strategic importance of Angola or Grenada—the primary motivation for Soviet expansion was the ideological need to retain some sense of forward motion outside the USSR. Many of the putative "socialist" and "communist" revolutions Moscow supported were nothing of the kind and in the end would amount to little when the homeland of the Revolution fell upon hard times. But to an ideological state like the USSR, even so small a nation as Grenada or so poor a country as Ethiopia became priceless, sought as one more medal to pin on the Soviet chest and to fend off the gnawing doubt, the "revolutionary inferiority complex," as Georgii Arbatov dubbed it, that the Soviet system was a failure both at home and in its appeal abroad.[4]

What this meant in practice is that once the Soviets moved away from their area of immediate empire in Europe, they were limited in their ability to discriminate among revolutionary movements. Originally, of course, the sparks from the Bolshevik inferno were supposed to float west and ignite similar fires in Germany. The German revolt, like others in Eastern Europe in the interwar period, was crushed quickly. Later, with the end of World War II, the averting of communist regimes in France, Italy, and Greece, and the establishment of NATO and the Warsaw Pact, Europe was to all intents and purposes played out as a theater of future revolution. If the Soviet Union was to be the patron of Marxist-Leninist uprisings, it would have to find them elsewhere, and accordingly, the Soviets took an interest in activities all across the Third World. Some of these movements were of questionable ideological character, coming as they did from such backward societies that an abstraction like "Marxism-Leninism" had about as much meaning to the average person as astrophysics. But Moscow was so anxious to bring these disparate revolutions under its wing—and later, to keep China from doing the same—that it invented a new term, calling such regimes "of socialist orientation" rather than "socialist" per se.[5]

This increasing Soviet tendency to intervene in world events "even if these developments are territorially remote," Gromyko told the Supreme Soviet in 1969, was driven by a sense of obligation imposed by "responsibility to the Soviet people and our internationalist duty."[6] Gromyko's language was more than boilerplate, since Soviet moves are almost inexplicable otherwise; later analyses have tried to paint a veneer of realism on Soviet policy in the Third World without much success. In his analysis of Soviet policy in Africa, Odd Arne Westad notes that too much evidence points away from realist explanations, including the fact that "the Soviet officials who designed the intervention in southern Africa were driven by ideas of promoting their model of development abroad."[7] Indeed, there is nothing so damaging to realist theories of international politics than leaders who refuse to act like realists, and chief among them was the powerful Kremlin ideology chief, Mikhail Suslov, described by Dobrynin as "convinced that all struggle in the Third World had an ideological basis: imperialism against communism and socialism. Under the slogan of solidarity, he and his zealous followers in the Party managed to involve the Politburo in many Third World adventures."[8]

Not only did Soviet involvement in the Third World add little, in any strategic sense, to the Soviet global position, but aid to such financial sinkholes as Cuba and other clients helped to ruin the Soviet economy in the bargain. At times, this created situations that verged on comedy. The Soviets felt it was important, for example, to maintain the illusion that the USSR and Cuba were two friendly socialist states trading oil for sugar. The Cubans, unfortunately, were having trouble coming up with enough sugar to meet their end of the bargain, and this resulted in a convoluted scheme in which the USSR guaranteed financing for Cuban sugar purchases—from capitalist France, no less—so that the Cubans could meet their quota of sugar deliveries *back* to the Soviet Union. This in turn meant that the Soviets were not only giving the Cubans cheap oil, but were running a risk of having to pay off the sugar debt to the French in hard currency if the Cubans defaulted.[9] (Put another way, the Soviets were backing foreign loans so the Cubans could trade French sugar for Soviet oil at below-market prices.) Although massive weapons sales to the Third World offset some of these costs, the burden was so grave that increasing Soviet entanglements around the world became a nearly suicidal policy in the long term. Yakovlev, looking back at the costs of the relentless search for new clients, wrote in 1994 that the damage to the USSR was so severe he hoped the new Russia would learn from its mistakes: "God save us from what was called internationalism in the Bolshevik manner."[10]

This drive to expand, so strong that it could produce such impressive levels of self-delusion in Moscow, was neither the product of a particular leader nor of some nebulous historical hangover from Russia's imperial past. (The cliché about the Russian lust for "warm-water ports" was heard in the West so often during the Cold War that the Soviets could be forgiven if they wondered whether they *should* have oriented their foreign policy around water temperatures.) Expansion, like violence, was part of the Soviet identity, an expression of a "long tradition of 'Red imperialism' that had existed since the earliest days of the Communist International, establishing an absolute duty to aid the international proletariat."[11]

While the Soviets never lost sight of the primacy of Europe in their foreign policy, neither were they able to shed their attachment to revolutionary regimes in the Third World. Support for these regimes spoke to the core of the Soviet identity as a revolutionary state, and there was no way to brush their entreaties aside and still lay claim to being the Marxist Vatican. Indeed, the Soviet leadership was often so keen to believe that their assistance was required by genuine revolutionaries that they would find them—or create them—even where they did not exist. Yakovlev is scathingly critical of the fact that the Kremlin would attach itself to almost anyone in the Third World who declared a "socialist orientation," noting that "the friends of the Soviet Union included 'Africa's first Marxist,' and later emperor-cannibal Bokassa, the Ugandan tyrant Idi Amin, the merciless murderer from Ethiopia Haile Mariam Mengistu. It's possible to go on enumerating names from, I hope, days that are long behind us. The choice of company," he adds bitterly, "was the most reactionary, the most sinister."[12]

In Ethiopia, for example, the victory of Soviet-supported forces in Angola led the Kremlin to believe there was now a tide of revolutionary momentum in Africa, and the "lessons" of Angola inspired them to assist Mengistu's coup, a decision that meant an eventual investment of over one billion dollars worth of military aid.[13] Not only did the Soviets accept the preposterous idea that the Ethiopian coup was somehow a class struggle, but Soviet advisors even busied themselves (as they had in other less developed countries) trying to create an actual communist party. Nearly 200 Ethiopians were brought to Moscow in the late 1970s to "take courses on party building, organization of labor unions, women's and youth movements, solving nationality and other issues," while in 1978, a handful of Soviet officials were sent to assist the Ethiopian regime in "creating a vanguard party of the working class."[14] It was "important," Brezhnev told Mengistu during a 1977 meeting in Moscow, "in order to advance the revolutionary process, to create a party of the working class," and to "activate the international affairs of Ethiopia with the aim of foiling the encroachments of imperialist and other reactionary forces."[15]

The Soviets were certain that Ethiopian leader Mengistu was not only a Marxist, but that he was actually fighting hostile nationalist elements in his own leadership—this, at a time when Mengistu and his fellow coup plotters were so ignorant of ideologies, according to one that defected to the United States later, "that at one point in the early stage of the revolution delegations were sent to Tanzania, Yugoslavia, China, and India to shop for one for Ethiopia."[16] No doubt Mengistu would have declared himself almost anything if it meant keeping Soviet aid coming, but it is nonetheless startling to note the importance the Soviet leaders attached to an ideological issue that had so little to do with the actual situation on the Horn of Africa.

In the end, there is no better confirmation of the ideological nature of Soviet expansion (and of American resistance) than the fact that countries that were once the focus of competition between the two most powerful states on earth have since fallen into irrelevance. Sub-Saharan Africa in the twenty-first century is collapsing under the weight of disease, hunger, and ethnic wars of horrifying proportions, but the United States has shown little interest in it under presidential administrations of either party. Russia, for its part, only began to renew contacts in earnest with former Soviet allies after the election of President Vladimir Putin in 2000, but even Putin's government has not sought to return to areas that the USSR once deluged with weapons, advisors, and proxy forces.[17] It is hard to disagree with Dobrynin's bemused look back to the 1970s: "In retrospect, I cannot help being surprised at the amount of energy and effort spent almost entirely in vain by Moscow and Washington on these so-called African affairs. Twenty years later, no one (except historians) could as much as remember them."[18] Likewise, a Russian historian of the Vietnam War considers it "strange and inexplicable that the interests of the great powers could clash in this small country which played so minimal a role in the strategic balance of forces at the time," an observation that could now be made about any number of Third World nations.[19]

WHY MOTIVATIONS MATTER

Even if it is now undeniable that Soviet expansion was more a matter of ideology than geopolitics, it is nonetheless fair to ask why motivations in general should matter at all in prosecuting a cold war. Is it all that important to know that an enemy state's motivations in a particular area are driven by ideology rather than resources or military access? If anything, ideological expansion should be the least important kind of move to counter; if the area under attack has no actual strategic value, it should hardly be worth contesting over something as intangible as ideology. In the Soviet case, it could be argued that U.S. policy should have been formulated in accordance with U.S. interests—which, if defined narrowly, were not threatened by events in remote corners of Africa or even Southeast Asia. A cold calculation of interest would ask only if the Soviet Union is stronger or in a better position to make the United States weaker by being in a particular location, and whether the disparities are so great or the object at issue is so valuable that it is worth the deaths of U.S. servicemen. By this reasoning, it should matter considerably less whether Moscow is merely seeking oil or sugar or if it is also hoping to indoctrinate Cubans or Angolans in the works of Lenin. (In fact, a realist calculation should encourage the opponent to waste time and manpower on pointless errands like trying to imbue semiliterate subsistence farmers with an appreciation for the finer points of dialectical materialism.) Why, then, even raise the issue of the ideological nature of Soviet expansion?

Ideologically motivated aggression presents a special danger for Western policymakers because it falls outside the kinds of more routine patterns of interstate conflict to which Westerners are accustomed. This kind of expansion is different in that it is not negotiable; it is not limited; it carries special dangers for coalition politics; it inflicts unique, chal-lenging economic costs for the aggressor; and finally, it raises a moral dilemma that realist-minded leaders would more often than not rather ignore.

The attempt to subvert another state for ideological reasons cannot be countered with reasonable negotiation, no matter what the hopes of legalistic Westerners. In the absence of ideological competition, issues in peripheral areas would not only be otherwise limited or resolvable, but they probably would not arise in the first place. Even nominal allies, after all, can find themselves in dire conflicts over everything from resources to the rights of ethnic groups. Britain and Iceland have fought periodic "cod wars" over fishing rights; Greece and Turkey in the modern era have been in a state of continual hostility over Cyprus (among other things) for decades. But these are problems that are by their nature self-contained: only the most paranoid Greek really thinks that Turkey hopes to march its troops through the streets of Athens like their Ottoman predecessors, and Iceland's territorial claims of fishing waters are hardly a threat to Britain's way of life. Even the ludicrous claims to ownership of entire bodies of water by dictators like Moammar Quadhafi are, in effect, limited to the issue at hand. (Osama bin Laden's designs on the Middle East or China's claims over Taiwan are more ominous, since they are likely only the first in a series of escalating demands.) Even nakedly expansionist powers, if they seek greater territory for no better reason than self-aggrandizement or to resolve some ancient border dispute, are primarily a threat only to their neighbors. They tend not to seek wider conflict, and their actions are not meant to speak to any greater significance than the real estate at issue.

Ideologically motivated aggression, by contrast, does not occur over some discrete event or resource; the Soviets did not seek to control other states because of disputes over borders or cod fishing. Nor should willingness to avoid a world war—one need not be completely suicidal to be expansionist, after all—be confused with a willingness to compromise. "Undoubtedly the Soviets wished to avoid a confrontation with the United States," Russian historian Ilya Gaiduk has written. "But this does not mean they had abandoned their plans to win superiority over 'imperialists' in the worldwide struggle."[20] To convince the Soviets to abandon their cause would have been as pointless in the 1960s and 1970s as it would be now to try to convince al-Qaeda or the hard-line Iranian clerics that they should let go of what they see as a holy struggle against the West.

If nothing else, an understanding of the ideological motivations of the opponent should make clear the limited opportunity to resolve the situation by diplomatic means. There is no instance where communist thrusts were blunted by cooperative diplomacy, since there was nothing the West could offer, short of outright bribes and concessions, that would be worth the ideological costs of foregoing a potential addition to the socialist commonwealth. "We hold that support to the peoples' revolutionary struggles cannot be sacrificed for the sake of relations between governments," Chinese Foreign Minister Zhou Enlai said in 1971. "Only traitors do that."[21]

Another important consideration is the open-ended agenda of ideological expansion. A regime like the Soviet Union does not seek conquest because it adds to the overall power of the state, but rather as a means of creating a staging area for the propagation of its social system to the *next* target, to "bring about internal changes in other states that it has already achieved in its own domestic sphere."[22] This is, of course, a simple exposition of the domino theory: that each fallen government increases the likelihood that another will fall as well. Critics of American foreign policy and particularly of American involvement in Vietnam have tried to caricature the domino theory in various ways, from self-serving propaganda meant to cover U.S. sins in the Third World to outright paranoia about communist bugbears. It is unfortunate that concern about communist expansion was labeled so infelicitously, making it easier to dismiss: even the fact that dominoes did indeed fall in

Laos and Cambodia (and nearly fell across Central America a decade later) was not enough to sway those who believed that the Soviet Union and China had no interest in a broader war against the West.

This kind of sophistic waving away of the intentions behind communist interventions in the Third World was more excusable at the height of the Cold War, before the scope of Soviet and Chinese involvement in "nationalist" wars of "liberation" became clear. The word "nationalist" itself became a totem among opponents of the domino theory, even though inviting communist participation in nationalist fronts as a concession turned out to be especially dangerous; as Mao Zedong told Laotian communist leader Kaysone Phomvihane in 1970, the "purpose of organizing a coalition government is to destroy the coalition government," noting that there is "no reason to believe" in a permanent power-sharing arrangement.[23]

Soviet involvement in such struggles was a coherent strategy against the "Main Adversary," as the United States was called in Soviet documents, with no eventual end foreseen to it. Former KGB agent Vasilii Mitrokhin describes the report prepared for the Central Committee by his service's chief, Aleksandr Shelepin.

> On July 29, 1961, Shelepin sent Khrushchev the outline of a new and aggressive grand global strategy against the Main Adversary designed to "create circumstances in different areas of the world which would assist in diverting the attention and forces of the United States and its allies, and would tie them down during the settlement of the question of a German peace treaty and West Berlin's proposal." The first part of the plan was to use national liberation movements around the world to secure an advantage in the East-West struggle and to "activate by the means available to the KGB armed uprisings against pro-Western reactionary governments." At the top of the list for demolition Shelepin placed "reactionary" regimes in the Main Adversary's own backyard in Central America, beginning in Nicaragua where he proposed coordinating a "revolutionary front" in collaboration with the Cubans and the Sandinistas. Shelepin also proposed destabilizing NATO bases in western Europe and a disinformation campaign designed to demoralize the West by persuading it of the growing superiority of Soviet forces.[24]

Shelepin's plan was quickly approved as a Communist Party directive, and as Mitrokhin points out, "elements of it, especially the use of national liberation movements in the struggle with the Main Adversary, continued to reappear in Soviet strategy for the next quarter of a century."[25] Many in the West have since derided the idea that the Kremlin was following some detailed and inflexible long-range plan; but this sensible objection should not be confused with the more unreasonable conclusion that the Soviets were therefore following no plan at all.[26]

Among themselves, communist regimes argued not over whether revolutionary movements should be aided, but only whether enough was being done to support them, and it is typical of the narrow vision of so many critics of "dominoes" that what was obvious to communists was impenetrable to Westerners. During a series of meetings in Moscow in the summer of 1963, for example, the Chinese charged that the USSR was unwilling to risk greater involvement in Third World revolutionary struggles. The Soviets contested the Chinese view and used as an example of their commitment to revolutionary movements the massive amount of arms they had transferred to Algeria's rebels the year before:

> You [Chinese] fabricated an undoubted falsehood to the effect that the USSR did not aid the Algerian people's war of liberation. Here are the facts. In the most decisive period of the war, from 1960–1962, we supplied free to the People's Liberation Army of Algeria 25 thousand rifles, 21 thousand machine guns and sub-machine guns, 1300 howitzers, cannons and mortars, many tens of thousands of pistols and other weapons. Over 5 million rubles' worth of clothes, provisions and medical supplies were supplied to Algeria by Soviet social organizations alone. Hundreds of wounded from the Algerian Liberation Army were saved and treated in the Soviet Union. Soviet wheat, sugar, butter, conserves, condensed milk, etc., streamed into Algeria.[27]

Nor did Soviet leaders consider each nation in isolation: the point was to assemble revolutionary regimes like patchwork across regions. Marshal Nikolai Ogarkov, during a 1983 conversation with Grenadian officers in Moscow, welcomed Grenada into the Soviet fold in Latin America, noting that "over two decades ago there was only Cuba in Latin America, today there are Nicaragua, Grenada, and a serious battle is going on in El Salvador."[28]

In a similar vein, Fidel Castro and East German party chief Erich Honecker—leaders of states then deeply involved in proxy fighting in the Third World—happily contemplated a situation in a 1977 discussion in which African wars could be used to "inflict a severe defeat on the entire reactionary imperialist policy [of the United States]." As Castro envisioned it: "If we succeed in strengthening the revolution in Libya, Ethiopia, Mozambique, [Yemen], and Angola, we have an integrated strategy for the whole African continent."[29] No "domino theorist" could have said it better.

Another aspect of the nature of Soviet expansionism was that it potentially had a more alarming affect on friends and allies in a way that ordinary expansion or conflict did not. When Argentina invaded the Falkland Islands in 1982, for example, Washington's reluctance to choose sides openly could not overly worry American allies elsewhere, since there was no reason for other nations to be concerned that the outcome of the Falklands War would affect them. Argentina, for its own reasons, wanted a set of South Atlantic islands, and win or lose, the matter would end there. A failure to confront an ideological opponent with open-ended goals, however, raises questions about where the enemy will strike next—since it is certain that it will in fact strike again—and whether a coalition will at some point rescue its smaller members.

While the Europeans may have needed no elaborate guarantees that U.S. troops would fight in the German forests, smaller and more remote allies were less sure. "If the Americans decide to pack it up because their position is untenable in South Vietnam," Lee Kwan Yew of Singapore said in 1966, "and if the Thais . . . decide not to resist . . . then it is very pertinent what happens to the 500 armed communists wandering around the borders of Thailand and Malaysia. And if Malaysia cannot be held, then Singapore must make adjustments accordingly."[30] As Douglas Macdonald later wrote:

> Indeed, when the Americans "packed it up" in Vietnam and Cambodia in 1974-1975 the Thais moved toward "neutralism" and unceremoniously threw the United States military out of their country, even refusing the Americans an intelligence listening post. The Thais publicly stated that the Americans could not be trusted (especially condemning the U.S. Congress) and that an American presence in Thailand would only invite communist intervention without providing a guarantee of American protection, which could no longer be trusted.

"If the United States had not responded in some precipitous fashion to the threat to Thailand [posed by Vietnam]," Macdonald sensibly asks, "why should other regional Small Powers [have had] confidence in it as a protector?"[31]

Although in later years some scholars questioned whether great powers really drew conclusions about each other's resolve from their actions in the international system, it is now evident that the superpowers in fact did watch each other closely for signs of weakness and sought opportunities to humiliate each other by poaching allies.[32] No attempt at a careful realist cataloging of the globe can fail to take into account the effect of losses in less important areas: it is no comfort to the Japanese to say that a communist takeover of South Korea is not all that important or to West Germans or Italians to say that ceding Africa to the Soviet Union would never, ever mean ceding Europe. While this does not mean that the United States could have fought to overturn every communist government in the world, it does suggest that allies will be more likely to draw conclusions from the response to expansion-ist enemies rather than to those with more limited goals.

None of this is meant to deny the value (or the reality) of geostra-tegic thinking, and one important reason to oppose an ideologically expansive power, of course, is that it is only sensible to deny the enemy resources that will make it a more powerful and difficult opponent. Soviet gains in the Third World, as one analysis pointed out in the late 1980s, "provide the capacity to respond to the security needs of client states and to monitor the military activities of the United States in regions as far from Soviet territory as the South Atlantic and the Southwest Pacific," and there is no reason that such a capability should come cheap.[33]

There is another advantage gained, however, when a state like the USSR is faced with escalating costs of expansion, one that is directly related to the nature of the regime. The Soviet Union, insofar as it sought to woo clients rather than to capture them, claimed to offer a superior economic model that replaced capitalist excess with more equitable social distribution and promised a quick transition from agrarianism to industrialism. As we now know, much of that impressive economic performance was in fact a sham, an illusion created by the profligate use of raw materials and other natural resources, including gold and diamonds that were sold to generate precious hard currency.[34] Thus, it was not only prudent to deny the Soviets those strategic resources that would strengthen their military capacity, but also to increase the costs of maintaining the fiction of a productive and efficient industrial econ-omy. If the Soviets want to give the Cubans cheap oil for French sugar (or to send their dearly bought Western grain to Mongolia or Vietnam), that kind of ruinous foolishness should be encouraged and in fact can be made even more expensive a scheme by ensuring that nothing is done, even through inadvertence or negligence, to make Soviet access to oil, sugar, grain, or anything else any easier than need be.

This is a point with both strategic and ideological import. A nation encumbered with a malfunctioning economy has difficulty projecting power. A global presence is expensive and requires costly investments in transportation and other sorts of infrastructure (not to mention a navy to police and service clients and friends). Allowing the Soviets to govern an empire unfettered would have been to forego the opportu-nity to bring relative American strengths, particularly maritime power, to bear. Western wealth, along with the far greater ability to project power, allowed the United States and its allies to engage in a competi-tion with the Soviets at relatively less cost and damage to their econo-mies. This continually forced the Soviets into making hard choices between internal priorities and external revolutionary commitments that would become increasingly difficult to defend even in their own

minds. "It is necessary to remember," Soviet policy analyst Andrei
Kortunov wrote in 1990,

> that the tens of billions of rubles which are annually extorted from our
> economy are a million unbuilt apartments, kilometers of unlaid highways,
> nonexistent schools and hospitals, sanitoria and libraries. It has become a
> sad paradox that according to many indices—length of life, level of infant
> mortality, even sometimes the level of consumption—we find ourselves in
> a worse position than some of the countries we are helping.[35]

While Americans have a tradition of complaining about foreign aid
(and then giving it anyway), they were not faced with this kind of stark
choice between foreign guns and domestic butter. The U.S. presence in
the Third World not only increased the costs of Soviet involvement at
relatively less cost to Americans, but also made the fiction of Soviet
economic strength—itself a cornerstone of the regime's ideological
pretensions—that much harder to sustain.

But there is a final and ultimately more pressing reason to consider
the meaning of the ideological nature of Soviet expansion: the moral
dimension of Soviet conquest. At the outset of World War I, the average
villager in central Europe might not have cared very much if, at the end
of it all, he found himself living in the Russian Empire rather than the
Austro-Hungarian Empire, or if the indigenous resident of a colony in
Africa had difficulty seeing how life would change very much if his
shores were suddenly being visited by German rather than British
warships. But communism, in any of its national varieties, is synony-
mous with misery, and to fall within Moscow's orbit all too often meant
becoming a smaller version of the impoverished Soviet police state.
Indeed, the Soviet Union was perhaps not the worst of the communist
dictatorships; it probably mattered little, however, to the innocent millions slaughtered and starved across Europe and the Third World
whether they were being murdered by Chinese "dogmatists" or Soviet
"revisionists," but only that they might have lived had they not had the
misfortune to be the target of communist aggression.

Critics will no doubt interject here to suggest that life under colonial
Western rule or even as an ally of the West (as in the Shah's Iran, for
example) was hardly a daily excursion into joy and plenty. Americans
and those acting on the behalf of the American-led coalition subverted
governments, countenanced torture, and engaged in outright military
conquest of recalcitrant states, particularly in Latin America. Nothing
excuses the mistakes and excesses of the Western powers, and there can
be no argument that the desperate and protracted nature of the Cold
War at times led the United States and its allies to act like the thing they
were fighting against. (While some see the Sicilian Expedition as a

warning to Americans about imperial overreach, others point out the monstrous treatment the Athenians meted out to the Melians—"the strong do what they can and the weak suffer what they must," the Athenians told the inhabitants of Melos before inflicting genocide on them—as the object lesson in the ways war can corrupt even a noble democracy.) But there are three objections that must be borne in mind, and they are as relevant to the twenty-first century as they were to the twentieth century.

First, mass murder is not an aberration among ideological states, but a tool of governance. This is so obvious it seems almost pedantic to repeat it, but it is a point that at times has been forgotten with the collapse of the USSR. (It is a point that many leftist intellectuals shied away from before the end of the Cold War, lest Soviet crimes taint socialism by extension.) To say that the Western powers did terrible things during four decades of war is true, but it is as true as saying that the armed forces of the Allies committed war crimes and atrocities during World War II: it is a fact, but it does not then allow the Allies and the Axis together to be submerged in a moral murkiness that confounds the attempt to distinguish one from the other. Much of what the West inflicted on nations caught in the crossfire of the Cold War was done out of stupidity, desperation, or plain bad judgment. Occasionally—such as the plots to kill Castro—it did things out of sheer malice. But all of them were acts of war, and this was a cardinal difference from the kind of horror the Soviets visited on their "allies." Rather than being designed to further the struggle with the United States, the Soviet Union was trying to recreate itself, to clone its system, even if that meant *weakening* its allies through purges and other forms of terror. The Soviet aim was to extinguish not only Western forms of government, but the values and beliefs that undergirded those governments, and ordinary human beings quite naturally did not wish to submit to the destruction of their own liberty.

This is why, whatever the crimes of the West, most people would have chosen the relative freedoms of life across the Iron Curtain rather than endure the transformation of their own societies. It should be elegant enough testimony to this point that the USSR itself was torn apart by its own citizens, but it bears noting that the Soviet coalition, even in Eastern Europe, was one held together by force and coercion. The reluctance of so many in the West to oppose the expansion of communism reflected, as Jean Francois Revel later complained, the fact that democratic civilization during the Cold War was "the first in history to blame itself because another power is working to destroy it."[36] Although it became fashionable to equate Soviet and American imperialism, there is a reason that the barbed wire and guard dogs were on the *eastern* side of the Berlin Wall. It is now more than clear that most people, given the choice, would reject the Soviet system, and there was ample moral (as well as strategic) reason to help them do so during the Cold War.

WHAT THE HELL IS VIETNAM WORTH TO ME?

For all of the practical and moral arguments that can be marshaled to support contesting the world with an ideological opponent, they seem to pale when placed against the tremendous human cost of the single largest attempt to do so during the Cold War: the American war against communism in Southeast Asia. Lyndon Johnson, ruminating over the deepening crisis in Vietnam in 1964, put it bluntly to McGeorge Bundy:

> I was just looking at this sergeant of mine [a military aide to the president] this morning. Got six little old kids over there . . . and I just thought about ordering his kids in there and what in the hell am I ordering him out there for? What the hell is Vietnam worth to me? What is Laos worth to me? What is it worth to this country?[37]

It is too easy now, with the Cold War part of a previous century, to answer simply and unequivocally that the terror inflicted on millions of Vietnamese and the heartbreak visited on thousands upon thousands of families of American servicemen was "worth it."

It is equally irresponsible, however, to ignore the fact that the spread of an inhumane ideology was slowed and a price exacted on its Soviet and Chinese patrons. At the very least, it is past time to return Vietnam to its proper context, as a central act in the Cold War. The attempts since the fall of Saigon to redefine U.S. involvement in Vietnam as an intervention in a local matter, or a crass American attempt at imperial expansion, or even as a misguided attempt to honor an unwise commitment to a corrupt ally depict the men who died there only as casualties in an Asian quagmire rather than on a Cold War battlefield. Among the many things that are now clear in retrospect is that Vietnam was a communist coalition struggle, not a civil war, the Vietnam conflict inflicted severe costs on the communist nations that fought it, and it may well have had a greater impact on the Cold War than previously thought. With this in mind, the conventional wisdom that has since labeled the war as a pointless adventure that inflicted (in Henry Kissinger's words) a "cost out of proportion to any conceivable gain" should be reconsidered.[38]

VIETNAM AS A COALITION WAR

There are few myths in the wake of the Cold War as commonly accepted as the idea that the conflict in Vietnam was a civil war, a purely

internal matter, rather than a war against a communist coalition with
larger aims. It is a tenacious image, as evidenced in a 2000 article by
journalist Neil Sheehan.

> In the spirit of John Kennedy's grandiose inaugural address, we saw
> ourselves as the new Romans holding back the barbarians at the frontiers
> of our beneficent empire. It was all delusions. The Vietnamese were no
> one's pawns and they never threatened us. They simply wanted us to go
> home and leave them alone.[39]

In later years, Robert McNamara would say that he failed to understand
nationalism in Vietnam, which led to Robert Conquest's retort that,
"No, what he failed to understand was Communism (though he no
doubt misunderstood nationalism, too)."[40] For many Americans, particularly younger ones, Vietnam has receded into memory as a kind of
grand mistake, in which U.S. forces were sent, like rookie police officers,
into a domestic quarrel in a bad part of town. That the war in Vietnam
was directly related to the Soviet-American conflict of 1945–1991 is
something that probably would not even occur to most Americans in
the twenty-first century.

But the nature of the war is of crucial importance: if Vietnam was
merely an Asian civil war that the Americans foolishly recast into a test
of wills with the communist world, then it is hard to justify any kind of
intervention, much less so the lives finally lost or the total material
effort expended. But if it was really only one theater of many in a world
at war, then the question becomes one of whether fighting is better than
surrender, of what price should be paid to slow the enemy's advance,
and perhaps even to avoid having to fight another day in another place.

The attempted takeover of South Vietnam could only be considered
a "civil" conflict in the most narrow interpretation. As Brian Crozier has
written: "Technically it was a civil war in that the same people, speaking
the same language and with the same culture and history, lived on both
sides of the artificial dividing line agreed to at the 1954 Geneva conference. In reality, it was an international war between the Communist
world and the West."[41] It is difficult to reach any other conclusion, given
the comments of Soviet, Chinese, and Vietnamese leaders of the time.
The question of the degree to which Ho Chi Minh or his lieutenants
were "nationalists" rather than "communists" has become a staple of
revisionist histories of the war, in which Ho is depicted as a nationalist
in temporary alliance with the Soviets and the Chinese to realize what
were strictly Vietnamese goals. But this distinction between nationalist
and internationalist aims is an artificial one, as Stephane Courtois has
written: "Communism was never incompatible with nationalism or
even xenophobia, particularly in Asia. Unfortunately, beneath the sur-

face of this apparently amiable and unanimously accepted [Vietnam-ese] nationalism there lurked a Stalinist form of Maoism that followed its prototypes extremely closely."[42]

China, in particular, saw in Vietnam an opportunity both to establish a series of new communist regimes and to enhance the PRC's position in the communist world. When Ho Chi Minh asked for help in building roads in Sino-Vietnamese border areas in 1965, Mao added, "Because we will fight large-scale battles in the future, it will be good if we also build roads to Thailand."[43] As one analyst of the Chinese archives later concluded, "Mao certainly planned to expand the revolution in Viet-nam not only to the rest of Indochina, but also to other countries in Southeast Asia."[44] Nor was this idle talk: over the course of the war, China stationed over 300,000 troops in the North, losing 1,100 killed and nearly four times that many wounded.[45] President Johnson's fear of Chinese intervention turned out to be well-grounded, as "there would have been a real danger of a Sino-American war [in Vietnam] with dire consequences for the world" if the United States had invaded the North early in the war.[46] Chinese radicalism on the issue of Vietnam would not abate until the country was deep in the throes of the Cultural Revolution, when Beijing looked to better relations with the United States once the Sino-Soviet conflict was at the brink of open war.

As for the North Vietnamese themselves, if they were nationalists, they were hiding it well. Khrushchev, in his previously suppressed memoirs, had profound admiration for Ho Chi Minh: "You had to revere this man, really go down on your knees before him in gratitude for his selfless contributions to the Communist cause, to which he gave all his strength and abilities."[47] But even Ho was a more careful diplo-mat than his successor, Le Duan, whose commitment to international revolution could never be mistaken for nationalism. "We think that we should have a moral obligation before you and the international Com-munist movement," he told his Chinese hosts in a 1966 meeting in Beijing.

> We keep on struggling against America until the final victory. We still maintain the spirit of proletarian internationalism. For the sake of the international communist movement and international spirit, it doesn't matter if the process of socialist development in the south of Vietnam is delayed for 30 or 40 years.[48]

Five years later, his enthusiasm was unabated: "We want to smash the U.S.-Japan alliance as well as the alliance between the U.S., Japan and the regional bourgeois class. We have to establish a world front that will be built first by some core countries and later enlarged to include African and Latin American countries."[49]

Like the Chinese, the Vietnamese worried that Moscow—and Khrushchev specifically—was too timid to confront the United States. Worse, they saw any accommodation with the West as a betrayal of principle, as Gaiduk later explained.

> Le Duan and his colleagues [in 1964] did not avoid criticism of the Soviet position on such issues as peaceful coexistence with the West, Soviet assistance to India in her conflict with China, refusal to help the Chinese build nuclear weapons, and the lack of support for national liberation movements. The Vietnamese believed there was a real danger of nuclear war and that peace could be defended solely by means of revolutionary struggle. Peaceful coexistence with capitalist countries worked against the intensification of this struggle "to throw back imperialism and overthrow it piece by piece."

This attitude led the Soviets to conclude that the Vietnamese leaders at the time "actually exclude[d] an opportunity to pursue a policy of peaceful coexistence."[50]

In one sense, Vietnamese intentions were irrelevant once the two communist giants threw their efforts into the struggle. Even if there were leaders in the North for whom the war was only about national unification (and such men were not the most prominent voices), Soviet involvement in particular meant that the war in Southeast Asia would necessarily take on the nature of an ideological struggle between East and West. But in any case, as historian Stein Tonnesson has written, revelations since the end of the Cold War make plain that "the domino theory accurately reflected Communist intentions."

> Communist leaders in China, Vietnam, Cambodia, and elsewhere certainly intended to expand communism. They believed strongly in the fraternity of communist movements and states, and saw it as a matter of obligation and pride to use victories in one country to sustain and enhance revolutionary movements in the next. Hanoi and Beijing wanted dominoes to fall as much as Washington wished to keep them standing. The domino theory, then, was absolutely correct—as far as beliefs, hopes and intentions were concerned.[51]

Although Tonnesson argues that the theory was also wrong, in the sense that it underestimated the tensions that would arise within the communist coalition—"fraternity had its limits," he rightly points out—it is difficult to reconcile the ambitions of the North Vietnamese leaders and their benefactors in Moscow and Beijing with any reading of the war as a nationalist struggle into which the United States blindly interposed itself.

Still, the natural affinity between the two radical members of the communist coalition would in fact wane as Mao became more unpredictable and China descended into the madness of the Cultural Revolution. Not that Mao was ever easy to deal with or understand: "Fighting a war of attrition," he told Pham Van Dong in 1967, "is like having meals."

> It is best not to have too big a bite. In fighting the U.S. troops, you can have a bite the size of a platoon, a company, or a battalion. With regard to the troops of the puppet regime, you can have a regiment size bite. It means that fighting is similar to having meals, you should have one bite after another. After all, fighting is not too difficult an undertaking. The way of conducting it is just similar to the way you eat.[52]

Although the Vietnamese used to say that they were fighting the war with "Moscow's technology and Beijing's strategy," they came to rely more on Soviet weaponry than on Mao's increasingly bizarre or conflicting strategic advice. Although the North Vietnamese, and particularly their southern comrades in the National Liberation Front, initially tended to find more ideological sustenance in Beijing's hard-charging attitude rather than Moscow's more plodding approach, in time the reliable pipeline of Soviet arms became more important than the unpredictable advice of their Chinese patrons.

And what of the main communist coalition partner, the USSR? The irony of Soviet involvement is that although the Vietnam war quickly became an arena of confrontation between the Soviet Union and the United States, it is a conflict that Moscow did not want, but for ideological reasons found that it was one it could not escape.

THE RELUCTANT ALLY: THE USSR

The test of wills and commitment between the United States and the Soviet Union in Vietnam was one Moscow would have just as soon avoided had it not been thrust upon the Kremlin leaders by their "allies" in Beijing and Hanoi. (Cuba, too, was troublesome throughout the 1960s and 1970s: Dobrynin claims that "the behavior of our allies in two major trouble spots in our relations with the United States—Vietnam and Cuba—systematically blocked any rational discussion of other problems that were really of key importance to both of us.")[53] The Americans could only guess at Soviet concerns about supporting the North in its struggle, but in any case such private reluctance was irrelevant: the public commitment to Hanoi was a commitment of Soviet prestige and resources to the direct defeat of an American ally, and after 1965 the Vietnam war would, in Moscow's view, have to be played out according to an ideological commitment to "proletarian internationalism," even if that meant tussling with the Americans on one side and the Chinese on the other. But no matter what their later efforts, it now appears that the Soviets were eager to avoid a conflict over Vietnam, in order to better use what they hoped was a coming détente to further their interests in Europe.[54] (This focus on Europe, in fact, would be the cornerstone of Chinese criticisms that portrayed the USSR as just another great power trying to protect its own imperial possessions.)

Soviet reticence was understandable. By 1964, Soviet leaders were fed up with lives of fear and uncertainty, both at home and abroad. They were, almost to a man, survivors of the Stalin era, many of them members of the so-called Class of '38 who had risen to their posts when their predecessors were executed in the dictator's purges of 1936–1938. They had survived the purges only to find themselves fighting for survival again in World War II. After Stalin's death, they no longer had to fear for their lives on a daily basis, but the eventual winner of the succession struggle, Khrushchev, turned out to be mercurial, to say the least, and the patience of the Kremlin bureaucrats was sorely tested by his risky gambles in foreign policy and chaotic economic and political schemes at home. In October 1964, they retired Khrushchev and sent him packing to his dacha. While no less committed to the expansion of the Soviet system throughout the world, the new leadership sought to avoid the sort of unnecessary risks that in their eyes Khrushchev was too prone to run. Better relations with the West, they believed, would help them to realize their expansive goals gradually and more safely (a point discussed in more detail in the next chapter).

The Americans, too, were hopeful that the new team in Moscow would continue the steps taken in the wake of the Cuban missile crisis to improve relations, but there was also a clear streak of foul temper in the nation following Kennedy's assassination. Republican presidential candidate Barry Goldwater was talking tough on Vietnam and other foreign issues, so much so that it inspired real fear in no less a communist leader than Fidel Castro. In a strange moment in the Cold War, Castro was so worried about Goldwater that he sent a private message to Johnson in 1964, saying that "if there is anything I can do to add to his [i.e., Johnson's] majority (aside from retiring from politics), I shall be happy to cooperate," even if that included allowing Johnson to take some sort of violent action against Cuba to avert charges of being soft on communism.[55] Regardless of who won in 1964, the impending fall of South Vietnam faced America with the implications of its own accession to global leadership, and neither Goldwater nor Johnson (or for that matter, even JFK, earlier) could well argue for America's role as leader of the Free World while accepting outright communist defeats of allies, even if minor ones, in the Third World.[56]

Whatever the superpowers' hopes for improved relations in 1964, however, events outside of the traditional European arena of confrontation forced both the Soviets and Americans to choose between ideological commitments and diplomatic harmony. Less than five months after Khrushchev's ouster, the United States committed large numbers of forces to the conflict in Vietnam, a move that in Soviet eyes derailed an emerging détente that some think might have been achieved even under Khrushchev.[57] Until 1964, the Soviet Union remained "chiefly an observer of developments in Vietnam," but this would change when the Americans escalated the conflict and increased their involvement (including the humiliation of bombing the North while Soviet Prime Minister Aleksei Kosygin was visiting Hanoi).[58] The Soviets, by virtually all accounts, had no wish, as Leonid Brezhnev once put it, "to sink in the swamps of Vietnam," but they were incapable of resisting what they saw as an ideological challenge posed by the military involvement of the world's preeminent imperialist power in a communist revolutionary struggle.[59]

This is not to say that the Kremlin leadership, under either Khrushchev or Brezhnev, regarded Vietnam as unimportant, but rather only that they were hesitant to do anything that drained resources away from the primary area of confrontation in Europe. Pressure to react came not only from the Chinese, who were more than eager to score Moscow for being unwilling to face down the Americans, but even from within the Soviet leadership and particularly the military.[60] According to senior Soviet leader Anastas Mikoian, the 1965 bombing combined with the U.S. invasion of the Dominican Republic that year, "really resonated in the [Politburo] and the government. Many were noticeably agitated." The defense minister, Marshal Rodion Malinovskii, gave a speech shortly thereafter.

It was asserted that we should not be limited by anything we were already doing to help Vietnam, and that after the Dominican events we should expect action directed against Cuba. Thus we should actively counter the Americans. It was proposed that in the West (that is, in Berlin and on the border with Western Europe) a military demonstration should be carried out, and to send certain units—airborne forces and others—from our territory to Germany and to Hungary. [Malinovskii] emphasized that we must be ready to strike West Berlin. Later, he added his own comment that "in general, in connection with the emerging situation, it follows that we are not afraid to run the risk of war. [ne boiat'sia idti na risk voiny]."

"Malinovskii's words," Mikoian wrote (in a previously unpublished section of his memoirs) "staggered me."[61] The Vietnamese campaign against the South in 1964 had triggered an American response, and this in turn had presented the Soviets with a challenge they could only walk away from at the risk of abandoning their most central convictions.

Despite this early, angry call to run such immediate risks to halt the American counterattack in Southeast Asia, the war quickly became a draining, long-term proposition for the USSR. Although Soviet propaganda would score significant points among U.S. allies in Europe by portraying Washington and not Moscow as a bellicose imperial power, Vietnam still posed political and economic challenges. The Soviet military presence in Vietnam was never large—in another moment where the Cold War was a bit hotter than we thought, however, Soviet air defense personnel in the North actually shot down U.S. planes; the political and material commitment was far more burdensome than it seemed at the time. Kosygin in particular thought that Vietnam was hobbling other areas of the Soviet economy and objected repeatedly to aid to the North.[62]

But even when the Soviets provided assistance, it rarely translated into goodwill or obedience in Hanoi, not least because of the drumbeat of Chinese criticism. "Soviet aid," Deng Xiaoping sniped to the Vietnamese in 1965, "is aimed at serving their own strategy," which was true but could hardly be counted as a criticism since it was a strategy of aiding a revolutionary struggle against the United States.[63] The costs of the war were so evident that the Soviet embassy in Vietnam even suggested to Moscow in 1967 that one condition that could force Hanoi to seek terms with the United States would be if "socialist countries were to declare *that they could no longer bear the ever growing burdens of the Vietnam War* owing to dangers involved in the protracted and expanded war" [emphasis added].[64] The actual costs of aid are hard to determine, especially since the war had an indirect effect of bolstering the Soviet military's claims to more resources in general, but estimates of direct Soviet assistance run to as much as over one-half billion dollars per year at the height of the conflict, money that the Soviet economy could ill afford.[65]

Moreover, Soviet diplomacy with the West was continually hamstrung by the demands of its junior coalition partner in the North and its deadly Chinese competitor. The never-to-be détente of the early 1960s may have been aborted by a rain of American bombs in Vietnam, but later efforts by Moscow to create a more hospitable climate for its plans constantly ran afoul of Vietnamese and Chinese ideological militancy. The Chinese, for example, would use their discussions with members of other socialist parties to deride the Soviets for being unwilling to run the kinds of risks in Berlin that Malinovskii had once suggested and that had so alarmed Mikoian and others in the Politburo.

The demand on Moscow to turn up the heat on the Americans in Europe in order to support the struggle in Vietnam was a consistent Chinese practice in their conversations with fraternal parties during [the mid-1960s]. In the discussions with the Japanese Communist Party delegation in March, Liu Shaoqui and Deng Xiaoping urged the Soviet Union to "resort to brinkmanship" and create "greater tension in the west" to counter Washington's expansion of the Vietnam War while Peng Zhen, Mayor of Beijing, stated emphatically: "If the Soviet Union was really desiring to support Vietnam in the struggle, it would create a tenser situation in West Berlin, to stop the United States boldly withdrawing its troops from West Germany to Vietnam. This would be more effective than missiles."[66]

The Soviets, understandably, were less enthusiastic about courting world war in Europe, where so many communist gains could be lost, in order to satisfy demands by the Asian comrades that verged, at least in China's case, on the near hysterical.

Détente, in a strange mirroring of the debate emerging in the West, became a term of derision, with every effort to improve relations between Moscow and Washington taken as a sign of an impending Great Power sellout of Vietnam and other revolutionary regimes. "Nixon's policy of détente," Hanoi warned,

is aimed at achieving the objective of dividing the socialist camp in an attempt to weaken the revolution. In implementing a policy of "détente" with the big countries, the U.S. imperialists are scheming to "control" the socialist countries in their movement to develop the revolutionary offensive, while the United States is continuing its limited counteroffensives against the revolutionary movement in various areas and small countries.[67]

In other words, any improvement in Soviet-American relations was by definition an ideological betrayal, and a foolish acquiescence in an American trap to boot. This was unfair to the Soviets, who were simply making the point that they could get more done (as will be seen in the next chapter) in the absence of continual East-West tensions and, of course, without the added distraction of a thermonuclear war. Hanoi would come to regret its militant support of the Chinese line when Nixon would visit Beijing in 1971, but for most of the war, the Soviets would find themselves constantly having to defend their ideological rectitude against charges of heresy and weakness from their fraternal "allies."

The net effect was to ideologically encumber Soviet diplomacy, making it almost impossible for the Soviets to seek a more advantageous relationship with the United States. Nixon, for his part, knew that severing the Soviet commitment to Vietnam was the ideological and material prerequisite for any kind of credible American withdrawal, but he was enraged by what he saw as combined Soviet, Chinese, and Vietnamese intransigence (so much so that in 1971 he vowed more bombing of the North while pounding his desk and shouting "We're gonna level that goddamned country!")[68] Thus the war delayed by several years Soviet hopes for détente, while helping to drain the Soviet treasury and dividing Moscow's attention between the Vietnamese situation and other, more important areas, including Europe. The war in Vietnam, as it turned out, inflicted direct economic costs on the Soviet Union and strained the already burdened Soviet economy, complicated alliance relations in the communist world, and temporarily subverted Soviet plans to take advantage of the West's continual hopes for better relations. Whether this was worth the cost America paid will forever be debated, but the undeniable damage done to the USSR must be taken into any such reckoning.

THE COMMUNIST VICTORY OF 1965:
A COUNTERFACTUAL POSTSCRIPT

One reason the lessons of Vietnam remain so controversial is that there is no way to know if the Western coalition would have been so much worse off if nothing had been done to stem the communist advance in 1965. As Michael Lind points out, even with the casualties sustained in Vietnam—which were less than the United States took in three months on the Western Front in World War I—America and its allies still won the Cold War with less blood spilled than in the previous world wars.[69] But could those tens of thousands of men have been saved and the Cold War won anyway?

We cannot know exactly what would have happened if the communist star had been raised over Saigon a decade earlier than it was. We do know, however, what happened after the fall of the South in 1975. Kissinger described it well:

> Although, in a strict sense, the only dominoes which fell were Cambodia and Laos, anti-Western revolutionaries in many other areas of the globe began to feel emboldened. It is doubtful that Castro would have intervened in Angola, or the Soviet Union in Ethiopia, had America not been perceived to have collapsed in Indochina, to have become demoralized by Watergate, and to have afterward retreated into a cocoon . . . had South Vietnam fallen in the early 1960s, the communists' attempted coup in Indonesia, which nearly succeeded in 1965, might have overthrown the government and produced another strategic disaster.[70]

Even in 1975, the Soviets expected a similar rash of misfortunes to follow America's defeat. *Izvestiia* crowed (less than a month after

Saigon's fall) that America was now in a precarious position and that things would only get worse as U.S. allies lost faith.[71]

What if a communist victory had produced a similar reaction in 1965? The West might have found itself facing a surge of communist expansion in Asia and Africa, financed by a Soviet Union that was economically more willing to make sacrifices than it would be ten years later, unencumbered by squabbles between Moscow, Beijing, and Vietnam, and aided by what would almost certainly be a collapse of faith among Third World nations that the United States would intervene on their behalf. A communist victory in 1965 might not have averted the intense Sino-Soviet clashes of the late 1960s, but it would have undercut Chinese claims of Soviet weakness and at the least would have removed one more issue of contention between the communist superpowers.

It is also possible that an invigorated communist movement in the Third World would have intensified Soviet and Chinese competition in the region, with deadly results. Journalist David Pryce-Jones recalls a 1967 meeting with Milovan Djilas in which the old Yugoslav dissident warned him what was at stake.

> "I know nothing about you," Djilas said, "you may be a spy or provocateur. But if you have any influence, use it to tell the Americans that they must win the war in Vietnam." America alone, he argued, had the strength to stand between the Soviet Union and China. If it withdrew, if it failed, in his revision of the domino theory, then Vietnam and the rest of Asia would fall to one or other of the two great Communist powers. A merciless battle for supremacy would ensue.[72]

Another possibility is that the fall of the South would have led the Soviets to indulge their belief that the United States was wounded and capable of being defeated in other areas, perhaps closer to home. Either outcome would increase the likelihood of World War III, especially if Western leaders saw Vietnam in 1965 as one more loss to the communists after China in 1949 (and the near miss in Korea in 1950) and steeled themselves to never allow another such defeat no matter what the risk. The communist victory in 1965 could well have been the beginning of a chain of events of apocalyptic proportions.

But what about a more optimistic scenario? One thing that is certain is the American defeat in Vietnam encouraged the Soviets to expand their reach and to foolishly overextend themselves at a time when they should have been tending to an economy badly in need of repair, as Gaiduk writes:

> Inspired by its gains and by the decline of U.S. prestige resulting from Vietnam and domestic upheaval, the Soviet leadership adopted a more

aggressive and rigid foreign policy, particularly in the third world. The lessons of Vietnam had a diametrically opposed effect in Moscow. Instead of seeing the U.S. defeat in Indochina as a warning against similar adventures of their own, Soviet leaders, blinded by Marxist-Leninist philosophy and by the conviction that the revolutionary trend of history was on their side, believed that where imperialism had failed they would certainly succeed. . . . This belief led in the 1970s to Soviet involvement in the turmoil in Africa and the Middle East and eventually to the tragedy of Afghanistan that became one of the reasons for the collapse of the Soviet regime.[73]

Kissinger agrees, noting:

From America's failure, Moscow drew the conclusion which the advocates of the domino theory had so feared—that the historical correlation of forces had shifted in its favor. As a result, it tried to expand into Yemen, Angola, Ethiopia, and ultimately, Afghanistan. But in the process, it found that geopolitical realities applied just as much to communist societies as they did to capitalist ones. In fact, being less resilient, Soviet overextension produced, not catharsis, as it did in America, but disintegration.[74]

If the collapse of South Vietnam baited the Soviets into a suicidal overextension, why should America have sacrificed so many thousands of men just to delay the inevitable Soviet collapse by ten years? Why not abandon the South, accept a communist victory in 1965, and let the Soviets mindlessly squander blood and treasure chasing a pipe dream around the rest of the Third World?

One answer is that the Soviets, as formidable as they seemed in 1975, were actually less able to sustain the kind of effort they extended at the time than they might have been a decade earlier. It is true that in 1965, the Soviet Union was poorer and had a smaller economy, but there was still at the least the illusion of dynamism in the economy. There is no telling what a decade *without* the burden of the Vietnam War and *with* the benefits of an earlier détente might have done to bolster the Soviet system. A greater Soviet naval reach would have arrived in Southeast Asia much earlier—as Gaiduk points out, "a strong foothold in Asia" was one undeniable outcome of the war—and if the other Asian dominoes, perhaps joined by Thailand, had fallen that much sooner, all of Asia, from the Soviet Far East to Indochina, would have been under communist control. One thing, admittedly, that would have slowed the Soviets in the 1960s was the lack of a power projection capacity, and the West should be grateful that Nikita Khrushchev's obsession with nuclear weapons so badly hobbled the development of Soviet naval power and airlift capabilities.

Again, it is irresponsible to say with complete conviction (and in hindsight) that the lives of so many Americans were justly expended in the war in Vietnam or for that matter in any of the Cold War's peripheral conflicts. Only World War II, the "good war," easily passes the test of necessity, with America and the democracies literally fighting for their lives against a genocidal regime on one shore and a racist empire on the other. But no consideration of Vietnam and no future consideration of engaging in peripheral war can afford to lose sight of the fact that more is at stake in each contest with an ideological power than a particular piece of territory. Lind depicts the Cold War as no different in character from the earlier struggle against the totalitarians that spawned it and Vietnam as its more dire moment:

> Indochina was the Dunkirk of the American effort in the Cold War. The Vietnam War will never be understood as anything but a horrible debacle. At the same time it cannot be understood except as a failed campaign in a successful world war against imperial tyrannies that slaughtered and starved more of their own subjects than any regimes in history.[75]

If the American intervention in Vietnam staved off an earlier Soviet thrust into the Third World, held China at bay, or bought time for other nations to resist the efforts of either of the communist superpowers, it may even be too much to say that it was a "failed campaign," although if it was a success, it was one gained at a ghastly price. Whether Vietnam was the West's Dunkirk or America's Sicilian Expedition, it was an unarguable tragedy—but perhaps also an unavoidable one.

TOMORROW'S PERIPHERY: THE COLD WAR AND DISTANT WARS IN THE TWENTY-FIRST CENTURY

The American war in Vietnam was neither well-conceived nor well-executed—but those are another set of debates entirely, and they will not be rehearsed here. What the experience in Vietnam, as well as in other areas the Soviets tried to capture during the Cold War, does suggest is the possibility of forcing an ideologically driven opponent to pay the costs of its policies. (Certainly, this is a lesson many critics of the war feel *Americans* should learn.) The Soviet Union declared Moscow to be the fountainhead of communist revolution, and in short order the Kremlin found itself presented with what should have been a foreseeable problem: once you proclaim yourself the surrogate father to all Marxist orphans, you cannot be surprised when the waifs show up—or are left—at your door. Such was the case with Vietnam: the Soviets were ideologically bound to support North Vietnam, if for no other reason than that it was a communist entity fighting what it claimed to be a struggle of national liberation against imperialist aggression—not to mention the fact that the Chinese were more than willing to step in and reap the credit as the superior revolutionary power if the Soviets demurred.

The story of Vietnam is actually many stories, of course, but one of them is a lesson for American policymakers that the democracies are not alone in being willing to pay a high price for their beliefs. Vietnam and other Third World entanglements killed thousands of American and allied soldiers, but the West, perhaps unknowingly, inflicted more damage than it knew on the Soviet enemy. The struggle in the Third World and the Soviet Union's increasing desperation to hold onto its position there, Aleksandr Yakovlev wrote, turned into "gigantic expenditures and, especially tragically, human victims, about whom to this day if we speak of them, we speak of them under our breath."[76]

At first glance, relentless conflict with proxies across the Third World seems the least likely aspect of the Cold War to reappear in the new century. The very idea of a "periphery" has a Cold War connotation, as the term came to refer broadly to any area that was not in Europe or North America. Today, it could be taken to mean any third area contested by two nuclear-armed powers that is not central to the interests of either. (A confrontation with China over Taiwan, for example, cannot be considered a "peripheral" engagement, at least not to the Chinese, in the way that confrontation over the Spratley Islands or even North Korea might be.) What relevance, then, does the history of the Soviet-American conflict in such areas have to cold wars in the twenty-first century?

It is admittedly improbable that a single opponent will create outposts of a hostile system across the planet in the near future. There is so far no ideology that is contesting the dominance of liberal capitalist democracy on a global scale. Even China, an immense nation nominally committed to the same revolutionary communist ideology as the Soviets were, is not actively seeking allies or converts far from its own borders. Conservatives in particular are prone to point this out, since many of them feel that they were at the forefront of the rhetorical campaign against the USSR and now worry that the scale of the Cold War is being lessened by comparisons with the current American troubles with China (not to mention that such talk endangers lucrative dealings with the People's Republic that are unfortunately supported by conservatives and liberals alike). "China is not the Soviet Union, let alone Nazi Germany," *National Review* protested in early 2001. "China doesn't have an alternative ideology with global appeal. It isn't fighting the United States on every possible front worldwide, and couldn't do so even if it wanted to."[77]

This last point is true but irrelevant. (And China *does* in fact espouse an alternative ideology, one in whose name it killed thousands of Americans in Korea, even if its global appeal has since fallen.) Although the People's Republic is not yet capable of challenging the United States in peripheral areas or even in Taiwan, this says nothing about whether China or anyone else might one day attempt to fight the United States on secondary fronts, through allies, proxies, clients, or other agents of mischief. It also says nothing about the wide reach of terrorist organizations that may, in the future, be part of shadow governments in failed states which in turn could be used as platforms to destabilize other regimes near and far. If these states or entities decide to increase the scope and scale of their power by shifting the struggle against the United States to distant theaters—if, to take but one example, Islamic fundamentalists in one part of the world armed and supported a rebellion in another that in turn threatened Western interests—then American leaders will find new relevance in the old dilemma of when and how to intervene. (It is in peripheral struggles, after all, that the most American lives were placed at direct risk of hostilities during the Cold War, and even now more U.S. servicemen are endangered in small wars and failed states than in confrontations with America's main opponents.) This is all the more vexing a problem if intervention is to be contemplated against a client supported by a nuclear-armed opponent—that is, if nuclear deterrence means that the threat cannot be directly resolved at the source.

While the kind of hopscotching of the map that took place between the superpowers during the Cold War is improbable, proxy warfare (to say nothing of direct combat) in a peripheral area with a nuclear-armed opponent is increasingly likely. In such an event, policymakers must ask themselves about the motivations behind the aggression, in order to determine whether there is a real likelihood of a negotiated peace or whether a compromise in the particular instance will set the stage for the enemy's further expansion. Amidst the tragedy and violence created by the Cold War in the Third World, it is important to bear in mind that there was no way to avert Soviet expansionism, no way to negotiate its limits, and no alternatives but to accept it or to oppose it, either by force of arms in a particular theater or by indirect political and economic attacks on the Soviet ability to sustain such interventions. To do otherwise would have been to encourage more encroachments, for there is a terrible difference—as the attacks of terrorists constantly remind us now in the twenty-first century—between a country in search of treasure and a regime in need of converts.

In the early 1970s, the American approach to the overall escalation of the Cold War and to the quagmire in Vietnam in particular was to seek a kind of cease-fire, a "détente," with the Soviet Union. As it evolved into an attempt to negotiate the non-negotiable, it was a failure, but initially it was a policy based on more modest hopes. In the next chapter, we turn to the evolution of détente and its lessons for the future.

NOTES

1. A. N. Yakovlev, *Gor'kaia chasha: Bol'shevizm i Reformatsiia Rossii* (Yaroslavl': Verkhne-Volzhskoe, 1994), p. 193.

2. Anatolii Dobrynin, *In Confidence* (Seattle: University of Washington Press), p. 404.

3. Dobrynin, p. 404.

4. Georgii Arbatov, *Zatianuvsheesiia vyzdorovlenie* (Moscow: Mezhdunarodnye Otnosheniia, 1991), p. 217.

5. See Yves Santamaria, "Afrocommunism: Ethiopia, Angola, and Mozambique," in Stephane Courtois, et al., *The Black Book of Communism* (Cambridge, MA: Harvard University Press, 1999).

6. Quoted in Linda J. Titlar, "Image and Perception in Soviet and Russian Foreign Policy," unpublished doctoral dissertation, University of Maryland, 1995, p. 66.

7. Odd Arne Westad, "Moscow and the Angolan Crisis, 1974–1976: A New Pattern of Intervention," *Cold War International History Project Bulletin* 8–9, http://cwihp.si.edu/.

8. Dobrynin, p. 404.

9. Titlar, pp. 179-180.

10. Yakovlev, p. 194.

11. Santamaria in Courtois, et al., p. 685.

12. Yakovlev, p. 190.

13. See Odd Arne Westad, "The Fall of Détente and the Turning Tides of History," in Odd Arne Westad, ed., *The Fall of Détente: Soviet-American Relations during the Carter Years* (Oslo: Scandinavian University Press, 1997), p. 20.

14. "Document: Soviet Foreign Ministry, Background Report on Soviet-Ethiopian Relations, 3 April 1978," available at the Cold War International History Project, http://cwihp.si.edu/default.htm.

15. "Document: CPSU CC to SED CC, Information on Visit of Mengistu Haile Mariam to Moscow, 13 May 1977," *Cold War International History Project*, http://cwihp.si.edu/.

16. Ermias Abebe, "The Horn, the Cold War, and Documents from the Former East Bloc: An Ethiopian View," *Cold War International History Project Bulletin* 8–9, available online at http://cwihp.si.edu/.

17. In 2001, the Russians even shut down their intelligence facility at Lourdes, Cuba, as an unjustifiably expensive installation. Economy is now more important than Cold War geographical advantage, apparently.

18. Dobrynin, p. 407.

19. Ilya V. Gaiduk, *The Soviet Union and the Vietnam War* (Chicago: Ivan R. Dee, 1996), p. xi.

20. Gaiduk, p. 131.

21. Odd Arne Westad, et al., eds., *77 Conversations Between Chinese and Foreign Leaders on the Wars in Indochina, 1964–1977* (Washington: Woodrow Wilson International Center for Scholars, Cold War International History Project Working Paper No. 22, May 1998), pp. 77, 179.

22. Nigel Gould-Davies, "Rethinking the Role of Ideology in International Politics During the Cold War," *Journal of Cold War Studies* (1) 1, Winter 1999, p. 103.

23. Westad, et al., ed., *77 Conversations*, p. 172.

24. See Christopher Andrew and Vasilii Mitrokhin, *The Sword and the Shield: The Mitrokhin Archive* (New York: Basic Books, 1999), p. 181. This document is

discussed in detail in Vladimir Zubok and Constantine Pleshakov, *Inside the Kremlin's Cold War: From Stalin to Khrushchev* (Cambridge, MA: Harvard University Press, 1996), pp. 252–255.

25. Andrews and Mitrokhin, p. 181.

26. A typical comment: "Early views that the Soviet Union had a clear blueprint for world domination have been discredited." David S. Painter and Melvyn P. Leffler, "Introduction: The International System and the Origins of the Cold War," in Melvyn P. Leffler and David S. Painter, eds., *Origins of the Cold War* (London: Routledge, 1994), p. 2.

27. "Stenogram: Meeting of the Delegations of the Communist Party of the Soviet Union and the Chinese Communist Party, Moscow, 5–20 July 1963," Cold War International History Project, http://cwihp.si.edu/.

28. "Pentagon Unveils Document on Grenada-Soviet Meeting," Subject File "Grenada," Soviet ("Red") Archives, Records of Radio Free Europe/Radio Liberty Research Institute, Open Society Archives, Budapest, Hungary. Russian scholar Karen Khachaturov (the chairman of the Russian Committee for Cooperation with Latin America) disputes the idea that the Soviets wanted a strong Marxist ally in Nicaragua, arguing that "one Cuba was enough for Moscow," but even if the point is taken that the USSR did not instigate the revolutions in Nicaragua or Grenada, it was ideologically helpless to resist aiding and protecting them later. Interview with Karen Khachaturov, Moscow, February 3, 2000.

29. "Transcript of Meeting between East German leader Erich Honecker and Cuban leader Fidel Castro, East Berlin, April 1977," Cold War International History Project, http://cwihp.si.edu/.

30. Quoted in Robert O. Tilman, *Southeast Asia and the Enemy Beyond: ASEAN Perceptions of External Threats* (Boulder, CO: Westview, 1987), p. 137.

31. Macdonald made this point in a roundtable exchange via Internet, February 11, 2000. See H-Net discussion logs, http://www2.h-net.msu.edu/~diplo/.

32. "Decision-makers do not consistently use another state's past behavior...to predict that state's behavior," Jonathan Mercer has argued. "Adversaries rarely get reputations for lacking resolve." The entire Cold War, apparently, is the disconfirming case. Jonathan Mercer, *Reputation and International Politics* (Ithaca, NY: Cornell University Press, 1996), pp. 9–10.

33. Roger Kanet, "The Evolution of Soviet Policy," in Edward Kolodziej and Roger Kanet, eds., *The Limits of Soviet Power in the Developing World* (Baltimore: Johns Hopkins University Press, 1989), pp. 50–51.

34. Dmitrii Volkogonov, *Lenin* (New York: The Free Press, 1994), pp. 338–340.

35. Quoted in Titlar, p. 176.

36. Jean Francois Revel, *How Democracies Perish* (New York: Doubleday, 1984), p. 7.

37. Michael Beschloss, ed., *Taking Charge: The Johnson White House Tapes, 1963-1964* (New York: Simon and Schuster, 1997), p. 370.

38. Henry Kissinger, *Diplomacy* (New York: Simon and Schuster, 1994), p. 698.

39. Neil Sheehan, "Why the US Was Fortunate to Lose the War," *The Boston Sunday Globe*, April 30, 2000, p. M20.

40. Robert Conquest, *Reflections on a Ravaged Century* (New York: Norton, 2000), p. 234.

41. Brian Crozier, *The Rise and Fall of the Soviet Empire* (Rocklin, CA: Forum, 1999), p. 245.

42. Jean-Louis Margolin, "Vietnam and Laos: The Impasse of War Communism," in Courtois, et al., pp. 565–566.

43. Westad, et al., eds., *77 Conversations*, p. 87.

44. Stein Tonnesson, "Tracking Multidimensional Dominoes," in Westad, et al., eds., *77 Conversations*, p. 37.

45.Qiang Zhai, *China and the Vietnam Wars, 1950–1975* (Chapel Hill: University of North Carolina Press, 2000), p. 135.

46. Zhai, p. 156.

47. *Khrushchev Remembers: The Glasnost Tapes* (Boston: Little, Brown, 1990), p. 155.

48. Westad, et al., eds., *77 Conversations*, p. 97.

49. Westad, et al., eds., *77 Conversations*, p. 179.

50. Gaiduk, p. 8.

51. Tonnesson, p. 35.

52. Westad, et al., eds., *77 Conversations*, p. 105.

53. Dobrynin, p. 136.

54. Gaiduk, p. 18; interview with Aleksandr Orlov, Moscow, Russia, February 5, 2000.

55. "If the President feels it necessary during the campaign to make bellicose statements about Cuba or even to take some hostile action—if he will inform me, unofficially, that a specific action is required because of domestic political considerations, I shall understand and not take any serious retaliatory action." Castro sent the message through Lisa Howard of ABC News, February 12, 1964. The transcript of Howard's report from the White House files may be viewed at the National Security Archive, at http://www.gwu.edu/~nsarchiv/NSAEBB/NSAEBB18/09-01.htm.

56. Kennedy's beliefs about Vietnam are still debated, but David Kaiser has recently argued that the doomed Vietnam policy of the 1960s predated JFK, and that Kennedy actually resisted greater military involvement in Southeast Asia. See David Kaiser, *American Tragedy* (Cambridge, MA: Harvard University Press, 2000). Whatever Kennedy's intentions about Vietnam, however, his rhetorical commitment to aiding anticommunist movements is undeniable.

57. Aleksandr Orlov of the Military History Institute suggests that this nascent Soviet-American détente had been considered in Moscow as early as 1963, but that the commitment of troops to Vietnam rendered the issue moot. Interview.

58. Gaiduk, pp. 5, 30.

59. Dobrynin, p. 143; Interview with Vladimir Matiash, Moscow, Russia, February 3, 2000.

60. Matiash, interview.

61. Anastas Mikoian, *Tak bylo* (Moscow: Vagrius, 1999), p. 619.

62. Interview with Ilya Gaiduk, Moscow, Russia, February 4, 2000.

63. Westad, et al., eds., *77 Conversations*, p. 87.

64. Gaiduk, p. 110.

65. Matiash, interview; also see Douglas Pike, *Vietnam and the Soviet Union: Anatomy of an Alliance* (Boulder, CO: Westview Press, 1987), p. 139. In the ten years after the war, Vietnam's overall economic reliance on the USSR became more pronounced and more expensive. See Sheldon Simon, "The Soviet Union and Southeast Asia," in Edward Kolodziej and Roger Kanet, eds., *The Limits of Soviet Power in the Developing World* (Baltimore: John Hopkins University Press, 1989), pp. 155–156.

66. Zhai, p. 14.

67. Quoted in Stephen J. Morris, "The Soviet-Chinese-Vietnamese Triangle in the 1970s: The View From Moscow," Washington, D.C.: Cold War International History Project Working Paper #25, April 1999, p. 16.

68. Transcribed by J. Kimball in April 2000 from White House Tapes, First Chronological Release, February 1971—July 1971, Nixon Presidential Materials,

National Archives, available at H-Diplo logs, April 22, 2000, http://www2.h-net.msu.edu/~diplo/.

69. Michael Lind, *Vietnam: The Necessary War* (New York: The Free Press, 1999), p. 282.

70. Kissinger, p. 698.

71. V. Osipov, "Problemy zapadnogo al'iansa," *Izvestiia*, May 29, 1975, p. 3.

72. The New Criterion online edition, "Remembering Milovan Djilas," David Pryce-Jones, 1999, http:/www.newcriterion.com/archive/18/oct99/djilas.htm.

73. Gaiduk, p. 250.

74. Kissinger, p. 701.

75. Lind, p. 282.

76. Yakovlev, p. 195.

77. Richard Lowry, "China Trade—Without Guilt," *National Review*, May 14, 2000, p. 39.

5

The Limits of Détente

Détente would never have resulted in the tearing down of the Iron Curtain.

—Valentin Falin, 1992

DÉTENTE AND ENGAGEMENT, THEN AND NOW

After nearly twenty-five years of acrimony (and several of outright combat in Korea and Vietnam), the West and the communist world embarked on détente, an attempt to scale back tensions and increase communication and cooperation. These efforts succeeded in covering the Cold War with a veneer of cordiality but changed little else, as the Soviets and the Americans saw different things in détente from the outset. Détente itself might not be worth dwelling on were it not that Western governments seem so intent on pursuing it with a new set of opponents after the Cold War. Whether under the guise of "engagement" or "strategic partnership" or other rubrics (including campaigns to build overly inclusive future coalitions against terrorists and their sponsors), the essence of policies that seek cooperation over confrontation will be much the same as détente: to enmesh states that oppose the status quo in the daily life of the international community and to give them a stake in the existing system, in the hope that it will not only keep the peace, but also help them to "develop" or "progress" or "grow."

Détente, like "appeasement," has become something of a pejorative term in the political lexicon now, fairly or not. In its time, détente was derided, as "engagement" often is now, by turns as naive or amoral, depending on whether it was seen as an attempt at civilizing the Soviets or as an American sellout of friends overseas in order to secure a respite at home. Détente's defenders, for their part, argued that it was nothing more or less than a realistic appraisal of what was possible given the existing power relationship between the United States and the Soviet Union at the time, just as those now favoring engagement with China, North Korea, or other international malefactors argue that policies of neocontainment amount to little more than psychological denial of the limits of U.S. power and a misunderstanding of how to elicit better behavior from such regimes. A reasonable case can be made that détente was an amalgam of approaches, and to praise or criticize any one policy called "détente" is to miss the complexity of the U.S.-Soviet relationship in the 1970s.

Still, some of the opprobrium surrounding the concept of détente is deserved. No matter how irresistible its origins or how sensible it may have seemed at first, by the time it was discarded it was in fact as bad a policy as its detractors claimed. The problem then, as now, is that there was no common understanding between America and its opponents about the meaning of détente. At a basic level, the Americans saw détente as a means of managing a great power relationship, a way to regularize the Soviet-American competition and make it less unpredictable and therefore less dangerous. In this, the Soviets concurred, but they did not see such a regularization of international life as an end in itself. Rather, Moscow saw détente as a *strategy*, a means of furthering Soviet goals without risking the loss of their achievements in an accidental or precipitous war. A 1967 report to the Politburo by Foreign Minister Andrei Gromyko was clear in this regard:

> On the whole, international tension does not suit the state interests of the Soviet Union and its friends. The construction of socialism and the development of the economy call for the maintenance of peace. In the conditions of détente it is easier to consolidate and broaden the positions of the Soviet Union in the world.[1]

Or as a senior Communist Party official put it while discussing détente in a private meeting with a group of Soviet academics in 1973, "it is appropriate to recall the words of Marx in one of his letters, that in politics you may conclude alliances with the Devil himself if you are certain you can cheat the Devil."[2] It should not have come as a surprise to Americans that what they thought was a modus vivendi with Moscow amounted to little more than a shift in Soviet strategy away from direct military competition with the United States and Europe and toward a more active (and at times, more violent) role in international life elsewhere.

However, it is important to think about both the uses of détente from the Western perspective as well. To what extent did the relaxation of tensions in the 1970s benefit the United States and its allies, and is there a role for "détente" or something like it in fighting and winning a cold war? Although (as will be seen in the next chapters) a more confrontational approach to the Cold War yielded significant results later, the experience of the 1980s does not irresistibly lead to the proposition that relentless hostility is therefore the only strategy available in a cold war. Indeed, some have argued that it was the alternating cycles of confrontation and accommodation and the consequent unpredictability of American policy that undermined the Soviet Union's ability to respond coherently or adeptly to Washington's challenges in the 1980s, although it bears noting that "unpredictability" is, by definition, almost impossible to pursue as a conscious and consistent policy.[3]

One reason to consider the experience of détente is that at times there may be no alternative to it. As flawed as détente was, the Western allies had little latitude to pursue any other course; even if American and European leaders were willing to adopt a consistently confrontational line in the 1970s, it would have been materially and socially difficult to sustain it. The American war in Vietnam produced a retreat abroad and disorder at home, with the public increasingly unwilling to think about foreign affairs, much less to risk the lives of their sons for it. The economy, the one area where the West was unarguably superior to the Soviet system, was a mess, with a combination of rising resource prices and fumbled economic policies already pointing the way to what would be called "stagflation," in which the U.S. economy experienced all the pain of inflation but none of the benefits of growth.

Worse, money and military might were not the only things in short supply: from late 1972 onward, Washington was racked by scandal, and by the late summer of 1974, the United States would be led for the first time in history by a president and vice president who are both unelected. The damage done to American leadership was evident, and U.S. alliance policy was further complicated by the fact that NATO members in places like Turkey, Greece, and Portugal were becoming more obsessed with internal problems than meeting a Soviet threat that many of them thought largely imaginary. By 1975, the strains within NATO had reached a point where President Gerald Ford went to Europe to reassure the Atlantic Alliance that while "on occasion . . . America may seem to stray somewhat off course," the United States would "continue to be a strong partner"—a statement that could only raise more doubts by virtue of the fact that Ford felt the need to say it.[4] At the end of the Cold War, President George H. W. Bush warned Americans in his 1989 inaugural address that the United States had "more will than wallet," but this was a better description of the early 1970s—with the possible exception that there was little to draw upon even in the way of will.

Détente, of course, was not specifically a response to the ragged state of the American economy or the violence done to the social contract during the Watergate scandal, and in fact the end of détente came about in part because the Soviets overestimated the degree to which internal disorder in the United States freed them from some of the constraints of the superpower competition. But even in its more immediate origins—specifically, the Soviet attainment of nuclear parity and the consequent American understanding that the Soviet Union could not be isolated militarily or politically—there were elements of détente that were useful to the West in the longer term struggle with the East. The relaxation of tensions for a time broadened the Soviet-American competition to include more than arms, where the Soviets could still muster a quantitative edge, and moved toward ideas and culture, the Achilles' heel of ideological states and one of the many places (the economy and technological capacity being among the others) where the West always held a decisive advantage. Indeed, many of the social and cultural openings to the Soviet Union later exploited by Western policy were initially breached during détente.

Moreover, during the era of détente, Soviet leaders came to value a certain standing and prestige they were given in the international system; although Henry Kissinger and Richard Nixon failed to coax the Soviet Union into becoming a status quo power, they did help to deepen Moscow's craving for international respect and legitimacy. (Even despots can chafe at constant castigation for being what they are.) American policy, through a series of treaties and other, less formal, recognitions of Soviet status, helped to continue the process begun by the Western Europeans in which the Soviets became, if not a status quo power, at the least a power led by men who were keenly aware of how they were perceived within the status quo itself.

In the first years of the twenty-first century, America is enjoying significant prosperity of a kind that makes the economic travails of the 1970s seem a distant memory. (Public carping about the so-called "energy crisis" of 2001, which nudged gasoline prices up, must seem almost quaint to older Americans who remember the oil shocks and gas lines of a quarter century earlier.) But prosperity, like the preeminent American military position at the turn of the century, is not a fact but a policy that is as sensitive to international change—as evidenced by the economic downturn spurred by the September 2001 terrorist attacks, for example—as any other. While it is unlikely in the foreseeable future that the United States will fall to the economic and military depths it experienced under Richard Nixon and Jimmy Carter, the experience of détente could nonetheless provide valuable insights should the West again find itself at a temporary disadvantage against a more robust or aggressive competitor.

In any case, there is a more worrisome problem than relative economic decline: the question of how to deter and contain rising powers that do not value peace or the international status quo as the United States does. These powers might be states with whom America shares almost no common experience; in this regard, it is important to remember that by the time détente emerged between the Soviet Union and the United States, both superpowers had not only previously had the opportunity to work in tandem (dating back to the Grand Alliance of World War II), but also had been chastened by crises ranging from Berlin to Cuba. Future attempts at détente may have to be undertaken with opponents who are more radical and with whom the United States has had less contact than the Brezhnev-era USSR. Whatever the eventual failings of détente, it is still worth asking what might be taken from the experience of the 1970s—and what might be avoided.

YOU JUST CAN'T HAVE THIS KIND OF WAR: NUCLEAR WEAPONS AND THE ADVENT OF DÉTENTE

The environment in which détente came about was not one that either its supporters or its detractors could choose, but instead was driven by technological developments that made the reliable delivery of large numbers of nuclear weapons possible. "According to American data, the U.S.A. and the USSR have built up enough weapons to destroy each other many times over," Richard Nixon told Leonid Brezhnev upon meeting him in 1972. "We have come to the same conclusion," Brezhnev replied.[5]

This is not to say that technological change irresistibly produces strategies or that decision-makers were helplessly propelled along the path of détente by the missile age, but rather that the East-West conflict, by the late 1950s, was taking place in a very different strategic environment than the one in which it began. Détente came to mean many things, but the wellspring of the basic idea was the simple fact of an emerging parity in long-range nuclear missiles and the consequent price of war. Images of conflict in the immediate postwar decade, in which both sides apparently envisioned a Red Army sweep of Europe followed by something like World War II with nuclear bombs, quickly gave way to the realization that World War III would be something a bit bigger than Stalingrad or the Bulge and that the tense peace between East and West might have to be more enduring than either side initially thought possible.[6]

In 1949, the Soviet Union ended the American atomic monopoly; four years later, the Soviet hydrogen bomb was tested less than a year after the appearance of its American counterpart. These early bombs were few in number and difficult to deliver, and while there was no shortage of fear and panic over a Soviet atomic attack, there was still little grasp of "nuclear war" as destruction on a planetary scale. But with the coming of the missile age, it was not long before the horrific meaning of hundreds of missile-delivered bombs began to sink in. In 1957, President Dwight Eisenhower rejected the alarmist prescriptions of the secret review of American defense policy, the Gaither Report (which warned the Soviets would have an intercontinental nuclear missile advantage over the United States by 1959 and advocated a crash program of missile construction), saying that "you just can't have this kind of war. There aren't enough bulldozers to scrape the bodies off the streets."[7]

All in all, the 1950s were anxious years for the Americans where the Cold War was concerned, even if they are now remembered as a kind of golden era of peace and prosperity. (The Gaither Report, for example, was leaked to the *Washington Post*, which said it "shows an America exposed to an almost immediate threat from the missile-bristling Soviet Union"; former defense secretary Robert Lovett said that reading it was like "looking in the abyss and seeing Hell at the bottom.")[8] The decade had begun with the mayhem of Korea and gotten progressively worse, and not just because of the development of Soviet nuclear weapons. In 1955, the Soviets responded to the rearming of Germany in NATO by forming the Warsaw Pact, and the following year Soviet troops crushed the Hungarian revolt while the British, French, and Americans were busy bickering over the Suez crisis. The problem of Berlin continued to fester, with Moscow continually threatening to reach its own arrangements with a regime the other Allies did not recognize and thus, in effect, to spark a new European war. The October 1957 launch of *Sputnik* created a national panic in the United States, with physicist Edward Teller making the hyperbolic claim that America had now lost a battle more important than Pearl Harbor.[9]

The Americans were losing the arms race, or so many thought, and the putative "missile gap" became an issue in the 1960 election. (The gap, Eisenhower rightly complained, was a fiction, pushed by what he saw as "sanctimonious, hypocritical bastards," but it was a fiction that had a firm hold on the public imagination at the time.)[10] The Soviets, masters of what was thought to be a nearly monolithic empire from the Baltic coast to the Soviet and Chinese Pacific shores, seemed to be ascendant. Led by Nikita Khrushchev, the man who had no compunction about threats to "bury" the United States—he had meant that primarily in economic terms, but the nuance was understandably lost on many Americans—and spoke of cranking out missiles like "sausages," the Soviet Union was a now an apparently fearless opponent.

The 1960s, which began with the U-2 incident and the building of the Berlin Wall, did not promise to be much better. (His confidant and colleague, Anastas Mikoian, later claimed that Khrushchev's hotheaded reaction to the U-2 shootdown in particular helped to "bury détente" for the time being and to prolong excessive Soviet defense spending just as the Kremlin was hoping for better relations with the United States.)[11] Although Khrushchev's blustery hijinks, as it turned out, were intended to mask the fact that the missile gap was in fact a *Soviet* gap, this did not make his thunderings any less alarming. Khrushchev did not intend to remain behind the United States in nuclear weapons or delivery systems: to the contrary, he was unswerving in his intention to make the USSR more, rather than less, dependent on nuclear arms.

Desperate as he was to reduce the burden of defense expenditures on the Soviet budget, Khrushchev had committed the Soviet Union to a shortsighted but cost-saving strategy much like the American concept of "massive retaliation," in which nuclear weapons would be the ultimate arbiter of any armed conflict between East and West. Central to this strategy was a doctrinal declaration that a war of any size between the superpowers, even a so-called local war, would inevitably become a nuclear war.[12] Consequently, the Soviet defense establishment was reconfigured for nuclear conflict, right down to the closure of lines of jet fighter aircraft and the dismantling of surface naval vessels (useless, of course, in the one-day war represented by an intercontinental nuclear missile duel) in the docks of Leningrad.

But to hold the United States at bay with Soviet nuclear weapons meant that Khrushchev needed the ability to deliver a fast, reliable nuclear strike against American cities. He also needed to convince skeptics among his colleagues in Moscow that conventional arms were the weapons of the past and that nuclear warheads were those of the future. "Right now," he boasted to Mao Zedong in 1958, "with our intercontinental missiles, we have America by the throat."[13] But the Soviet intercontinental arsenal was smaller than that of the United States, and Soviet bomber aircraft were drastically inferior to the American fleet. The answer to Khrushchev's problems, or so he thought, was to use Cuba to place the Americans under the same kind of immediate threat that U.S. weapons in Europe posed to the Soviet Union.

Few events in the Cold War have been analyzed at more length and with less profit than the Cuban missile crisis. Endless studies have shown, with ostensible finality, that the lesson of Cuba is to stand firm, to negotiate, to capitulate, to communicate, to empathize, to threaten, and on and on. These debates have become a matter more of religion than anything else and will not be rehearsed here. Perhaps the only lesson to be drawn from the events of October 1962 is that no opponent should think that any American administration will ever accept, even at the risk of war, the stationing of enemy nuclear missiles 90 miles from the United States. Much has been made of the "secret deal" that would eventually remove American missiles from Turkey as part of the cost of a Soviet retreat, but even Khrushchev's colleagues did not think it much of a deal and told him so as they removed him from office:

> Not having any other way out [charged one of the speakers at a special meeting of the Central Committee in 1964], we had to accept every demand and condition dictated by the U.S., going as far as permitting U.S. airplanes to inspect our ships. At the insistence of the United States, the missiles, and most of our forces there, had to be withdrawn from Cuba. . . . This incident damaged the international prestige of our government, our party, our armed forces, while at the same time helping to raise the authority of the United States.[14]

A Chinese delegation a year earlier had made the same accusation: "The facts are that under threat from the United States you were obliged to remove your missiles. . . . Besides that, you also conduct propaganda among the peoples of the world, convincing them to believe in some sort of promise by Kennedy, and thereby you adorn American imperialism."[15] In the end, the Kennedy administration declared the situation intolerable, the Soviet Union reversed itself, and the outcome was perceived as an American victory, even in Moscow and Havana.

In terms of détente, the more important aspect of the Cuban crisis is that it drove home the point that American nuclear supremacy was no guarantee of peace and that America itself was vulnerable to attack. In the 1962 nuclear war plan, which envisioned a spasmodic emptying of the U.S. arsenal in an attempt to eradicate enemy nuclear forces, American planners admitted that some fraction of the Soviet nuclear inventory, even without the Cuban missiles, would survive and strike the United States, killing millions and causing catastrophic damage.[16]

It also reaffirmed that the Soviet Union was a direct threat to the United States, not just to its neighbors in Europe or Asia. (The shoe-banging and bellicose grandstanding that might have made Khrushchev seem a somewhat comic figure in the late 1950s probably seemed a lot less funny to people stocking fallout shelters in 1962.) This trip to the brink of war was followed by a kind of mini détente, in which it was "understood that both superpowers would continue the ideological struggle," including continued actions against each other's clients in the Third World, while "committ[ing] themselves to finding nonmilitary solutions to their problems."[17] The most prominent achievement of this short thaw was the 1963 test ban treaty and the installation of the "hot line," but these were mechanical rather than fundamental issues. This more cordial atmosphere was an unnatural condition for two states determined to contest global supremacy and did not last much past Kennedy's assassination and Khrushchev's removal.

In any case, Khrushchev's Cuban gamble had solved nothing in terms of Soviet nuclear inferiority, and once he was deposed, his successors set about engaging in a major military buildup and overhaul of military doctrine. This reform of defense policy, undertaken in the main from 1965 to 1967, was meant to remedy both the missile gap and the breach in Soviet civil-military relations opened by Khrushchev's crude attempts to subdue the more expensive conventional branches of the Soviet armed forces. Although the Soviets would never succeed in matching U.S. military power system for system, particularly at sea, the modernization and expansion of their nuclear missile forces was a major success, and by the early 1970s, the description of a "missile-bristling" USSR was actually one that could be applied to both superpowers.

Even before the full impact of this post-Khrushchev military reorganization was evident, U.S. and NATO policymakers could not escape the realization that by approximately 1970, Western nuclear superiority would be a thing of the past and that in the interim the Soviet and American arsenals would grow to immense sizes. Parity turned Eisenhower's belief that "you just can't have this kind of war" into a more urgent need for both sides to avoid such a conflict at almost any cost. A lot had changed since 1957, and a nuclear war in 1970 with an exchange of thousands of weapons would create a lot more problems than the lack of bulldozers for the bodies.

Aside from the fact that a war between the superpowers would lay waste to the entire Northern Hemisphere, however, there was now no military sense in a first strike because of recent technological and quantitative developments. First, missiles had moved from insecure launch pads to more sturdy silos and submarines, thus drastically reducing the probability that they could be destroyed by an enemy strike. While any attack against silos would require great accuracy, no one really knew how accurate missiles were under actual wartime conditions or whether they would survive their transpolar flight and fall where they were aimed. In theory, manned bombers were far more accurate, but relying on them was based on the shaky assumption that they could survive the initial attack and enemy air defense measures—and an even shakier assumption that there would be anything of military value left on either side to hit some eight or ten hours after World

War III began with ICBM strikes. Second, the sheer numbers of missiles had grown to the point where it was virtually impossible to destroy them all in one salvo. The third development came later in the decade: the arming of missiles with multiple warheads, an innovation that made a preemptive strike more tempting (since there were fewer targets to hit on the ground as opposed to the many more that would appear in flight) but also made any reliable defense against an attack impossible given the technology of the time.

Taken together, these developments meant that each superpower now had a "secure second strike capability," which meant that no matter which side launched or was struck first, enough weapons would remain not only to do great damage to the attacker, but in fact to destroy it. The Americans gave a name to the fact that each side could now fully hold the other hostage and embraced it actively as a matter of policy: "mutual assured destruction" or MAD.

There is a great deal more to the nuclear theology that surrounded the advent of parity—this was, after all, the period in which nuclear strategy became a specialized, almost incomprehensibly complex endeavor. But however tangled the plans and scenarios that tumbled from military organizations and think tanks on both sides of the Atlantic, the fact of MAD was inescapable. The Soviets grudgingly accepted MAD as a reality, if not a desirable situation: it ran counter to an approach to the nuclear arms race that Volkogonov described as "dictated by a class mentality," one that demanded a "struggle for parity, and no concessions on anything so long as there was a possibility to achieve superiority."[18] The Americans, in the person of Secretary of Defense Robert McNamara, presented MAD as an inherently stabilizing phenomenon that ought to be encouraged and maintained.[19] Soviet objections and American enthusiasm were beside the point: parity existed, regardless of what anyone in Moscow or Washington thought of it. Unless one side or the other could find a magic bullet and break the nuclear impasse, there was no way to contemplate eradication of enemy forces without accepting suicidal levels of damage and casualties in return.

The fundamental political reality of parity, then, was that the Soviet Union and the United States had to learn to live with each other, and this in turn was the strategic cornerstone of détente. "A wholesale assault on the communist system under conditions of nuclear parity," Kissinger was to write later in defending détente, "promised to be long and bitter."[20] Soviet leaders, who had labored under conditions of conventional military superiority but nuclear inferiority, began to breathe easier as the perceived threat of a U.S. first strike receded.[21] (Still, the decreased likelihood of nuclear war actually worried some in the Warsaw Pact who preferred to keep the peace with nuclear terror rather than to shift to more expensive conventional arms.)[22] This did not mean war was unthinkable; both sides dutifully prepared for Armageddon on the chance that a crisis, miscalculation, or other unforeseen circumstance could raise the possibility of nuclear conflict even if neither side wanted it. Foreshadowing differences that would emerge over détente, there was a clear divergence between the Soviet and American understanding of the nuclear dynamics driving détente in the first place. The Americans, harking back to Bernard Brodie's comment that nuclear weapons meant "the end of strategy as we know it," interpreted MAD to mean that nuclear weapons did little else but deter the use of other nuclear weapons or, at worst, that they would enforce a kind of intrawar deterrence by being a source of punishment in kind for every nuclear weapon used in intercontinental combat. The Soviets, by contrast, maintained that a nuclear war would be war like any other, a war in the classical sense as even Clausewitz would understand it, undertaken for political aims and capable of producing a meaningful victory.[23] (Brezhnev would repudiate this position publicly in 1977, but the Soviet General Staff would cling to the idea of "nuclear victory" into the 1980s.)[24]

Conflicting ideas about "victory" after a nuclear war were not enough to undermine the pressure felt by both superpowers to seek a kind of breathing space after the acrimony and crises of the 1950s and 1960s. Although derailed first by the war in Vietnam and then again by the Soviet invasion of Czechoslovakia, by 1969, the superpowers were heading for a relationship that acknowledged them to be equals, accepted the international status quo insofar as it related to the postwar settlement in Europe, and accepted the ghastly reality of nuclear war. These three precepts would, as it turns out, survive the era of détente itself, at least until 1981. The problem with détente was not in these explicit assumptions the superpowers shared, but rather in the implicit ones each held separately.

THE UNITED STATES AND THE PERMANENCE OF DÉTENTE

Détente was the product of differing U.S. views of the Soviet Union and of differing opinions about what, if anything, to do about growing Soviet power. It was not so much a policy as a collection of policies, many of which did not share fundamental beliefs. Some saw the Soviet Union as aggressive but rational and therefore amenable to negotiation and compromise or, at the least, to pursuing their interests with a minimum of fuss and rhetoric. Others saw the United States as the source of just as much mischief in the world, if not more, as communism and saw détente as a welcome respite in the Cold War that belatedly recognized Moscow's defensiveness in the face, as Harry Gelman has written, of American "excesses."

> [S]ome felt more dangerous tendencies might come to the fore in the Soviet leadership and in Soviet policy if American policy were overly provocative. According to this reading, Americans should empathize with Soviet perceptions of a hostile and dangerous United States and not provoke dangerous confrontations by contesting Soviet policy too vigorously.[25]

But whether détente was seen as a tool for managing tensions or an atonement for overly aggressive Western policies in the past, all advocates of lessened tensions apparently agreed on one thing: détente should be permanent, and efforts to disturb it were a threat to the peace, either because they would interfere with the careful balancing act of the realists or they would convince Moscow that there was no point in dealing peacefully with hotheaded Americans. Even after the word "détente" was banished from the White House under Gerald Ford, the essential goal of maintaining the relationship with the Soviet Union would remain, although the term itself was to remain unspoken. This would not change until 1979, when Jimmy Carter and later Ronald Reagan would abandon any pretense of common interest with the USSR beyond that of avoiding war.

That détente, in the American vision, had no obvious end in sight is not surprising, given that it had no obvious beginning, either. Initially, détente was a child of necessity rather than a conscious policy, as the Americans found themselves in the position of having to catch up with political developments among their allies. West German Chancellor Willy Brandt, upon election in 1969, pursued a line first explored by the French of circumventing the stagnant relationship between Moscow and Washington in the 1960s and bettering relations with the Soviet Union as a European, rather than Atlantic, initiative. Brandt was seeking greater contact with and access to East Germany, and so he repudiated the so-called "Hallstein Doctrine," under which the Federal Republic of Germany had refused to maintain relations with any nation save the USSR that recognized East Germany as a legitimate state.

In Kissinger's account, the Nixon administration was uncomfortable with Brandt's *Ostpolitik*, but realized that the Hallstein Doctrine was "unsustainable" and that support for progress on the overall German question might finally ease the decades old Soviet-American standoff over the status of Berlin.[26] Beyond that, however, it was unclear what direction or form détente was supposed to take. Kissinger claims, in a passage that could serve as a realist's credo, that he and Nixon saw détente a means of protecting American interests while dealing with the new realities of power in the 1970s:

Nixon's new approach to foreign policy challenged American exceptionalism and its imperative that policy be based on the affirmation of transcendent values. America's challenge, as Nixon and his advisors saw it, was to adapt these traditional verities to the new international environment. America's domestic experience had led it to interpret the international order as essentially benign, and its diplomacy as an expression of goodwill and a willingness to compromise. Nixon's foreign policy, on the other hand, perceived the world as composed of ambiguous challenges, of nations impelled by interest rather than goodwill, and of incremental rather than final changes—a world, in short, that could be managed but could be neither dominated nor rejected. In such a world, no clear-cut terminal point beckoned, and the solution to one problem was more likely to turn into an admission ticket to the next one.[27]

Détente, then, was an ongoing process, not a goal in itself, "a foreign policy geared to staying power as much as to salvation," in Kissinger's words. Nixon saw "no contradiction in treating the communist world as both adversary and collaborator: adversary in fundamental ideology and in the need to prevent communism from upsetting the global equilibrium; collaborator in keeping the ideological conflict from exploding into a nuclear war."[28]

Underlying this exposition of détente is an implicit admission both of its ad hoc origins and its eventual permanence in the minds of its advocates. Brandt, at least, had specific ends in mind, while the Nixon administration sought only to manage the Soviet Union as a "geopolitical phenomenon" and avoid destroying the planet. (Kissinger warned in 1974 that efforts to use détente as a means of changing Soviet internal policies was to risk "what must remain our overriding objective—the prevention of nuclear war.")[29] It was difficult to see in the American approach where détente could lead to a particular situation in which its goals could be proclaimed to have been "achieved"; indeed, even to pose the question in this way would run counter to what Nixon and Kissinger apparently intended the policy to mean. Kissinger pointedly describes critics of Nixon's policy as "more concerned with ideology than with geopolitics," and describes the later debate over détente as a contest between "proponents of foreign policy as strategy and foreign policy as crusade."[30]

In the short term, a lowering of Soviet-American tensions suited America well enough, for reasons that ranged from the political upheavals in Washington to the disarray in the economy. Fighting the Soviet Union on everything from arms control to the Third World (including Vietnam) would have been costly and unpopular. But there was little thinking beyond the short term; as Nixon, Kissinger, and Ford practiced it, détente remained a strategy that delayed or deflected but did not resolve fundamental issues between the United States and the

Soviet Union. While this may have been useful to the United States in
the immediate circumstances, the fact that the Kremlin found this ad
hoc approach to détente to be perfectly suited to Soviet ends should
have been a cautionary sign.

For the USSR, an American foreign policy that emphasized mitigating
day-to-day frictions while leaving aside the larger ideological conflict
was not only acceptable, but even desirable, and if Nixon had not
offered it, the Soviets might well have sought it anyway. The architects
of détente might argue that this is true but not relevant. Kissinger's
irritation at critics like Senator Henry Jackson who argued, in effect, that
Nixon and then Ford were being played for saps by the Soviet Union is
understandable, not least because he and other supporters of détente
had never asserted and did not believe that the Soviets had agreed to a
more cooperative relationship out of anything but their own self-interest. "The real issue," Kissinger argued, "is whether détente also served
America's purposes."[31]

This raises the question of what, in fact, America's purposes were.
Unstated in all this is why the Soviets and the Americans were in a
confrontational relationship in the first place. Realist assumptions
about the interests of generic great powers had displaced the problem
of Soviet ideology, and so détente, as a realist solution, displaced other
approaches by default. The Americans assumed the permanence of the
enemy's regime and took the tense equilibrium of the Cold War as
something to manage, rather than to solve. To abjure direct attacks on
the opponent in the name of avoiding a planetary holocaust is only
prudent. To assume that the agreement of the enemy in this regard,
however, is equivalent to an understanding about the role of war and
the value of peace is a strategic error of the first order. The Soviets
understood this; the Americans did not.

THE SOVIET UNION: DÉTENTE AS STRATEGY

There could be no greater threat to American or Soviet interests than
a nuclear war, and in this sense, the Soviets and the Americans shared
a common understanding of the value of détente. The Soviets, however,
saw the stabilization of international life during the Cold War as creating
a more congenial environment for the conduct of war short of nuclear
violence, a direct contradiction of the growing American sense that
détente reflected an overall conceptual convergence between the superpowers. That is, Moscow saw détente as a strategy, an instrument that
would further Soviet goals, and not as some fundamental reordering of
international politics. Through the entire period, as Robert Conquest
writes,

the Soviet "ideological" offensive went ahead. At home in the USSR, there was a continuous flow of propaganda (the viciousness of whose tone is still not sufficiently appreciated abroad) against the internal evils and the international aggressiveness and militarism of the West, blanketing the country with harsh abuse and plain lies. Abroad, every possible medium was employed to blacken the Western governments and their friends, to assist their enemies, and to undermine their military defenses and their political will.[32]

The Americans cannot with any justice claim to be surprised by this, even if they acted as though the Soviet pursuit throughout the 1970s of their ongoing struggle with the West were some sort of betrayal of a mutual understanding. Soviet leaders and writers at the time were blunt in their admissions that détente meant only a military détente, a set of steps and agreements to lessen the probability of all-out nuclear war. The "ideological struggle," as it was commonly referred to in the Soviet press, would go on, as would the Soviet dedication to contesting peripheral areas with the United States.

This delineation and use of a military détente as a strategy, as opposed to a broader conceptual reconciliation, was understandable in ideological terms, and in retrospect, it is hard to imagine how the Soviets could have seen détente in almost any other light. The Soviet worldview was, unlike its American counterpart, teleological: the Soviet Union was a state with a destination at a specific point in history, while the United States was a state intent on perfecting a destiny it felt it had already gained at its founding. For the Americans, peace and prosperity were the desired order of things; while for the Soviets, these were conditions whose value was only measurable against the contribution they made to the eventual achievement of the state's ultimate goals.

A dispassionate observer might comment that by 1972, the Soviet Union was in fine shape: a regional empire, a wide set of alliances across the globe, relative prosperity, and the respect of the international community as a power coequal to the United States. To assume, however, that this was enough for a state committed to revolutionary dynamism—even if that dynamism had nearly been suffocated in the domestic sphere by years of repression and stifling political orthodoxy—is to miss the regime's constant need to revalidate itself in its own eyes and those of its citizens and allies. (Even when the American economy was at a standstill and the Soviets were arguably at their height of their power, for example, the regime's insecurity about comparing living standards was tangible.)[33] To accept détente as a fact of life rather than a strategy would have contravened essential tenets of Soviet ideology, and Soviet spokesmen, particularly among the military, were always harshly critical of any attempt to remove ideology from discussion of the East-West relationship as attempts to poison Eastern minds with "bourgeois" Western political views.[34] The idea that détente later fell victim to ordinary great power politics and that its collapse could be equally blamed on Moscow and Washington was a charge that met with special hostility on the part of Soviet commentators, who instead presented the end of détente as a kind of morality play in which dark imperialist forces triumphed over more sensible and peaceful people.[35]

The Soviet approach to détente was strongly colored by the opportunities that Moscow saw in the West's hopes for better relations. The Soviets did not survey their position in the 1970s and sigh with relief that they had finally arrived at some plateau of safety, but assumed instead that they were now the ascendant power and that the United States was in decline. The Kremlin did not see détente as a flexible American accommodation with a changing world order (the way Kissinger hoped it would be seen); rather, they drew the conclusion that it was the direct result of American weakness and the fading allure of the American system. Disarray in NATO helped to confirm this Soviet diagnosis, with disagreements between Washington and Brussels seen as heralding the end of NATO in any useful military sense. By 1975, Soviet writers were openly talking about a "crisis of trust" in the Atlantic Alliance that was driving the United States back toward North America literally and figuratively.[36]

Looking back in 1980 over the previous decade, Soviet foreign policy spokesman Henry Trofimenko wrote that détente, like the "Nixon Doctrine" of shifting defense burdens to regional allies, was a policy of necessity for Washington, driven by

> a comparatively realistic conclusion drawn by official Washington from the lessons of Vietnam and, in a broader sense, from an analysis of a new world balance of power, which had shifted away from the United States. . . . [I]n spite of the endeavor to maintain what military-power position the United States still had, it proved to be the first and only doctrine in a long line of U.S. doctrines proclaimed since World War II which postulated not stepped up confrontation with the Soviet Union and the other socialist nations but a shift to negotiation with them, and acknowledged the fact that U.S. capabilities were limited in the area of shaping the international situation.[37]

Nixon's sensible policies, Trofimenko sadly adds, fell victim to the "political-financial clique" of the northeastern American elite. (How this shadowy group deposed the Californian Nixon to install the Michigander Ford and then got stuck with the Georgian Carter is a mystery; Trofimenko's evaluation is obviously based on first ideological principles rather than what actually happened in American politics between 1974 and 1977.)[38] This reading of the United States, when combined with the restless need to expand (Arbatov's "revolutionary inferiority complex"), drove the Soviets to see détente as an opportunity for more global gains rather than as a new understanding of the rules of international politics.

The relative clarity of Soviet goals, compared with the fuzzy melding of *realpolitik* and idealistic pedantry that characterized American aims, should make evident the advantages that Western confusion offered to the East. Craig Nation has summed up Soviet aims in détente concisely, and they are revealing in themselves:[39]

1. To stabilize the arms race once approximate strategic parity with the United States was achieved.
2. To win international acceptance of the postwar security order in Europe.
3. To create a more propitious climate for East-West trade and technology transfer.
4. To neutralize the threat of U.S.-Chinese collusion by giving the West a greater stake in positive relations with the USSR.

To this, one could make the obvious addition of avoiding a general war with the United States, of course. Note, however, that not one of these aims is even remotely related to the overarching American view of détente as an instrument for keeping the peace and altering the Soviet perception of the value of the international status quo. Indeed, these four goals could be restated thus: (1) To lock in a nuclear balance while leaving the Soviets in a commanding position in Europe; (2) to force the West's final approval for the takeover of Eastern Europe after 1945 and thus to legitimate the Soviet conquest of the region; (3) to salve the increasingly worrisome wounds in the Soviet economy with Western goods and know-how while making no fundamental political concessions to get them; and (4), to feign friendship with one enemy in order to divide a possible alliance it might make with another.

The Soviet version of détente, as a strategy, was a great success. Nuclear parity and MAD were enshrined so firmly at the heart of the Soviet-American relationship—at least in Western eyes—that even in the early twenty-first century, Washington's plans for national missile defenses were still hampered by concerns in both East and West over the 1972 Antiballistic Missile Treaty. The Soviet imperium in Europe went unchallenged for another twenty years and collapsed only within 18 months of the final collapse of the USSR itself. The record on trade and technology is more mixed, but at the least the Kremlin could rest assured that the West would not make things harder than they already were. Only where China is concerned did Moscow fail, and even there, had the Soviets been more willing to cooperate with the Nixon administration on Vietnam, it is possible the Sino-American rapprochement in 1971 could have been delayed or undermined.

The Americans had hoped to alter Soviet behavior and to create a more benign international environment, to turn the Cold War from a condition of ongoing crisis to one of businesslike competition. The Nixon administration doggedly pursued nuclear arms control on Soviet terms, despite repeated Soviet support for aggression in various hot spots and the tightening of restraints on liberties at home. The result, by the time Kissinger and Gerald Ford left Washington in 1977, was a Soviet resurgence that left Moscow and its empire in a commanding position and the United States scrambling to meet challenges at almost every level of the Soviet-American conflict, from strategic nuclear arms to proxy wars on the periphery.[40] The Soviet version of détente, as a strategy for decreasing the likelihood of war while simultaneously pursuing Soviet goals aggressively in areas outside of Europe, was an undeniable success—certainly more so than its American counterpart.

THE FAILURE OF LINKAGE

If the Soviets succeeded in separating the military aspects of détente from the overall ideological struggle, it was in no small part due to the fact that the Americans let them. This was not the original intent behind the bettering of relations; Nixon and Kissinger came to the White House promising to enforce the notion of "linkage," in which progress in arms control and other areas dear to Moscow had to be matched by better Soviet behavior in other areas. The theory seemed simple enough: if the Soviets value progress on one issue, they must compromise on another. "Crisis or confrontation in one place," Nixon told Congress in 1969, "and real cooperation in another cannot long be sustained simultaneously. . . . We must seek to advance on a front at least broad enough to make clear that we see some relationship between political and military issues."[41] The Soviets were clearly eager to continue negotiations on strategic arms, and Nixon hoped this would give him leverage to make headway on regional issues such as the Middle East and with regard to ongoing Soviet assistance to Vietnam.[42] Insofar as the Americans saw in détente a strategy to further U.S. interests, linkage was its primary instrument. But if détente and linkage are to be judged by their effects on Soviet behavior, they were resounding failures. What went wrong?

John Gaddis has cataloged the shortcomings of linkage from the American side, including the fact that it was based on rosy assumptions of Soviet intentions, that Nixon and Kissinger oversold it to the public and to Congress, and that the U.S. foreign policy bureaucracy was not structured to engage in the sort of centralized control over rewards and punishments that linkage envisioned.[43] But with regard to the nature of the Soviet opponent, it was flawed at a higher level, based as it was on a poor understanding of American strengths and weaknesses relative to those of the USSR. Worse, it embodied the classic war-gaming mistake of planning for the convenience of what one would like the enemy to do, rather than the more thorny possibilities of what the enemy is capable of doing.

A fatal problem with linkage is that Soviet and American decision-makers were not governing in the same social environment, nor were they managing the same types of coalitions. The Kremlin could maintain a rhetorical commitment to peace with little consequence at home, primarily by altering the flow of information about American policies. Moscow's "allies," particularly those that faced NATO directly on the Western front, were satellites, having learned in 1956 and 1968 the risks of crossing their imperial masters. If there was no progress on arms control, it could be laid at Washington's door with little fear of contradiction. Even where there may have been popular Soviet support for better relations—the extent of such support is unknowable now—there was no way for that support to find political expression. In any case, Moscow set about preparing itself for the impact of détente in ways that Washington did not or could not.

> From the opening stages of the movement toward détente, the defensive reaction of the Brezhnev leadership had taken two forms. One was an effort to tighten ideological discipline within the Soviet Union, to strengthen controls in order to withstand the subversive effects anticipated from greater contacts with the West. The other was a sporadic effort to demonstrate—to one's peers and retainers—that Soviet opportunities to advance abroad were not being sacrificed to détente.[44]

The Americans, by comparison, found that the public had little stomach for the hardball politics of linkage. Arms control had already found a hallowed place in the public imagination, and public support in the United States and Europe could hardly be expected for a stance that risked the future of talks aimed at reducing nuclear weapons by linking them to the fate of oppressed groups in the USSR or a Soviet intervention in some part of the world most people would have trouble finding on a map.

The Soviets were aware that arms control was a winning issue and linkage was a loser, in the world's eyes, and made sure to consistently practice a kind of reverse linkage in which they would claim that progress on crucial issues of war and peace was only possible if Washington would stop playing games with more trivial issues.[45] Jimmy

Carter in particular would feel the full effect of this ploy when the
Soviets would use SALT II, which he dearly wanted, to deflect Carter's
human rights demands.

Another weakness, perhaps the most important one, of linkage is
that the Soviets figured out early on that the policy was in effect an
American bluff and that Washington had not thought through the
problem of what to do if Moscow called it. When the Soviets pressed
ahead and acted as though "linked" questions were in fact separable,
Nixon and Kissinger gave in to their own realist predilections rather
than disrupt the full range of Soviet-American relations over any one
issue. Andrei Gromyko paid a left-handed compliment to the White
House's willingness to back away from its stated commitment to
linkage in his memoirs.

> Fortunately for the world, Kissinger did not practice what he preached
> with total consistency. Thus most of the successes he eventually achieved
> in combination with the Soviet side—particularly in the field of nuclear
> arms control—occurred because Washington did *not* make agreement in
> one area conditional upon agreement in another [emphasis original].[46]

(When Kissinger later offered to join the decidedly anti*realpolitik*
Reagan administration, Gromyko acidly observed that "to ignore principles, as Kissinger had frequently done, is a game that takes its toll.")[47]

Linkage was a game of chicken played in full view of the world, and
while the stakes were something less than life or death—no one was
going to go to war over dissidents in Russia or Cubans in Africa—the
Americans were nonetheless loath to engage in it. In the end, the realists
of the 1970s could not bring themselves to inflict the costs of their own
policies on Moscow, and the project fell apart. The effect of this, as the
Soviets themselves admitted even at the time, was to free up resources
for Soviet involvement in the Third World by lowering the immediate
costs of Soviet-American confrontation, including in the arms race.[48]

Indeed, when Senator Jackson pushed in the early 1970s for the most
explicit kind of linkage by tying trade relations to human rights, Kissinger and Nixon opposed it. Kissinger has since argued—as advocates of
trade with China do now—that opponents of détente like Jackson
missed the point, which was supposedly to restrain Soviet *international*
behavior, not to change Soviet domestic arrangements, and that any
claim Nixon had gone soft on communism because he would not make
linkage so broad a concept was patently unfair.[49]

> On several occasions during the Brezhnev era, Nixon and his associates
> confronted the Soviet leadership when the Soviet will to power had not
> yet eroded. And we found them to be formidable adversaries. . . . After

Vietnam and in the midst of Watergate, we found ourselves in the position of a swimmer who, having just barely escaped drowning, is being urged to cross the English Channel and is then accused of pessimism when he displays a lack of enthusiasm at the prospect.[50]

The Soviets, for their part, sensed this reluctance, and as each "link" between American policy and Soviet behavior was broken, they became more daring in their attempts to undermine the entire concept.

This was unfortunate, because Jackson and others had hit upon an important Soviet vulnerability, as Dobrynin later wrote:

In the closed society of the Soviet Union, the Kremlin was afraid of emigration in general (irrespective of nationality or religion) lest an escape hatch from the happy land of socialism seem to offer a degree of liberalization that might destabilize the domestic situation. So the crucial difference in the Soviet and American approaches to the issue was that while the Americans wanted to export to the Soviet Union its free humanitarian and commercial values, the Soviet government simply wanted the commercial benefits of trade, but not the political values.[51]

It was precisely this link, between respect for Western values and the benefits of Western trade, that Kissinger and Nixon would not enforce. By 1976, when a major crackdown on dissident activity was undertaken, Moscow had little reason to fear that its own behavior could imperil the things it hoped to achieve in the Soviet-American relationship. "Linkage" and realism cannot coexist; as John Newhouse pointed out, linkage as it was practiced "infuses superpower exchanges with righteous indignation," exactly the kind of emotionalism that the Nixon administration hoped to avoid and tried to avert.[52]

Kissinger's comment, however, reveals another flaw in the policy of linkage, which is that it took Soviet power as a given rather than a problem. To say that the Americans were wary of assaulting the Soviets before their will to power had "eroded" raises the question of how such "erosion" is accomplished in the first place. This is a central question in thinking about the role of détente in a cold war, raising as it does the choice between active measures designed to undermine the enemy's power or a more passive strategy that inconsistently exploits whatever weaknesses might occur naturally.

The Americans chose the passive option. It is difficult to be overly critical of such a policy, since alternatives to it were costly: the two primary areas in which the Soviets were vulnerable to Western challenges were arms and trade. An all-fronts arms race, in which both NATO and Third World allies were rearmed in numbers and quality, would have strained the Soviet budget in response (this was in fact the post-1981 strategy) but would also have been a difficult burden on an already faltering U.S. economy. Halting trade would have been of questionable value and difficult to enforce, but at the least would have complicated Soviet efforts to gain access to various Western technologies. In any case, both of these were left unexploited in the 1970s; then, as now, the adherents of détente held to the view that the enemy was a permanent fact of life and that commercial and military treaties would do more to mellow a dogmatic and repressive opponent than arms races and trade embargoes.

Another problem with linkage is that although it exposed the Soviet vulnerability on human rights in particular and the state-society relationship in general, Nixon and the later détentists had no interest in exploring it because to do so conflicted with their own instincts. "I cannot remember an occasion when he launched into a digression on the differing social structures of our states," Gromyko recalled of Nixon. "He always presented himself as a pragmatist uninterested in the theoretical aspects of an issue, a man who preferred to keep discussions on a purely practical level."[53]

This antipolemical reflex set the tone for a general American disengagement from ideological assaults. In this period, for example, Radio Free Europe and Radio Liberty were forced to adopt the position that they had "no mandate to advocate the establishment or disestablishment of any particular system, form of state organization or ideology in the areas to which they broadcast." Thus, when such broadcasts could survive Soviet jamming long enough to be heard, they were deprived of any polemical edge so as not to offend the Kremlin authorities who were trying to block them anyway, leading Walter Laqueur to later write: "With instructions like these, it seems a miracle that the radios survived at all."[54]

And yet, while Nixon avoided making human rights a deal-breaker in Soviet-American relations, negotiations were taking place that would later place the issue at the heart of the Cold War. If détente had one unarguable success, it was to entice the Soviets into signing the Helsinki Accords, an agreement that would hold the USSR to a standard of behavior that would inevitably conflict with both its revolutionary ideals and its more pragmatic need to maintain an empire by force. As Stephen Sestanovich puts it, détente's "claim to have begun digging totalitarianism's grave is weak. All the same, this was the moment when the Soviet Union agreed to treat human rights as a principle of East-West relations—an act of real importance for the disaster to come."[55]

HUMAN RIGHTS AND THE RENEWED COLD WAR

Although the renewal of Soviet-American hostility in the 1980s has come to be popularly associated with Ronald Reagan, in fact this harshest (and as it turned out, final) phase of the Cold War began under President Jimmy Carter in the late 1970s. Like Reagan after him, Carter was first and foremost a moralist rather than a realist; he placed human rights at the top of his foreign policy agenda during his campaign and did not sway from it after his election. Like Reagan, his approach to the question of human rights in the USSR was greatly influenced by his personal religious beliefs.[56] Whatever Carter's other failures as president, he and Reagan may share the credit (or blame, depending on one's view) for steering U.S. policy away from the futile treadmill of realism and toward active confrontation of the Soviet Union on ideological grounds.

The emergence of Jimmy Carter, with his explicit attachment to human rights as a foreign policy issue, could not have come at a worse time for the Soviets, as it followed a public Soviet commitment to human rights that the Kremlin had not intended to honor but, in the spirit of détente, could not avoid. In 1975, the Soviet Union signed the Helsinki Final Act, an East-West document that expressly demanded civilized behavior of the USSR (and from the other signatories) as the price of admission to civilized international society.

The Helsinki Accords were roundly criticized in the 1970s as just one more stack of paper that gave the Soviets something—in this case, greater legitimacy—for nothing. But in fact, the so-called Basket Three agreements (the first two covered political and economic issues) actually contained potentially explosive language that ranged across everything from reunification of families to increasing access to foreign media. Worse, Basket Three was not a notional commitment, but rather a concrete obligation that would be enforced by all of the signatories acting, in effect, as observers of the others. The significance did not escape the Soviet leadership, as Dobrynin recalls:

> Gromyko from time to time informed Brezhnev and others in the Politburo of the progress of the negotiations, but they paid little attention to the complex phraseology. To them, it all looked like the routine work of diplomacy.
>
> But when the treaty was ready and the third basket emerged in its entirety before the members of the Politburo, they were stunned. As opening day drew closer, the Politburo engaged in heated debates over the documents Brezhnev was to sign on behalf of the Soviet government—not much about the first or second baskets, but about the third. Many in the Politburo (Podgorny, Suslov, Kosygin, Andropov) had grave doubts about assuming international commitments that could open the way to foreign interference in our political life.[57]

Gromyko argued at the time that the propaganda rewards and economic benefits of signing the agreement outweighed any other risk, telling his colleagues that no matter what the language of Basket Three, "We are masters in our own house."[58]

The Kremlin could be excused for underplaying the threat represented by Basket Three, since it had long fallen out of fashion in Washington or Western Europe to make an issue of human rights. The Soviets had joined the Helsinki process in the spirit of using détente as a strategy, with no intention of adhering to its letter or spirit if it conflicted with Soviet goals. "From the very start," according to Dobrynin, "the Politburo's acceptance of the Helsinki humanitarian principles implied some noncompliance."[59]

This is not as sinister as it sounds. In 1975, the American global position was in disarray (the Final Act was just over three months after the fall of Saigon), and there was no reason for the Kremlin to think the United States was any more inclined to disrupt Soviet-American relations over the Helsinki Accords than it had been over anything else. At the time, President Ford was being attacked constantly as too easy on the Soviets, but strangely, this did not worry the Kremlin, who saw the whole U.S. foreign policy debate only in ideological terms. "Our embassy in Washington," according to Dobrynin,

> made sure that the Soviet leadership was well aware of the widespread anti-Soviet campaign in the United States [including criticism of Ford and détente] but Moscow did little to neutralize it. Moscow was strangely convinced that such campaigns were inevitable as a direct result of the ideological struggle between the different social systems.[60]

Brezhnev in fact wondered why Ford did not run as the peace candidate against "this obscurantist" Reagan in the primaries, thus showing a complete misunderstanding of the political situation in the United States at the time.[61] The Soviets concluded that insofar as Washington was capable of conducting a foreign policy in 1975, it seemed like it would be a continuation of the Nixon-Kissinger realist approach and would continue to veer away from overtly ideological issues like human rights.

THE LESSONS OF DÉTENTE

As with "engagement" in the late twentieth century, détente was a policy that drifted in conflicting directions because it had no clear goals other than a general desire to avoid war. On the one hand, it seemed to accept the immutability of the USSR and strove only to manage the inevitable tensions that would arise between the United States and the Soviet Union as, respectively, the dominant power and the challenger. On the other hand, it carried a pedantic undertone, a belief that the

Soviets would internalize the norms of the international system by participating in it, especially if their aspirations to legitimacy were taken seriously. This, as John Gaddis has pointed out, was the "patronizing" side of détente, a belief that the Soviet Union could be trained "like some laboratory animal."[62] Kissinger would no doubt argue that this attempt to constrain the Soviets by involving them as a partner in the international status quo only reflected the Nixon team's confidence that détente should have been allowed to stand the "test of time" rather than being subverted by Jackson and other hard-line anticommunists.[63] This is essentially the same confusion in American policy with regard to China and other challengers in the twenty-first century: realists press for engagement as a means of averting misunderstanding and managing tensions, with the most optimistic Westerners certain that there is little wrong with China that a decade of American fast food and Internet access cannot cure.

Based on an obstinate realism that refused to come to terms with the unyielding ideological agenda of the opponent, détente did little to slow Soviet advances in strategic arms (although it restrained American research), lessen the worrisome imbalance in Europe (although Soviet propaganda managed to strain relations between NATO and the United States), or halt Soviet forays into the Third World (even as the Americans retreated from it). Even Kissinger would admit later that "the Nixon administration veered too far in the direction of stressing what it perceived as America's geopolitical necessities."[64]

Moreover, the tangible benefits of détente to the Soviets helped to postpone the economic reckoning that continually threatened their system. "Why bother developing your science and technology when you can order entire plants from abroad?" Arbatov later asked.

> Who needs to find radical solutions to the food problem when it's so easy to buy tens of millions of tons of grain, and no small amounts of butter and other products, from America, Canada, and Western Europe? Who needs to salvage the dreadfully backward construction industry when you can invite Finnish, Yugoslav or Swedish companies to build or renovate the most important sites? Or when you can import the most scarce materials, the plumbing and fixtures from West Germany, the wallpaper and the furniture from other Western countries?[65]

It has since become fashionable to blame the Carter administration for rank incompetence and the Reagan administration for mindless aggressiveness, but both presidents inherited a Soviet opponent whose views toward America had been shaped in large part by the détentists. "Carter and his advisors," Gaddis has properly pointed out, not only "had the misfortune to come to power at a time when the Soviet Union was launching a new series of challenges to the global balance of power, but when the United States faced unusual constraints in trying to counter them."[66] These challenges were in no small part the result of what the Soviets, from their experiences with Nixon and Ford, had come to think was possible in dealing with the Americans.

In fairness, it should be asked whether détente's architects had realistic alternatives before them. Kissinger, in exasperation, once "challenged the challengers" on the issue in 1976:

> What do those who speak so glibly about "one-way streets" or "preemptive concessions" propose concretely that this country do? What precisely has been given up? What level of confrontation do they seek? What threats would they make? What risks would they run? What precise changes in our defense posture, what level of expenditure over time, do they advocate? How concretely do they suggest managing the U.S.-Soviet relationship in an era of strategic equality?[67]

To these questions could be added yet more about what Kissinger's detractors saw as limits, if any, on U.S. action in the 1970s. How many foreign deployments to remote corners of Africa or Asia, so soon after Vietnam, were they willing to send their sons on? (Congress answered some of these questions resolutely in turning down Ford's request for aid to anticommunist forces in Angola.) Although the United States does not yet face a coordinated attack on as many fronts now as it did in 1975 and the American economy is considerably more robust than it was, these are still the relevant questions that will arise if a nuclear-armed challenger decides to threaten the international status quo in the current era.

The last condition that Kissinger attached to his questions—"strategic equality"—is important in this regard. Nuclear parity drove the advent of détente, and it is too easy in the early twenty-first century to argue in retrospect that Nixon, Ford, or Carter should have thrown caution to the wind and tested the Soviet resolve to go to war. Even Reagan, as will be seen, for all the talk of protracted nuclear war (another concept that gained new life under Carter) did not intend to press the superpower confrontation to apocalypse. Given that direct confrontation was foreclosed by parity and that the United States had neither the money nor the military might to go head-to-head with the USSR even without the added risk of general nuclear war, what were the American leaders of the 1970s to do?

It is under such conditions, where military action is unfeasible or unpopular and other actions (such as large-scale aid to allies) might be prohibitively expensive, that a policy of détente can serve U.S. interests if it is approached in the Soviet sense—that is, as a strategy to pursue national goals by temporarily bettering relations with the enemy. There is nothing inherently flawed with "linkage," if that term is meant to be understood as nothing more or less than that something of value in one area must be earned by returning something of value in another. Even when in the throes of stagflation, the United States had much that the Soviets valued: concrete goods such as food and technology and less tangible but nonetheless important assets like respect and legitimacy. Washington could withhold trade as easily as it could recognition of Soviet aspirations, both without endangering American soldiers or courting a general war. (The Hallstein Doctrine, for example, may have become difficult to sustain. But there is a world of difference between a grudging admission that the GDR exists and a wholesale legitimization of Soviet gains in Eastern Europe, and there may have been more that could have been extracted from the Soviets for its abandonment.) The United States, in the early 1970s, did not have the capacity or the will to meet the Soviet challenge on its own terms, and so détente could have been approached as an asymmetrical strategy: by shifting East-West conflict away from military factors where the Soviets were dominant, America could change the nature of the competition and play to its privileged economic, scientific, and political position by using trade, technology, and legitimacy as leverage over Soviet behavior.

The problem is that the policy was neither conceived nor executed as an asymmetrical strategy and devolved quickly into a subtle form of appeasement. Nothing was held at risk; the Soviets not only refused to moderate their behavior in the Third World, but even escalated their efforts to the point where they endangered things they still valued, such as strategic arms control. Like relations between China and the United States in the 1990s, the Soviet-American relationship of the 1970s found Washington hoping that each American concession would provide the breakthrough that would finally halt the Soviet advance. Instead, the Soviets pressed on, emboldened by successes to the point where Defense Minister Grechko in 1974 would publicly embrace the global Soviet role the Americans had hoped they would forego.

> At the present stage the historic function of the Soviet Armed Forces is not restricted merely to their function in defending our Motherland and other socialist countries. In its foreign policy activity, the Soviet state actively and purposefully opposes the export of counterrevolution and the policy of oppression, supports the national liberation struggle, and resolutely resists imperialist aggression in whatever distant region of our planet it may appear.[68]

A year later (that is, only three years after SALT I), the Soviets evidently lost whatever small concern they might have had about "linkage" as it was practiced by Kissinger and Ford: 1975, Harry Gelman writes, was "the decisive crossover in Politburo attitudes toward the United States, away from the expectations of grandiose benefits from the bilateral relationship toward a more forthright flaunting of the pursuit of competitive advantage."[69]

If one alternative was to fulfill the explicit threats of linkage and actually to punish the Soviets for their behavior, another was to invoke the political equivalent of the Hippocratic oath and "first do no harm," that is, to eschew pursuing détente at all rather than to risk sending conflicting messages to Moscow. A policy that in effect continued the frosty relationship of the 1960s carried some risk, particularly in terms of coalition politics: the Europeans were committed to better relations with Moscow, with or without the United States, and the French pullout from NATO in 1966 had made clear that there were considerable limits on Washington's ability to control its allies. Still, a policy that offered few concessions but likewise expected little in return might have been less costly than one that offered much, expected much, and gained almost nothing. Certainly, détente did little to avert crises; the Soviet threat to move troops to the Middle East during the 1973 Yom Kippur War (whether a bluff or not) resulted in a U.S. nuclear alert and one of the most serious incidents since the Cuban missile crisis.

Another lesson of détente relates to the differences in managing domestic opinion in different kinds of states. As a means of conducting a cold war, détente requires even more steadfastness and clarity of purpose than confrontation. During crises, people rally to the side of their government; Americans in particular are inclined to put aside their differences with each other and with Washington if the lives of U.S. soldiers are in jeopardy. Managing public opinion over a protracted period of good relations, however, is more difficult in a democracy and especially so in one so prone to public optimism as the United States. In the 1970s, the Soviets had the advantage of being able to maintain a steady stream of anti-American propaganda aimed at its people while moderating its rhetoric in international venues. The United States has no such capacity, and any attempt at détente runs the risk of accidentally convincing the American public that whatever was at issue with the enemy is now resolved and all that remains is to press ahead with reduced numbers of arms and increased numbers of treaties.

The experience of the Soviet-American détente is to beware this imbalance and to resist overselling what few benefits might be expected from a lull in political hostilities. In 1999 and 2001, for example, Americans were surprised at the intensely hostile reaction of the Chinese over the accidental bombing of their embassy in Serbia, and later, the loss of a Chinese jet that downed a U.S. aircraft before crashing itself. Many in the United States reacted almost with a sense of betrayal, as though trade and public cordiality with the Chinese had eradicated any issues of substance between Washington and Beijing.

The issue of propaganda nonetheless illustrates the usefulness of détente as a means of gaining access to a population in a closed society. Despite the increased repression the Kremlin visited on its people in the hopes of inoculating them against Western influences, domestic Soviet propaganda efforts during and after détente often fell victim to Groucho Marx's classic line, "Who are you going to believe, me or your own eyes?" Contacts between Soviet citizens and the West, cultural exchanges, travel, the greater flow of information behind the Iron Curtain, and even the trickle of Western goods that made their way East all planted the seeds of doubt among the populations of the Soviet empire and induced a great deal of self-doubt and anxiety in the Kremlin itself. The Soviets were right to fear the sudden influx of information that would inevitably result from any reasonable adherence to the Helsinki accords. There was already too much dangerous information loose in the Soviet Union, as the former editor of *Ogonek* recalled in his memoirs, and détente could only make it worse.

> You can't imagine how much information there was around us, and how it was sorted, through so many channels! . . . An interesting detail: censors were always paid more than any of the chief editors. The state's bureaucrats knew that news is an important means of brainwashing and that the person working as a filter in that stream of news is much more important than the one who formally signs the pages in the newspaper.[70]

Winston Churchill once observed that "it is probable that Soviet governments fear the friendship of the West even more than they do our hostility," and this should be turned to the Western advantage when possible in dealing with would-be totalitarians. Thus, an object of détente with any repressive society should be to loosen the regime's grip. This is exactly what China and Iran, to take two examples, clearly fear in better relations with the United States. Open societies should demand openness as the price of détente; it is not only consistent with their principles, but promises to reap far greater rewards in the long term than treaties laden with meaningless niceties.

To seek a détente that is in one's own interests because of social, financial, or military constraints is not only understandable, but might even be advisable under certain circumstances. But the attainment of a reduction in tensions should never be mistaken for a fundamental alteration of the enemy's ideological precepts or eventual goals. As Mastny reports, there was no connection between détente and Soviet military planning, which required promulgating scenarios in which

NATO attacks first, something Mastny and others rightly deride as "so ludicrous that hardly any general in his right mind would consider it."

> As the extensive records of the exercises of the East German army show particularly well, the Warsaw Pact kept practicing the thrust into Western Europe, with or without nuclear weapons, in ever greater detail, the perfectionist East Germans even printing in advance occupation currency and preparing new street signs with congenial names. . . . The Warsaw Pact's preparations for offensive warfare at a time when the Kremlin was not only preaching détente but also regarding it to be in its own best interest were all the more disconcerting since the Soviet command was far better informed than before about NATO's true intentions and capabilities.[71]

Soviet leaders were candid that there could be no ideological truce between the superpowers, even if that admission was not taken particularly seriously by their opposite numbers in Washington. The central flaw of détente, then and now, is that it is a policy driven by Western perceptions and beliefs and particularly by a prejudice that ideology (whether it is Communism, aggressive hypernationalism, or religion) is no match for either the crushing realist pressures of the international system or the siren song of Western culture and material abundance.

By the time the Soviets invaded Afghanistan in 1979, they had inflicted so much damage on détente by their own hand that the concept fell into well-earned disrepute. As Arbatov later recalled,

> We, in essence, became participants in the "dismantling" of détente [at the end of the 1970s and early 1980s], actually helping the enemies of détente in the USA and other NATO countries to start the second "cold war." Moreover, the negative aspects of our foreign and domestic policies in those years had an obvious influence on the constellation of political forces and on the course of political struggles in the USA and other western nations; we strengthened the position of the right and the far right, even militaristic, circles. . . . It must be acknowledged that Reagan—the "early" Reagan, the hater and bitter enemy of the "evil empire" . . . along with a whole cohort of the most conservative figures, came to power not without our help.[72]

This "early" Reagan was not so different from the "later" Jimmy Carter; Soviet actions were so blatantly aggressive by the time of the election that no serious contender for the White House could be seen as anything other than harshly critical of Moscow.

What did change with Reagan's election, however, was American strategy toward the Soviet Union. Perhaps more accurately, Reagan accelerated a change in strategy already underway, as the last traces of détente were swept away, and the United States committed itself to a new course. Whether that new course was one of steadfast opposition to further Soviet expansion or reckless confrontation and courting nuclear war is still debated. The experiences of the late 1970s and early 1980s, however they are judged by partisans, nonetheless raise the twin questions of accommodation and confrontation. Until 1977, the United States tried the former and gained breathing space for itself at the cost of emboldening its opponent. As Jimmy Carter came to office, it hardly seemed possible that the Americans would be willing to reopen hostilities with the Soviet Union, but by accident as much as design, the new president would lead the United States away from détente and toward a policy of confrontation that Ronald Reagan would not create, but rather inherit.

NOTES

1. Anatolii Dobrynin, *In Confidence* (Seattle, WA: University of Washington Press, 1995), p. 157.

2. Quoted in Harry Gelman, *The Brezhnev Politburo and the Decline of Détente* (Ithaca, NY: Cornell University Press, 1984), p. 159.

3. Stephen Sestanovich, "Did the West Undo the East?" *The National Interest* 31, Spring 1993, pp. 33–34.

4. "Ford Assures Allies of U.S. Will," *International Herald Tribune*, May 30, 1975, p. 1.

5. Andrei Gromyko, *Memoirs* (New York: Doubleday, 1989), p. 281.

6. Steven Ross has detailed the American images of war in the 1950s as seen from the late 1940s in *American War Plans 1945–1950* (London: Frank Cass, 1996).

7. Quoted in John Newhouse, *War and Peace in the Nuclear Age* (New York: Knopf, 1989), p. 120.

8. Newhouse, p. 119.

9. Newhouse, p. 118.

10. Quoted in Newhouse, p. 122.

11. Anastas Mikoian, *Tak bylo* (Moscow: Vagrius, 1999), p. 605.

12. See Thomas Nichols, *The Sacred Cause: Civil-Military Conflict Over Soviet National Security, 1917–1992* (Ithaca, NY: Cornell University Press, 1993), chapter 3.

13. D. A. Volkogonov, *Sem' Vozhdei* (Moscow: Novosti, 1995), vol. I, p. 413.

14. Aleksandr Fursenko and Timothy Naftali, *One Hell of a Gamble* (New York: Norton, 1997), p. 354.

15. "Stenogram: Meeting of the Delegations of the Communist Party of the Soviet Union and the Chinese Communist Party, Moscow, 5–20 July 1963," Cold War International History Project, http://cwihp.si.edu/.

16. The 1962 SIOP even envisioned striking China and Eastern Europe, whether they were parties to the conflict or not. Newhouse, p. 162.

17. Fursenko and Naftali, p. 337.

18. D. A. Volkogonov, *Sem' Vozhdei* (Moscow: Novosti, 1995), vol. II, p. 164.

19. Lawrence Freedman writes that McNamara's refusal to hinder the Soviet attainment of an assured destruction capability was the most controversial aspect of his approach to deterrence, but short of building missile defenses— something technologically pointless in the mid-1960s—it is fair to ask just what McNamara was supposed to do to "hinder" Soviet capabilities that were due to

be in place in the near future regardless of American moves. Lawrence Freedman, *The Evolution of Nuclear Strategy* (New York: St. Martin's Press, 1983), p. 247.

20. Henry Kissinger, *Diplomacy* (New York: Simon and Schuster, 1994), p. 756.

21. In 1967, for example, Soviet military exercises began, for the first time, without simulated nuclear strikes, a sign that Moscow understood the new strategic stability afforded by the coming of parity. See Jeffrey Simon, *Warsaw Pact Forces* (Boulder, CO: Westview, 1985), pp. 27–41.

22. The chief of the Czechoslovak general staff warned in 1968 that the Soviets had been baited into accepting a more expensive theory of war and drawn into a conventional arms race that "we can't win [b]ecause their economy is vastly more powerful than ours." See "Informal remarks by Czechoslovak Chief of General Staff, Gen. Otakar Rytír, at a Confidential Meeting of General Staff Officials, Prague, 13 March 1968," available at the National Security Archive online, http://www.gwu.edu/~nsarchiv/NSAEBB/NSAEBB14/doc23.htm.

23. Nichols, pp. 152–157.

24. Nichols, pp. 157–159. Vladimir Batiuk, however, disagrees with this characterization and argues for a split that placed Soviet and American civilian leaders on one side of the issue and their respective military counterparts on the other—that is, the civilians who feared nuclear war on both sides had more in common with each other than with their militaries.

25. Gelman, p. 15.

26. Kissinger, pp. 735-736.

27. Kissinger, p. 742.

28. Kissinger, p. 742.

29. Quoted in John Gaddis, *Strategies of Containment* (New York: Oxford University Press, 1982), p. 315, and see Kissinger, p. 743.

30. Kissinger, p. 745.

31. Kissinger, p. 746.

32. Robert Conquest, *Reflections on a Ravaged Century* (New York: Norton, 2000), p. 170.

33. See, for example, V. Osipov, "Nashe mesto v mire," *Izvestiia*, January 24, 1976, p. 3.

34. A. Shevchenko, "Manevry ideologicheskikh diversantov," *Krasnaia Zvezda*, May 28, 1977, p. 3.

35. N. Khmara, "Chto skryvaetsia za kontseptsiei 'ravnoi otvetsvennosti,'" *Krasnaia Zvezda*, February 18, 1982, p. 2.

36. See, for example, "NATO: Krizis doveriia," *Izvestiia*, April 24, 1975, p. 4.

37. "Trofimenko Accuses Washington of Thwarting Détente," p. 4. Translation from June 1980 issue of *SShA*, Subject File "Razriadka," Soviet ("Red") Archives, Records of Radio Free Europe/Radio Liberty Research Institute, Open Society Archives, Budapest, Hungary.

38. "Trofimenko Accuses...", p. 6.

39. R. Craig Nation, *Black Earth, Red Star* (Ithaca, NY: Cornell University Press, 1992), pp. 256–260.

40. Gaddis enumerates this damning list in *Strategies of Containment*, p. 311.

41. Quoted in Kissinger, p. 717.

42. Newhouse, p. 214.

43. Gaddis, pp. 310–320.

44. Gelman, pp. 157–158.

45. Gromyko, pp. 282–283.

46. Gromyko, p. 287.

47. Gromyko, p. 287.

48. See Roger Kanet, "Reassessing Soviet Doctrine: New Priorities and Perspectives," in Edward Kolodziej and Roger Kanet, eds., *The Limits of Soviet Power in the Developing World* (Baltimore: John Hopkins University Press, 1989), p. 403.

49. Kissinger, p. 755.

50. Kissinger, p. 756.

51. Dobrynin, p. 268.

52. Newhouse, p. 313.

53. Gromyko, p. 283.

54. Walter Laquer, *The Dream That Failed* (New York: Oxford University Press, 1994), p. 127.

55. Sestanovich, p. 27.

56. Carter aide Gordon Stewart believes that the strongly religious natures of both Carter (a devout Baptist) and National Security Advisor Zbigniew Brzezinski (a Pole and a Catholic) made their partnership a more natural one than it may have seemed to outside observers and strongly influenced the White House's policy toward human rights in the USSR. Interview with Gordon Stewart, New York, May 30, 2001.

57. Dobrynin, p. 346.

58. Dobrynin, p. 346.

59. Dobrynin, p. 346.

60. Dobrynin, p. 366.

61. Dobrynin, p. 371.

62. Gaddis, p. 320.

63. Kissinger, p. 747.

64. Kissinger, p. 761.

65. Quoted in Sestanovich, p. 31, see also Georgii Arbatov, *Zatianuvsheesiia vyzdorovlenie* (Moscow: Mezhdunarodnye Otnosheniia, 1991), p. 250.

66. Gaddis, p. 350.

67. Kissinger, p. 760.

68. Quoted in Gelman, p. 160.

69. Gelman, p. 162.

70. Vitalii Korotich, *Ot pervogo litsa* (Kharkov: Folio, 2000), p. 132.

71. Vojtech Mastny, "Introduction: Planning for the Unplannable," in *Taking Lyon on the Ninth Day? The 1964 Warsaw Pact Plan for a Nuclear War in Europe and Related Documents*, http://www.isn.ethz.ch/php/documents/introvm.htm.

72. Arbatov, p. 241.

6

Jimmy Carter and the Mounting Crisis

I confess that I was genuinely puzzled by [Reagan's] fierce anti-Soviet attack. In retrospect, I realize that it had been quite impossible for me to imagine anything much worse than Carter.

—Anatolii Dobrynin

JIMMY CARTER, HUMAN RIGHTS, AND THE END OF DÉTENTE

It is the conventional wisdom, not just among conservatives, that President Jimmy Carter stumbled through four years of trying to deal with a Soviet Union at the height of its powers while guiding the United States to the depths of its own. Much of the criticism leveled at the Carter administration's foreign policy is justified: it was at times contradictory, overly idealistic, and often riven by internal dissent among senior policymakers. By the end of Carter's presidency, the growth of Soviet power and ambitions represented a mounting crisis in the Cold War, one for which the Americans seemed unprepared.

The late 1970s, however, saw American strategy against the Soviet Union take a purposeful turn toward confrontation. Carter's foreign and defense policies never gained the realist sophistication of Nixon's before him or the ideological certitude of Reagan's after him, but they represented a transition away from an American policy—détente—with which the Soviets were comfortable, and a movement toward another—

ideological differences over human rights—with which they assuredly were not. Carter never fully shed the realist assumption that major issues between the superpowers could be compartmentalized (as evidenced by his doomed pursuit of SALT II in the face of growing Soviet ire and a recalcitrant Senate at home), but he helped, even if at times only inadvertently, to bridge the gap between Nixonian *realpolitik* and Reagan's ideological crusade. Carter's approach, in the wake of détente, served notice that the United States might actually care about issues beyond those that affected the raw balance of power.

As the presidential campaign season opened in 1975, the Soviets could rightly be satisfied with their place in the world, a power nearly equal to the United States and apparently ascending. Soviet complacency, however, did not take into account someone like Jimmy Carter. Carter not only ardently believed in the cause of human rights, but intended to force the issue with the Soviets. Unschooled in foreign affairs, he came to office committed both to arms control and to human rights—a marriage of issues that, in fairness to the détentist Republicans who preceded him, anyone in the Nixon or Ford White House could have told him would be almost impossible to sustain. Carter never fully understood that moralizing on one issue would jeopardize progress on the other, and he continued to believe that he could castigate the Soviets on human rights but still manage to forge ahead on SALT II.[1] Much has been made of the feuding between Carter's top foreign policy advisors, Secretary of State Cyrus Vance and National Security Advisor Zbigniew Brzezinski, but it was Carter himself who made human rights the lodestone of his foreign policy, even if it annoyed the Soviets to the point of halting progress on arms control.[2]

It is perhaps an understatement to say the Carter approach to foreign policy "annoyed" the Soviets. Even before Carter took office, there were rumblings and worries about the Georgia governor. Valentin Falin, later the deputy foreign minister and at the time Soviet ambassador to Bonn, warned Moscow in December 1976 that Carter was going to be a handful and that his administration would be a throwback to the "spirit of the cold war."[3] Once Carter was in office, the Soviets soon found his tenacious attachment to human rights grating and even infuriating. Gromyko—in whose memoirs Carter is portrayed as little better than an untutored bumpkin in foreign affairs—accused Carter of "set[ting] out to undermine détente in Europe," and excoriated him for trying to follow the policy which Kissinger had invented but never enforced:

One absurdity followed another. Washington declared that henceforth it would base its Soviet policy on the principle of "linkage"—that is, the level of cooperation would be dependent on the Soviet Union's fulfillment of conditions, improperly set by the USA and relating to the USSR's own domestic concerns or those involving a third country. It was in this context that a campaign was launched in the USA alleging that human rights were being violated in the USSR and the other socialist countries. . . . Carter took a personal hand in the campaign of provocation. Sounding like a zealous TV commercial, he seemed to think it was his duty to raise the matter of human rights every time he met a Soviet representative. I endured it myself.[4]

This was ascribing too much premeditation to Carter; as one scholar of the Carter presidency has pointed out, this "was not the 'linkage' of the Kissinger era," but rather a kind of "commonsense linkage" in which the Soviets needed to grasp that arms control agreements would be impossible to sell to the American people if they became wary of Soviet behavior in the Third World. "Linkage was not a policy for Carter, but [rather] a reality that Soviet leaders had to understand."[5]

In fact, although Carter had campaigned on the issue of human rights—insofar as the 1976 election was about foreign policy, that is— the Soviets themselves had a hand in pushing Carter to take action early on. The increasing pressure on dissidents in the winter of 1976, even before the new president was sworn in, was a challenge, in the words of a Carter aide, that the new administration "clearly had to react to"; thus, despite the "perception early in the Carter administration...that the president was going out of his way to 'put a stick in the Russians' eye' on the subject of human rights, it was actually the other way around."[6] Soviet leaders, for their part, believed that Carter "was deliberately interfering in the Soviet Union's internal affairs in order to undermine the existing regimes in the Soviet Union and Eastern Europe," and inside the Kremlin, according to Dobrynin, "the reaction was indignation, irritation, and concern."[7] Not for the first time, the Soviets were uncomprehending of the consequences of their own actions.

Coming so soon after the signing of the Helsinki Accords, there was even a sense in Moscow that the USSR had been sandbagged on the whole human rights business and that the Western powers were deliberately coordinating an attack based on the issue. Nefarious institutions like Radio Liberty, the Western media, various Helsinki-related groups, and others all seemed to be part of the same conspiracy. Less than two months after Carter's inauguration, Radio Moscow was decrying the "hawks" who were using human rights to make "some people in Washington...pawns of those circles in the United States which utterly oppose the peaceful development of relations between peoples."[8] Within two years of the signing of the Helsinki documents, the Soviets had gone from seeing "human rights" as yet another diplomatic pleasantry to a more sinister view, which saw it (along with things like "the free flow of information" and other Helsinki-related phrases) as weapons aimed directly and consciously at Soviet control of Eastern Europe.

To some extent, Soviet concern was justified. If Carter had initially stumbled into confrontation with the Kremlin because he was genuinely unaware of the fear the Helsinki concepts generated in Moscow, he stubbornly refused to back away from the issue despite evident Soviet anger. A good example of this was Carter's decision to invite the first Polish pope, John Paul II, to the White House, an act conceived by Brzezinski and approved by Carter as a message unmistakably aimed at Red Square rather than the South Lawn. Carter even opened his remarks in Polish, an act intended as a shot across the Kremlin's bow with regard to Eastern Europe. (This was no low-cost publicity stunt or ad hoc photo opportunity; it cost Carter support among anti-Catholic southerners and earned a scathing private rebuke from evangelist Oral Roberts.)[9]

That Carter personally aggravated the Kremlin is undeniable. The question remains of whether Carter's foreign policy had any positive effect on the American position in the Cold War at the time. The Soviets literally ran amok during Carter's administration; his infuriation of them with his talk of human rights was complimented by their humiliation of him by ignoring it. But in fairness to Carter, Soviet advances after 1977 (as discussed in the previous chapter) were largely the result of momentum they had built up earlier. Many of the Soviet weapons programs and Third World adventures which were laid at Carter's door predated him, and the Soviets pressed on not because they thought Carter was a rube, but because they had become accustomed to doing pretty much as they pleased during the Nixon and Ford years so long as they showed interest in arms control negotiations. Certainly, the previous Republican administrations had done nothing to convey any seriousness about human rights. ("Mr. Minister," Kissinger once said to Gromyko regarding the Helsinki accords, "why are we quibbling over these forms of words? No matter what goes into the final act, I don't believe the Soviet Union will ever do anything it doesn't want to do.")[10] There is much for which Carter can be blamed, but a Soviet Union that believed there was no real danger of American opposition to its aggressive aims is not one of them.

Nonetheless, it is difficult to argue that Carter's human rights policies had any immediate effect other than to sour U.S.-Soviet relations and to doom any progress on SALT II. For critics of détente, of course, this latter outcome would be considered an achievement, and in a sense it was, even if it was not what Carter intended. The plain fact is that when it came to Soviet expansionism and Soviet military programs, there was no apparent difference between good relations and bad, between progress on arms control or a stalemate. As Carter's defense secretary Harold Brown told Congress in 1979, "when we build weapons, they build; when we stop, they nevertheless continue to build."[11] SALT II was not a dangerous treaty per se—the Soviets were not going to defeat the United States in a nuclear war with a few extra warheads—but depriving Moscow of the ability to predict the growth of the American arsenal as well as making clear that the Congress' views of Soviet behavior cannot be ignored in the arms control process were useful in themselves.

The synergy of the Helsinki process and a more ideologically driven American policy began to raise the costs of internal policing and threatened to complicate Soviet efforts to maintain control over their empire. The Kremlin spent a great deal of time and money insulating Soviet citizens from both specific Western influences and often harmless general news, and the increased attention on Soviet civil liberties from both the Carter White House and the Helsinki signatories—"in public, in public, in public. Always in public!" Dobrynin later complained of Carter's criticisms—made it more difficult for Soviet authorities to pursue such policies without risk or publicity.[12] This was an especially bitter pill because Brezhnev initially supported Gromyko's recommendation that Helsinki should be signed. Not only did Brezhnev want the glory of signing such an important document, but he also saw no danger in Basket Three. "But he was wrong," Dobrynin writes. "The condition of Soviet dissidents did not change overnight, but they were definitely encouraged by this historic document."[13]

Pressure on the Soviets on matters such as free expression, the free flow of ideas and information, and freedom of conscience were all the price of greater economic interaction and less opprobrium as a pariah, and this pressure turned out to be more of an immediate threat than armaments. Conquest describes the starkness of the dilemma Helsinki created for the Soviet leaders:

> [T]hough they might suppress the voices of dissent in the USSR itself, they could not take the KGB's advice and arrest them by the thousands, nor could they employ their full measures of repression against people in the world's eye. . . . [After Helsinki] they now had, and could do no more than contain, a dissident movement—something the USSR in its prime had never faced. And the times were ripe, the exhaustion of the Soviet idea so far gone, that this small beginning was already shaking the system.[14]

Nor should the expense associated with increasing dissident activity be underestimated. In the 1970s, the Soviets were willing to spare almost no effort in the war against people like Aleksandr Solzhenitsyn, who alone at one point accounted for over 20 operations involving KGB organizations across six countries.[15] As a KGB defector later wrote, no act of defiance was too trivial to investigate, and the "effort and resources employed to track down each and every author of an anony-

mous letter or seditious graffito criticizing the Soviet system frequently
exceeded those devoted in the West to a major murder enquiry."[16]
Gromyko once provided a glimpse at the level of Soviet anxiety provoked by the increasing flow of information in this period by announcing that if the West were to orbit a television satellite broadcasting in
Russian, it would be regarded as a hostile act and that the Soviets would
shoot it down.[17]

Moscow's patience with the whole business soon wore thin. Reagan
came to office and picked up on the subject of Soviet domestic abuses
where Carter had left off, and the Soviets in response put crushing
pressure on the few Soviet Helsinki watchdog activists left (the last
three members of such a group disbanded themselves in 1982), increased jamming of Western radio, halted emigration, and even cut the
number of telephone lines running to the West by some two-thirds.[18]
Soviet leader Yuri Andropov later paid tribute to the effectiveness of the
campaign on human rights in 1983, as Soviet delegates were headed off
to a European conference at Stockholm. Andropov admonished them
to hang tough: "If we are strong, we will be respected and nobody will
think of or remember human rights. If we are weak, all will fall apart."[19]

THE SOVIET ASCENDANCY, 1975–1980

For the first year or so of his presidency, Carter limited himself to
rhetorical attacks on the Soviet human rights record as his administration tried, haltingly, to counter various Soviet moves around the globe.
Soviet arrogance and overreach, however, chastened the new president,
and by 1980, the challenging tone of American rhetoric at the outset of
Carter's tenure was matched by military programs at its end that
represented a kind of eventual despair on Carter's part. Hesitant and
at times incoherent, the changes introduced by Jimmy Carter nonetheless were striking enough to the Soviets, who saw them for the long-
term threat they represented, even if they imputed to them a greater
cohesiveness and malice than was actually warranted. Whatever Carter
may have wanted to achieve with the Soviets upon his election in 1976,
by 1979, the Soviets had by their own hand made almost any course
other than confrontation impossible. Carter's strategic programs in
particular are important, since Soviet critics at the time argued that they
were "gladly" picked up by the new Reagan administration, a charge
that was both accurate and, to Soviet eyes, alarming.[20]

The confrontational strategy developed under Jimmy Carter and
expanded by Reagan was a reaction to Soviet moves taken in the wake
of détente, and it is important to recall the situation the Americans were
facing by 1981. In the half decade from the fall of Saigon to the 1980

presidential election, Soviet power and prestige grew so rapidly that even some in the Kremlin itself wondered aloud if capitalism was on its last legs and socialism was irrevocably ascendant. At the least, a degree of placid arrogance was setting in among the Soviet leadership, notably on regional issues. "I happened to be present at several meetings of the Politburo dealing with Angola, Somalia, and Ethiopia," Dobrynin later wrote, "and I can report that American complaints were not even seriously considered. The Politburo simply did not see them as a legitimate American concern and not a major factor in our relations with Washington."[21]

The Soviet expansion into the Third World, while disturbing in itself, had less of an impact on American thinking than the increase in overall Soviet military capability, particularly in strategic nuclear systems. Soviet advances were undeniable, as Arbatov later admitted:

[T]he thought of restraint, of moderation in military affairs, was absolutely alien to us. Possibly it was even our deeply rooted inferiority complex that constantly drove us to catch up with the United States in nuclear arms. . . . during those years we were enthusiastically arming ourselves, like binging drunks [*kak zapoinye*], without any apparent political need.[22]

These dramatic leaps in the size and quality of Soviet forces were largely the result of the reorganization of Soviet military affairs that took place in the wake of Khrushchev's departure, with many of the systems and concepts that reached fruition in the 1970s actually the products of work begun in the late 1960s. The SALT I agreement and the associated ABM Treaty, in the end, had managed only to avert further U.S. research into ballistic missile defenses; elsewhere, SALT had capped overall levels of nuclear arms but left the door open for a qualitative arms race that the Soviets pursued with vigor.

In particular, the 1975 Soviet deployment of the SS-18 intercontinental ballistic missile—a "heavy" ICBM armed with ten highly accurate warheads—generated the panicky mathematics of the so-called "window of vulnerability" debate in the United States: with over 3,000 warheads on the SS-18, the Soviets theoretically had acquired the ability to destroy all 1,054 U.S. land-based ICBMs using only a fraction of their forces. Whether the Soviets really believed they could do this and escape catastrophic retaliation from American submarines and bombers is doubtful, but the issue was a potent one in the 1980 contest between Carter and Reagan, if only because to many of Carter's critics it was symbolic of the unchecked growth of Soviet power.

The perception that the Soviets were amassing military power in order to hold the West at bay in the face of ongoing Soviet global expansion was strengthened when Moscow committed the blunder of modernizing Soviet nuclear forces in Europe. This one Soviet move (now known to have been forced upon the foreign policy establishment by the defense ministry) probably did more damage to Soviet diplomatic efforts than anything until the invasion of Afghanistan. Older, fixed emplacement, single-warhead missiles were replaced by the SS-20, a mobile, three-warhead missile with an extended range that placed all NATO European capitals under direct threat from Soviet theater nuclear forces. Dobrynin claims that Soviet military leaders were "mesmerized" by the improved performance of the new SS-20s and notes that in Politburo discussions political considerations were brushed aside in favor of purely military arguments.[23] (As a member of the diplomatic establishment defeated on this issue, Dobrynin may have an axe to grind with the Soviet military, but his account accords with others and helps to explain the Kremlin's political tone deafness on the whole issue.)

The additional military capacity bought by these weapons was questionable—U.S. officials felt they would do little more than "bounce the rubble" in a nuclear war—but the brazenness with which the Soviets fielded these improved arms created genuine apprehension in Europe.[24] Dobrynin denies that the weapons, as Zbigniew Brzezinski worried at the time, were meant to "Finlandize" Western Europe but admits that Brzezinski's logic was sound: "Of course, this scenario did not reflect any of the real plans or intentions of the Soviet government. But how could people in the West know for sure that Moscow would not be tempted to use the new leverage of its SS-20 missiles?"[25]

Former Soviet officials and Russian policy analysts almost universally point to the SS-20 deployments as a turning point, a decision that galvanized Western opposition and laid the groundwork for the Carter and Reagan challenges thereafter. "Stupid," was the simple and recent evaluation of one Russian foreign policy scholar, while another called the SS-20s "a gift to the Americans" that allowed U.S. leaders to reinvigorate NATO as a coalition.[26] Aleksandr Yakovlev has denigrated the deployment of so many weapons that "there weren't even enough targets for them" as "criminally provocative;" NATO's consequent willingness to deploy the advanced Pershing II missile in response to the SS-20s later led Dmitrii Volkogonov to charge that "Soviet strategists, with this short-sighted policy, had actually handed the Americans a knife to put at the Soviet throat."[27]

The timing of the SS-20 fiasco was especially unfortunate for the Soviets, who until that point stood to gain from some serious American missteps. Carter was trying to recover from the uproar over his fumbled decision on the neutron bomb, in which he had twisted European arms to accept so-called enhanced radiation weapons (or, as they were derided by Soviet critics, the perfect "capitalist bombs" that killed people but spared real estate) and then reversed course and decided not to deploy them after all. The Soviets invested nearly one hundred million dollars in various propaganda and disinformation efforts aimed at the neutron bomb, but their money might well have been better spent elsewhere.[28] It is an axiom of war as well as politics never to interrupt your opponent when he is busy hurting himself. But this is exactly what the Soviets did, and the neutron bomb disaster was eventually over-shadowed by the SS-20s and a general sense of the growing Soviet threat.

Soviet advances in the Third World also undermined Soviet diplo-matic efforts dating back to Vietnam to portray the USSR as the more peaceable superpower. These skirmishes, however, paled next to the invasion of Afghanistan. For years, Westerners argued among them-selves about whether the USSR was really a threat to anyone outside of its own Eastern European empire; in 1979, Brezhnev and his colleagues forcefully rendered that argument moot. Even the threat represented by the SS-18s and SS-20s was only a notional one and could be interpreted (as it was by many of America's critics) as a Soviet attempt to defend itself against a technologically superior American coalition. But with the invasion of Afghanistan, the weight of the Soviet military machine was brought to bear against an impoverished neighbor, leaving the Soviets playing the very role of imperial bullies that they had tried to hang on the Americans over a decade earlier in Vietnam.

In one sense, the late 1970s were as bleak a period in the Cold War as the United States had ever seen: the Americans were held at bay by a massive Soviet nuclear arsenal against which there was no defense, NATO was paralyzed by fear and internal dissention, and the Soviets had established a formidable presence across the globe, even in the American backyard of Central America. During the 1980 presidential election, this was the picture that the Republicans wanted to paint of the Carter years, and there was a good deal of truth in it, even if much of what Carter had to deal with was actually Nixon's legacy. (Of course, among the Reaganite wing of the party, there was no love for Nixon, either, and a special animosity toward Kissinger.)

Still, there were opportunities in the situation as it stood by 1980 as well. The Soviets were not just overextended; had their dilemma only been to supply and maintain a wide-ranging empire, that in itself would have been a challenge to the Soviet economy. In addition to the sheer material burden of their global position, however, there were now increasing political costs as well. Soviet diplomatic ham-fistedness (of which the SS-20s were a stark example) had eroded the gains of the early 1970s and renewed the sense of caution and even outright alarm among nations that previously had been less inclined to toe the American line. (Even the French, who referred to the SS-20s as *le grand menace*, re-emerged as a forceful voice in the anti-Soviet coalition.)[29] Now, the enlarged Soviet empire was not just an economic drain, but an ongoing diplomatic and military liability, a set of gains that had be protected from internal overthrow and rationalized to an increasingly anxious world. The Soviets had gained the full benefits of being a global super-power, but they were also now facing the full range of vulnerabilities and costs their global ambitions had created.

THE MOUNTING CRISIS AND AMERICAN RESPONSES

Jimmy Carter and Ronald Reagan remain paradoxical figures in the history of the Cold War. Carter, the ostensible liberal, came to office with expectations of curtailing the arms race so unrealistic that they worried many in the American defense establishment even before he was sworn into office. (He made a comment during a postelection briefing with U.S. military leaders to the effect that he could envisage strategic forces on both sides no larger than two hundred submarine-based missiles, which supposedly left the chairman of the Joint Chiefs "stunned speechless.")[30] By the time Carter left office, however, a slew of new American military programs were underway, and relations with the USSR were as bad as they had been in years. Reagan, by comparison, came to the presidency after years of thundering about the Soviet military menace; in his second term, however, he would sign an unprec-edented treaty banning an entire class of nuclear weapons in Europe and laying the foundation for further cuts in strategic arms.

The actual distance between the foreign policies of these two leaders between 1978 and 1981 is less than it may seem, exaggerated by the tendency of Americans to measure political eras by presidential terms and therefore to draw too strong a demarcation between administra-tions. To think of Carter and Reagan as so fundamentally different is to miss the larger point that each administration was grappling with essentially the same problem: a militarily robust and aggressively ac-tivist Soviet Union. To a large degree the story of the Reagan administration's crusade against the Soviet Union begins not in 1981, but in Jimmy Carter's White House four years earlier.

Indeed, although Jimmy Carter has often been referred to as a "born-again Cold Warrior" in the wake of the 1979 invasion of Afghanistan, the record shows that the Carter administration was moving toward more confrontational policies as early as 1977 (with his insistence on placing human rights at the center of U.S.-Soviet relations, a theme even in his 1976 campaign) and that the Soviets accurately recognized these moves. With Carter's election, Soviet spokesman Henry Trofimenko later wrote, "U.S. foreign policy was being returned by the strategists of U.S. imperialism 'full circle' . . . to an adventuristic, hegemonistic policy of 'shaping' of the external situation according to U.S. plans and schemes," and that as early as 1977 the Carter administration was seeking to "effect some 'limited test of power' with the USSR," as opposed to a "more balanced, less emotional" foreign policy being advocated by others.[31] Some historians have even suggested that "the Carter administration's increasing assertiveness towards the Soviet Union" hastened the breakdown of détente.[32] (Valentin Falin has even gone so far as to suggest that Carter's hawkishness pushed the Soviets into invading Afghanistan. There is no evidence for this charge, but it is indicative of the degree of hostility felt about Carter among some in Moscow even now.)[33]

Carter's views met only with Soviet intransigence and hostility, particularly on human rights, and these Soviet attitudes quickly shook the new president out of many of his illusions. As Odd Arne Westad points out, "For Carter, there is little doubt that his first encounters with the Soviets triggered a negative change in his image of his Cold War rivals." The administration's reaction was significant in scope and scale.

> Presidential Directive 18, which Carter signed on 24 August 1977, reveals the beginnings of this process [of reevaluation], by emphasizing "forward defense" and the creation of a rapid deployment force with a global reach. Carter also became more aggressive on defense spending from late 1977 on, initiating research on the B-2 bomber project and continuing the development of the MX and Trident programs, although the President may have hoped to scrap the latter two in response to more comprehensive Soviet arms reduction proposals. By 1979—although the SALT II agreement was nearing completion—Carter had accepted deployment of the MX missile system and the new long range theater nuclear weapons (cruise missiles and Pershing II) in Europe.[34]

Nor were such efforts limited to U.S. strategic programs; in 1978, NATO—in a move called "long overdue" by one senior European NATO commander—began conventional rearmament in earnest.[35]

These programs were not initiated in a rhetorical or diplomatic vacuum: as the Americans moved to improve relations with China—a clear warning to the Soviets that Carter would not shy from seeking U.S.-Chinese containment of the USSR—Carter gave a speech in June 1978 at the U.S. Naval Academy in Annapolis in which he harshly criticized Soviet behavior. The Soviet reaction was predictably negative, but getting the Kremlin to take notice was exactly the intention behind the speech. Brzezinski in particular was gratified that "the Soviets had obviously heard the displeasure expressed by the president regarding their actions at home and abroad and were likely to believe that Carter was serious when he raised the possibility of future confrontations."[36] Thus, American responses were coupled with a message, often garbled and inconsistently pursued but nonetheless on the record, that Washington intended to use both diplomatic and military means to oppose further Soviet offenses and encroachments.

To the Soviets, the most alarming area in which Carter would revamp U.S. strategy was on the issue of nuclear war. In the summer of 1980, Carter took an astonishing step: he issued Presidential Directive (PD) 59, in which he appeared to join the Soviets in their belief that a protracted nuclear war could be fought and added the condition that the United States sought to deny victory, "however they may define it," to the Soviets.[37] It was a move that delighted conservatives (who, as will be seen, adopted and expanded Carter's concepts during the Reagan administration) and a jaw-dropping disappointment to arms-control advocates even on Carter's own foreign policy team.[38]

This American move was, again, one that the Soviets largely had brought upon themselves. Since the early 1960s, the Soviet Union had taken conflicting positions on nuclear war, with declarations of the USSR's commitment to peace and its understanding of the impossibility of nuclear conflict alternating with dark warnings that victory in a global thermonuclear exchange was not only possible, but that the Soviet Union expected to claim it. To some extent, this was probably a conscious gambit meant to convince U.S. allies, on the one hand, that it was only America and not the Soviet Union that sought a third world war, while on the other hand making it plain to Washington that Moscow would not flinch in the face of the American nuclear arsenal, even if it meant almost complete destruction of both societies.

This schizophrenic rhetoric represented a genuine division in the Soviet leadership on the whole issue. In 1977, in his so-called "Tula speech" (named for the Moscow suburb in which he gave it), Brezhnev attempted to rule out victory in nuclear war as an impossibility, a position that reflected the civilian leadership's growing impatience with the political intemperance of the Soviet military, not to mention their unwillingness to sacrifice the entire USSR on the altar of a global war with imperialism. But Soviet military leaders, ever the more ideologically consistent members of the Kremlin inner circle, continued to maintain that nuclear "victory" was possible because the Soviet Union, due to its supposedly superior system of social and political organization, would emerge from the ashes of World War III more quickly than the capitalist powers and thus put an end to imperialism once and for all. Even under Gorbachev, who tried forcefully to put a stop to such talk, senior Soviet officers would challenge civilian thinkers ("vegetarian pacifists" Volkogonov called them before his anti-Soviet conversion) who argued, as Brezhnev had in 1981, that counting on victory in a nuclear war was "dangerous madness."[39]

Whatever the state of the Soviet civil-military debate, prudence demanded that the Americans take to heart those Soviet pronouncements that suggested the Soviet Union had fallen into believing a nuclear war could be fought and won. If Moscow was serious, then the credibility of the U.S. deterrent was eroding and the escalation of a crisis into a full-blown nuclear war was that much more likely. If Moscow was bluffing, then something had to be done to restore a certain amount of Soviet circumspection when trying to use the specter of nuclear war to political advantage. Whether the Soviets really believed that the accumulation of arms conferred such an advantage is difficult to say, but they did nothing to disabuse the Americans of that belief and even took a certain pleasure in it. "I even got the impression that whenever a new weapons system appeared that caused an outcry in the West," Arbatov later wrote, "we started to rejoice and say to ourselves: 'Why, look how strong and clever we are. We've managed to outdo and scare even the Americans and NATO.' "[40]

In any case, growing Soviet assertiveness on the issue of nuclear war called into question the previous tenets of Mutual Assured Destruction, which were now implicitly rejected in PD 59. The new American strategy was designed to deter a Soviet attack by responding specifically to Soviet strategy: if the Soviets really believed in various kinds of limited nuclear scenarios, Brzezinski "wanted them on notice that it would be a two-party game."[41] PD 59 assumed that what the Soviets valued most was not the lives of Soviet citizens, but continued control of Eurasia by the Communist Party of the Soviet Union. Accordingly, PD 59 created a kind of wish list of targets that not only envisaged striking the Soviet political leadership in its bunkers, but also a wealth of other locations ranging from military bases to important economic installations.[42] The actual execution of the strategy in PD 59 was problematic almost to the point of absurd, since striking so many targets and in the process "decapitating" the entire Soviet command structure rendered the whole idea of a "limited" nuclear war contradictory, but the point was to impress upon the Soviets that they were no longer alone in their blustery willingness to risk a nuclear exchange.[43]

Initial Soviet responses to Carter's policies in 1977 and 1978 tended to center on Moscow's irritation with the president's preoccupation with human rights, but after the Annapolis speech public Soviet pronouncements hardened considerably. These were not merely attempts to score propaganda points: Politburo documents indicate that within days of the Annapolis speech, the Soviet leadership reevaluated the threat posed by Carter. "A serious deterioration and exacerbation of the [international] situation has occurred," Brezhnev told the Politburo on June 8, 1978,

> And the primary source of this deterioration is the growing aggression of the foreign policy of the Carter government, the continually more sharply anti-Soviet character of the statements of the President himself and of his closest associates—in the first instance those of Brzezinski. Judging from appearances, Carter is not simply falling under the usual influence of the most shameless anti-Soviet types and ringleaders of the military-industrial complex, but is intent on struggling for his election to a new term as President of the United States under the banner of anti-Soviet policy and a return to the "cold war."[44]

To Moscow, Carter's moves were all of a piece, and Soviet writers argued publicly that it was fairly easy to connect the dots from things like human rights to an American desire to fight a nuclear war. *Red Star* decried the "militaristic psychosis" gripping Washington, but to judge by the tone of Soviet writings, it was Moscow that was verging on hysterical.[45]

Opinions on the source of Carter's confrontational policy varied. Some Soviet commentators saw the evil influence of the Polish émigré Brzezinski behind the puppet president, while others claimed that right-wing propaganda had "brainwashed" the American public and Carter was now forced to fight for the presidency by becoming as mindless a hawk as his opponents.[46] Many Soviet defense analysts discerned an overall increase in American aggressiveness and pointed to this change in the American temper—without really asking where it originated—as the motive force behind Carter's increases in the defense budget and the 1979 NATO "two-track decision" (that is, to "talk and deploy" rather than to refuse to suspend the deployment of theater ballistic missiles during negotiations over them with the Soviets). Several argued that the whole two-track affair showed that the Americans were preparing for a nuclear war in Europe that would destroy both NATO and the USSR but spare the United States.[47] (One Soviet officer caustically suggested that the Europeans knew this and would "wait for the new Republican administration to take office and see how it will formulate American nuclear policy.")[48] Whatever the differing emphases on it, however, the Soviets believed that the American challenge was unequivocal and dangerous and demanded a response.

By 1980, the Kremlin had given up on Carter not only as a possible lame-duck president, but also because they felt that his hostility to the Soviet Union was nearly implacable and that after Afghanistan little could be done to mend the Soviet-American relationship as long as Carter was in the White House. What this meant in the short term was there would be no way to avoid increasingly vocal Soviet military demands to match the slew of defense programs put in place under Carter. Arbatov believes this laid the foundation for the later American attempt to outspend the Soviets in an unrestrained arms race:

> [In the 1970s] we showed the Americans and NATO, more clearly than ever before, that we were going to keep up with any new military program, and not only duplicate it, but sometimes even respond to one program with two or three of our own. The Americans quickly understood that the USSR's gross national product was three or four times smaller than their own and that of their allies, and that this provided a reliable and, more important, completely safe opportunity to undermine the might of the Soviet Union, perhaps eventually to inflict a total defeat upon it through economic exhaustion in a hopeless military rivalry.[49]

Volkogonov has echoed this point, arguing that by 1980, many in the Soviet leadership were intent on plunging headlong into an American trap:

> The achievement of strategic parity between the USA and the USSR was regarded as an event of great historical significance. But less was said about the fact that America's economic potential was actually twice that of the Soviet Union, and that America had not [had] to make great efforts in this regard. In Washington, they had properly evaluated the situation: to win a duel, you don't need dozens of pistols, just one that is absolutely reliable. The White House and the Pentagon exhausted the USSR with an arms race into which Soviet leaders entered mindlessly.[50]

This was especially worrisome to Brezhnev and other Soviet civilians who were hoping to hold the line on further Soviet military expenditures; even in 1981, at the twenty-fifth Party Congress, Brezhnev tried to breathe life into the détentist line without success. The American military challenge, which the Soviets themselves had done so much to bring about, would have to be answered, and at great expense.

FROM CARTER TO REAGAN

This initial period of the renewed hostilities in the Cold War is important because it shows a direct link between changes in U.S. strategy and effects within the Soviet Union. Perhaps most interesting is that the experience of the Carter era undermines the image of the Soviet leadership as dispassionate realists, willing to wave away the rhetoric of their opponents as long as business was being transacted at the negotiating table. Even though the Soviets believed that much of Carter's policies was motivated by a need to appease the American right, they nonetheless assumed that Carter meant what he said and that he therefore represented a danger to the Soviet Union. This was a marked change from the years of détente, when the Americans would temper public pronouncements about things like linkage with back-channel assurances that the Soviets had nothing to fear. (After the crisis over the Yom Kippur War in 1973, Nixon called Dobrynin to Camp David and described the "previous week as just an unpleasant episode in our relations" and asked Dobrynin to "please inform the general secretary that as long as I live and hold the office of president I will never allow a real confrontation with the Soviet Union.")[51]

This period also suggested the Soviet vulnerability to an American military challenge. Elsewhere, I have argued that the senior leaders of the Soviet Armed Forces were among the most inflexibly ideological members of the Soviet elite, and while some have taken issue with that characterization, what is undeniable is that they were the most relentlessly and vigilantly anti-American elements in Soviet politics. The Soviet civil-military relationship was a dysfunctional one in which military demands were almost impossible to resist: aside from the reverence for military power among the generation of Soviet leaders who lived through World War II, senior Soviet military leaders phrased their claims on national resources in charged ideological terms that practically commanded agreement with them.[52] Thus, it was nearly impossible to resist military arguments for matching each American program with a similar Soviet program (or as Arbatov said previously, with *two or three* programs), thereby straining the already rickety Soviet economy. The use of harsh rhetoric combined with an asymmetric ability to fund military programs would be a centerpiece of the Reagan strategy, but it was begun and showed its first effects under Jimmy Carter.

The similarity between Carter and Reagan did not escape the Soviets, then or now. A recent Russian study of Carter's presidency reasonably argues that although Carter never fully succeeded in his own efforts on human rights, he "institutionalized" human rights as a central issue in U.S. foreign policy and in fact laid the groundwork for Reagan's more energetic challenges on the same subject later. The human rights campaign, the Russian study argues, when viewed in its entirety across both administrations played "a destructive role in the collapse of the USSR and the entire Eastern bloc."[53] Soviet leaders later saw almost no difference between the conservative Reagan and the nominally liberal Carter; it is telling that while some American voters saw Reagan as the antidote to Carter's supposed weakness and others saw Carter as the last ditch defense against Reagan's supposed aggressiveness, in Moscow the perception was quite different, with many in the Kremlin hoping that Reagan's election might bring a return of a more ideologically moderate Nixonian Republicanism to the White House.[54]

Still, one can only wish that President Carter's opposition to the Soviet Union had been as strategically conceived as Moscow thought. The president's inconsistent behavior, seeking negotiations on SALT one moment and then changing direction and digging in on the issue of human rights the next, did little more than convince the Soviets that Carter could not be counted on to engage in productive negotiations. When the president once interrupted a discussion with Andrei Gromyko about strategic nuclear arms control to raise the case of a dissident, Gromyko was irate that no less a figure than the President of the United States was raising the case of some "criminal" out of nowhere. "I asked the president straight out: 'Isn't it time to drop such ploys as utterly unproductive?' On that note, the discussion came to a close."[55] In the end, Carter's presidency was "an unpleasant surprise" to the Soviet leadership, according to Dobrynin, and by 1980, "Moscow so distrusted Carter that it could not bring itself to support him even against Ronald Reagan."[56] Indeed, Dobrynin himself admits that in 1981, he underestimated how difficult Reagan would be to deal with because at the time "it had been quite impossible for me to imagine anything much worse than Carter."[57]

The shift in strategy under Carter had infuriated the Soviet leadership, who now felt no need to negotiate with any seriousness with the United States on any number of contentious issues. They also became determined to match the incipient American arms buildup. Carter, having been forced to learn the bitter price of détente, planted the first seeds of a strategy that would need further nurturing. It would fall to Ronald Reagan to exploit Carter's decisive rejection of the failed strategy of détente. All that remained was to complete the transition to confrontation—without starting a war in the process.

NOTES

1. Former Carter aide Gordon Stewart claims that Carter, throughout his time in office, never fully grasped the tension between his stance on human rights and his position on arms control, as he approached both as moral issues rather than as geopolitical matters. Interview with Gordon Stewart, New York, May 30, 2001.

2. Stewart, interview.

3. Valentin Falin, *Bez skidok na obstoiatel'stva* (Moscow: Respublika-Sovremmennik, 1999), p. 335.

4. Andrei Gromyko, *Memoirs* (New York: Doubleday, 1989), p. 292.

5. Robert A. Strong, *Working in the World: Jimmy Carter and the Making of American Foreign Policy* (Baton Rouge: Louisiana State University Press, 2000), p. 104.

6. Strong, p. 95.

7. Anatolii Dobrynin, *In Confidence* (Seattle: University of Washington Press, 1995), pp. 388–390.

8. Radio Moscow, March 11, 1977, transcribed in "Moscow Sees Détente Threatened by Human Rights Campaign," Subject File "Razriadka," Soviet ("Red") Archives, Records of Radio Free Europe/Radio Liberty Research Institute, Open Society Archives, Budapest, Hungary.

9. Stewart describes the letter from Roberts to Carter as calling into question the president's faith at a very personal level. Interview.

10. Quoted in Odd Arne Westad, "The Fall of Détente and the Turning Tides of History," in Odd Arne Westad, ed., *The Fall of Détente: Soviet-American Relations during the Carter Years* (Oslo: Scandinavian University Press, 1997), p. 17.

11. Quoted in Henry Kissinger, *For the Record: Selected Statements, 1977–1980* (Boston: Little, Brown, 1981), p. 204.

12. Quoted in Westad, p. 17.

13. Dobrynin, p. 346.

14. Robert Conquest, *Reflections on a Ravaged Century* (New York: Norton, 2000), pp. 180–181.

15. Christopher Andrew and Vasilii Mitrokhin, *The Sword and the Shield: The Mitrokhin Archive* (New York: Basic Books, 1999), p. 320.

16. Andrew and Mitrokhin, p. 547.

17. Conquest, p. 188.

18. David Satter, "Soviets Limit Personal Liberties at Home as Relations with West Deteriorate," *The Wall Street Journal*, Subject File "Ideologicheskaia bor'ba," Soviet ("Red") Archives, Records of Radio Free Europe/Radio Liberty Research Institute, Open Society Archives, Budapest, Hungary.

19. Nina Tannenwald, ed., *Understanding the End of the Cold War, 1980–1987: An Oral History Conference* (Providence, RI: Watson Institute for International Studies, 1999), p. 15.

20. See Nikolai Ogarkov, "Na strazhe mirnogo truda," *Kommunist* 10, October 1981, p. 81.

21. Dobrynin, 405.

22. Georgii Arbatov, *Zatianuvsheesia vyzdorovlenie* (Moscow: Mezhdunarodnye Otnosheniia, 1991), pp. 237–238.

23. Dobrynin, pp. 430–432.

24. John Newhouse, *War and Peace in the Nuclear Age* (New York: Knopf, 1989), p. 326, see also Westad, pp. 17–18.

25. Dobrynin, p. 432.

26. Interview with Vladimir Matiash and Ivan Kuzmin, Moscow, February 4, 2000.

27. A. N. Yakovlev, *Gor'kaia chasha: Bol'shevizm i Reformatsiia Rossii* (Yaroslavl': Verkhne-Volzhskoe, 1994), p. 192; Volkogonov, *Sem' vozhdei*, vol. II, p. 163.

28. Conquest, p. 172.

29. See Thomas Nichols, *The Sacred Cause: Civil-Military Conflict over Soviet National Security, 1917–1992* (Ithaca, NY: Cornell University Press, 1993), p. 105.

30. Newhouse, p. 294.

31. "Trofimenko Accuses Washington of Thwarting Détente," pp. 7–9, 16. Translation from June 1980 issue of *SShA*, Subject File "Razriadka," Soviet ("Red") Archives, Records of Radio Free Europe/Radio Liberty Research Institute, Open Society Archives, Budapest.

32. Quoted in Westad, p. 17.

33. Falin, p. 362

34. Westad, p. 17.

35. The comment was made by Norwegian General H. F. Zeiner Gunderson. Charles Corddry, "NATO's Confidence Increases as Neglect Yields to Rearma-

ment," August 21, 1978, Subject File "NATO," Soviet ("Red") Archives, Records of Radio Free Europe/Radio Liberty Research Institute, Open Society Archives, Budapest.

36. Strong, p. 114.

37. The phrasing is Secretary of Defense Harold Brown's. See his Annual Report to Congress, Fiscal Year 1982, January 19, 1981, p. 38.

38. As John Newhouse later wrote: "That Jimmy Carter—a certified dove and the most rhetorically committed nuclear disarmer among recent presidents—should have signed off on so dubious a proposition is irony of a kind peculiar to the Potomac Basin." Newhouse, p. 285.

39. Nichols, pp. 157–159.

40. Arbatov, pp. 237–238.

41. Newhouse, p. 286.

42. For a severely critical discussion of the targeting in PD 59, see Robert Jervis, *The Illogic of American Nuclear Strategy* (Ithaca, NY: Cornell University Press, 1984).

43. Over several years of teaching courses on U.S.-Soviet relations, I have found that one metaphor students readily grasp about PD 59 is from the movie *Lethal Weapon*, in which Mel Gibson plays a slightly unhinged Los Angeles police officer. When a suicidal man takes to a roof and threatens to jump, Gibson—instead of trying to talk him down—handcuffs himself to the man and *agrees* with him: "Let's do it! Let's jump!" The man, of course, panics at being trapped with someone apparently crazier than he is, and eventually Gibson pulls him off the roof onto an waiting air cushion. Judging from the Soviet reaction to it, PD 59 was much the equivalent of the Americans joining the Soviets on the roof and offering to jump.

44. "Brezhnev speech in Politburo on foreign affairs issues, June 8, 1978," in Westad, ed., pp. 207–208.

45. M. Ponomarev, "Militaristskii psikhoz," *Krasnaia Zvezda*, May 12, 1980, p. 3.

46. "Trofimenko Accuses…", p. 3.

47. See Leonid Zamiatin, "Miru nuzhna voennaia razriadka," *Literaturnaia Gazeta*, December 26, 1979, p. 14; R. Simonian, "Opasnye kontseptsii 'evrostrategov' NATO," *Krasnaia Zvezda*, December 28, 1979, p. 3; N. Petrov, "Besperspektivnyi kurs," *Pravda*, June 16, 1980, p. 7.

48. M. Ponomarev, " Stavka na iadernyi shantazh," *Krasnaia Zvezda*, November 16, 1980, p. 3.

49. Arbatov, p. 235.

50. Volkogonov, *Sem' vozhdei*, vol. II, p. 37.

51. Quoted in Dobrynin, p. 300.

52. Vladimir Matiash, among others, has made this point, noting that the military's constant references to 1941 and their uncompromising ideological stance put the civilian leadership at an inherent disadvantage in disputes. Interview.

53. Oleg N. Shirokov, "Printsipy formirovaniia politika 'zashchity prav cheloveka' SshA i mekhanizm ee realizatsii na mezhdunarodnoi arene v kontse 60-x–70-e gody XX veka (istoricheskie aspekty problemy)," unpublished dissertation summary, Nizhny Novgorod State University *imeni* Lobachevskii, Nizhny Novgorod, Russia, September 2001, pp. 21–23.

54. Newhouse, p. 333.

55. Gromyko, p. 293.

56. Dobrynin, p. 455.

57. Dobrynin, p. 484.

7

The 1980s:
Fighting to Win or
Prolonging the Agony?

My idea of American policy is simple, and some would say simplistic. It is this: "We win and they lose." What do you think of that?

—Ronald Reagan, to an advisor, 1977

FROM DÉTENTE TO WAR: THE DEBATE OVER
AMERICAN STRATEGY IN THE 1980S

With the collapse of even the fiction of détente at the end of the
1970s, the United States and the Soviet Union moved to reassess
their positions in the Cold War. The Kremlin remained nominally
committed to détente, but its actions suggested little interest in it
other than as a symbolic policy. The Americans, for the most part,
drew the conclusion that the previous decade of improved relations
had done little more than to create a stronger, bolder USSR. With
the invasion of Afghanistan and the election of Ronald Reagan as
president of the United States, the rhetoric between Moscow and
Washington would escalate to unprecedented levels of recrimination
and accusation, as the superpower relationship headed into a phase
of outright hostility so vicious that it represented, in essence, an
acceptance by both sides of a state of war. The truce of the 1970s
was over: in the next several years, the Soviets and the Americans
would come as close to a military conflagration as they had since
the terrifying days of the Cuban missile crisis.

Few questions surrounding the Cold War are more hotly debated than the effect of this change in American strategy. The move toward confrontation included a revamping of U.S. plans to fight a protracted nuclear war, a revitalization of NATO, and a massive investment in new weapons systems of all types, all complemented by an explosion of rhetoric from the Americans of a kind the Soviets had never heard before. To Reagan's critics, this aggressive new line only strengthened Soviet resolve, courted nuclear catastrophe, and actually prolonged the Cold War. Others see Reagan's policies as nothing short of heroic, an effort taken in concert with those of a new wave of conservative NATO leaders that imperiled the Soviet economy, broke the Soviet will to fight, and destroyed the USSR itself.

These positions, part of an ongoing and testy partisan debate, have often been reduced to caricatures. It is an article of faith by many on the American right that Reagan single-handedly leveled the decisive blow to the Soviet colossus (one group of Reagan's admirers feels so strongly that they want monuments to the 40th president placed in *every county* of the United States). The contrasting image of the 1980s that has emerged among Reagan's critics is of a decade in which a bumbling old man nearly started World War III and was saved only by the vision of a new generation of Soviet leaders. To say the least, these are flawed views, and there is little in the way of recommendations for the future to draw from them.

PROLONGING THE AGONY?

The charge that a more aggressive approach to the USSR only strengthened Soviet resolve in the 1980s is especially interesting because in many cases, Reagan's critics did not bother to wait for the end of the Cold War to make it. To take but one example, a leading sovietologist of the time, Seweryn Bialer, warned as early as 1984 that Reagan had so wounded and enraged Moscow with his intemperate rhetoric that the USSR was now an even more determined and energetic opponent.[1] Bialer, like many sovietologists, took this view because he believed that the Soviet system was indestructible; as he wrote (with Joan Afferica) in 1982, less than two years into the Reagan administration,

> The Soviet Union is not now nor will it be in the next decade in the throes of a true systemic crisis, for it boasts enormous unused reserves of political and social stability that suffice to endure the deepest difficulties. The Soviet economy, like any gigantic economy administered by intelligent and trained professionals, will not go bankrupt. It may become less effective, it may stagnate, it may even experience an absolute decline for a year or two; but, like the political system, it will not collapse.[2]

This was a stunning misunderstanding of the fundamental weaknesses of the Soviet system, but Bialer was not alone in his confidence in the pluckiness of Soviet economic managers or in the belief that confrontation with the USSR was reckless and stupid. The popular media had already come to the conclusion that Reagan, not the Soviets, was behind the worsening of relations in the 1980s. Robert Conquest's search of the use of the word "bellicose" in reference to various leaders in the post-1979 period found that the word was applied to Reagan 211 times, Margaret Thatcher 41 times, and Brezhnev just five, a remarkable discrepancy in a period where the United States was at peace and the Soviets were engaged in actual hostilities in Afghanistan.[3]

In a similar vein, after the Soviet collapse George Kennan indignantly argued that no one person or party "won" the cold war and that the "general effect of cold war extremism"—that is, of the Reagan strategy—"was to delay rather than hasten the great change that overtook the Soviet Union at the end of the 1980s."[4] This was part of a general belief Kennan had held since the days of the "X" article that "no great country has that sort of influence on the internal developments of any other one," a position that logically cannot be squared with his argument that aggressive U.S. policies could *delay* change in the Soviet Union: either the Americans affected the timetable of Soviet change or they did not. (Kennan's answer, apparently, is that Washington could only have negative effects on Soviet politics.) In any event, why Kennan would accept that a superpower locked in conflict with its worst enemy could somehow be passively "overtaken" by change is unclear, but the lesson he drew is not: faced with an aggressive and paranoid dictatorship, accommodation and defensiveness are to be preferred over outright confrontation.

As more information emerged from the Soviet wreckage in the early 1990s, efforts intensified to deny any link between Reaganism and the Soviet collapse. Raymond Garthoff spoke for many in 1994 when he argued,

> The West did not, as widely believed, win the Cold War through geopolitical containment and military deterrence. Still less was the Cold War won by the Reagan military buildup and the Reagan Doctrine [of material support for anticommunist movements], as some have suggested. Instead, "victory" came when a new generation of Soviet leaders realized how badly their system at home and their policies abroad had failed.[5]

Garthoff's language is revealing: Soviet policies can "fail," but they are not "defeated," as though the USSR had been almost completely insulated from the efforts of its opponents—a claim even most Russians would not bother to make. But for sheer silliness, even this bold assertion could not match a 1994 article by Richard Lebow and Janice Stein, in which they confidently declared they had *proof* that Reagan prolonged the Cold War. Their source? A confirmation of the charge from none other than Mikhail Gorbachev.[6] What better way to prove that Reagan mishandled the Cold War than to ask the opinion of the defeated Soviet leader himself?

Of course, similarly overstated arguments can be found in Reagan's favor as well. Peter Schweitzer, for one, claims that the Reagan administration conspired with the Saudi Arabians to collapse global oil prices and thus to choke off the Soviet supply of hard currency from its oil sales, which in turn so mortally wounded the Soviet economy that Gorbachev had little choice but to turn toward the West and end the Cold War. ("This thing," he quotes CIA director William Casey as saying of the Soviet economy, "is so haywire that if we play our cards right, it's going to implode.")[7] But while it may be true that U.S.-Saudi collusion strained the Soviet economy, this explanation, like other "magic bullet" theories, does not take into account why the Soviets were in such dire straits in the first place. (It also imputes a coherence, to say nothing of brilliance, to American foreign policy that even Reagan's admirers have found hard to accept.)[8] While the end of the Soviet Union was probably inevitable, there was nothing predetermined about the timing or the peaceful nature of its demise, and it is no better an explanation to rest the American victory solely and personally on Ronald Reagan's shoulders than it is to argue that U.S. policy was at best only of marginal relevance (or solely a negative factor) in the last days of the Cold War.

What, then, was the Reagan administration's strategy, and what effect did it actually have on the end of the Cold War? The answer has profound implications for strategy in a future cold war: if Reagan's all-fronts offensive against the Soviets merely prolonged and destabilized an already dangerous situation, then the lesson is that such a conflict is won by conciliation and patience, secure in the belief that such regimes are not only unsustainable but can be gentled onto the path of peaceful change. But if American foreign policy in the early 1980s aborted the Soviet Union's attempts to bolster and repair itself by seeking a breathing space, a "time-out" from an ideological and military competition to which it was determined to return, then it stands to reason that the sooner such systems are confronted the better (for by their nature they cannot be "reformed" in any meaningful way) and that only military containment can ensure that they *im*plode rather than *ex*plode when they are finally and forcefully deprived of opportunities to prop themselves up.

THE STRATEGY OF OVERDOING IT

The Reagan administration's strategy incorporated Carter's responses to the Soviet challenges of the 1970s and expanded on them, adding a conscious element of design to a set of policies that been reflexive and ad hoc in character. Moreover, Reagan and his advisors made explicit the ideological nature of their counterattack, something that had been implicit in Carter's criticisms of Soviet human rights abuses but had never been fully developed into a sustained assault on the fundamental character of the Soviet system.

Although at first this was Reagan operating more on instinct than design, it eventually resulted in a more coherent, three-pronged strategy: first, on a material level, the Americans sought to force the Soviets into a ruinous arms race that they could not win and thus either bankrupt them or place them in a position of actual military inferiority. Arbatov has bitterly charged that this unprecedented military buildup did nothing but increase demands for more Soviet military spending and thus "heap more troubles on the heads of the reformers," but that was just the point: the object was to exhaust the Soviet treasury, not to encourage what the Reagan team and others saw as the oxymoron of "Soviet reform."[9] Second, on an ideological level, Reagan made it clear that the United States would not come to terms with the Soviet Union until the Soviets rejected their revolutionary ambitions, a position that confronted the Soviets with a dilemma: either they could remain true to their central principles and continue the struggle abroad (while risking internal economic collapse), or they would have to find a way to abjure their very *raison d'être* and abandon their global ambitions if they hoped to save their imperium in Eurasia. Finally, as the concrete expression of the ideological challenge, the Americans made clear their willingness to return to an activist role abroad and provide military aid to regimes resisting communism—and even to overthrow such regimes themselves if possible.

In the words of former Reagan advisor Stephen Sestanovich, this was a strategy of "overdoing it." Because Soviet policy "had made a mess everywhere" by 1980, there were now opportunities to overwhelm the Soviets by attacking, virtually without exception, across a wide range of vulnerabilities the Soviets themselves had created.[10] The United States would go on the offensive everywhere the Soviets had left themselves exposed but especially so in places where the Soviet empire was feeling the strain of imperial overextension, such as Poland, Afghanistan, and Central America. The arms race, traditionally the one area where the Soviets managed to be competitive, would take a drastic turn when Reagan decided to exploit both the massive productive capacity of the American economy and the extensive possibilities of the American scientific establishment to engage in a quantitative *and* qualitative arms race that was meant to establish—as administration officials candidly admitted—nothing less than complete military superiority in all categories. CIA official (and later agency director) Robert Gates has pointed out that this was not, at first, "a comprehensive policy to wage economic warfare against the Soviets," but rather "a broad consensus to make things as difficult as possible for the Kremlin."[11] The Americans accordingly increased their military power while also bringing their considerable economic and scientific advantages to bear on the conflict.

Perhaps worst of all from the Soviet perspective was that these actions could not be rationalized merely as more aggressive moves in a great game of international chess because the Americans had openly placed them in the context of a crusade, a global struggle with an "evil empire" that the president and his advisors made clear they intended to win. Early Soviet hopes that Reagan would turn out to be another Richard Nixon, a *"delovoi"* or "businesslike" leader who talked the talk of anticommunism but walked the walk of détente, were quickly and firmly dashed.[12] For the first time perhaps since Harry Truman, the Soviet Union was faced with an American president who was willing to match their own level of rhetoric and who was willing to take his accusatory case to the international community. Even the arrival of the more conciliatory Mikhail Gorbachev and the subsequent relaxation of Soviet-American tensions would not stop Reagan from later going to Germany and openly daring the Soviets to prove the supposed superiority and appeal of their own system by tearing down the Berlin Wall.

The collapse of the Berlin Wall would come a year after Reagan left office. In 1981, when the new president arrived, no American political figure of any stripe, perhaps except Reagan himself, would have thought it possible. But a lot would have to be done, politically and militarily, to get to a point where the President of the United States could credibly demand the demolition of the Berlin Wall. In this, Reagan owed Carter a debt for beginning a number of programs he could adopt as his own. Strangely, he might have looked back and realized his debt as well to a Soviet leadership so blind to the emerging anti-Soviet consensus in America and the West that they made Reagan's tasks that much easier to accomplish.

SHOCKING THE SOVIETS

It is important to understand that U.S. strategy in the late 1970s and early 1980s was directed at what could only semifacetiously be called a "cooperative adversary," a power that never misses an opportunity to miss an opportunity. If the Kremlin was frustrated with Jimmy Carter, it did practically nothing in the late 1970s to head off the threat represented by figures like Reagan or to obviate their criticisms.

Although the 1980 election was primarily driven by the disastrous state of the domestic economy under the Democratic administration, Reagan had also tapped into a sense among ordinary Americans that Soviet advances had weakened the United States and that improving U.S. military strength should be a priority. (In this, he was helped by the "Committee on the Present Danger," a highly visible group of defense intellectuals of both parties who were deeply critical of Carter's handling of the USSR.)[13] Reagan did not have far to go to undermine the incumbent president on the issue: Carter had been inexplicably told by his pollsters to emphasize "peace" as an issue after 1978 "just as the public were moving in the opposite direction."[14] When Carter's final humiliations in foreign affairs came in 1979 with the one-two punch of the Afghanistan invasion and the seizure of the U.S. hostages in Iran, it should have occurred to the Soviet leadership that further Soviet-American tensions could only help Reagan's election and strengthen his mandate in foreign affairs once he was in office.

To some extent, the Soviets probably did not bother with conciliatory moves toward Reagan because they likely assumed, quite sensibly, that no president who campaigned on improving American defenses (and against SALT II) would then do an about-face and cancel programs he had already blessed as necessary. More to the point, the Soviets were waiting to see what tone Reagan would adopt; after all, new weapons systems are of less concern if they are not linked to a willingness to use them. Nixon had overseen a period of significant American military and technological advances but had made clear his commitment to cooperation first and foremost, and so the competition in hardware, while taxing, was not viewed from Moscow as a direct threat to the Soviet-American relationship. In this regard, Reagan's early rhetoric and his initial appointments did far more than Carter's weapons programs to jolt the Soviets into an awareness of the new situation they faced in Washington.

Among the first of these shocks was a press conference Reagan gave within days of his inauguration that made Jimmy Carter's complaints about human rights seem almost stilted and polite. "I know of no leader of the Soviet Union since the revolution and including the present leadership," Reagan said, "that has not more than once repeated in the various communist congresses they hold their determination that their goal must be a promotion of world revolution and a one-world socialist or communist state, whichever word you want to use."

Now, as long as they do that and as long as they, at the same time, have openly and publicly declared that the only morality they recognize is what will further their cause, meaning they reserve unto themselves the right to commit any crime, to lie, to cheat, in order to attain that, and that is moral, not immoral, and we operate on a different set of standards, I think when you do business with them, even at a détente, you keep that in mind.[15]

Soviet observers were stunned; even at their worst, American presidents rarely blasted the entire Soviet leadership with ad hominem attacks on their character, and certainly not within days of assuming office.[16] The report in the *Washington Post* tried to mitigate Reagan's attack by suggesting, with no small amount of condescension, that the president was a tad behind the times. "Soviet experts pointed out that the appeals for world revolution and a one-world communist state," it editorialized in the news story reporting the speech, "disappeared from Soviet speeches in the mid-1960s." This was inaccurate and even disingenuous—the Soviet "experts" remained nameless, no doubt to their present relief—but in any event, it could do nothing to soften the impact of the president's words in Moscow.[17]

Reagan's early cabinet-level appointments were also cause for anxiety. There was great concern about the choices of academics Richard Pipes and Jeane Kirkpatrick, both uncompromising anticommunists, as advisors; although ironically, there was some hope in the Kremlin that Reagan's pick as secretary of defense, Caspar Weinberger, would actually be a moderating influence on the right-wing cabal supposedly forming in Washington.[18]

The Soviets, it should be noted, were not the only ones who worried about extremists making their way into the White House. CIA official Gates, himself a longtime Washington insider, later wrote that

the handful of people who wrote that the United States could spend the Soviets into the ground on defense and thereby speed bringing the system to its knees were dismissed by most in Washington as right-wing kooks. And, I must admit, I, along with [Central Intelligence] Agency colleagues, agreed with that conventional wisdom.[19]

What was worrisome to the Soviets was not that such people existed, but that they were not being stopped—in effect, that America had reached a point where such "kooks" were now the majority. Soviet leaders simply did not understand Reagan or the foundations of his popularity, and for the first five years of the president's tenure, they never really grasped the role they had played in creating him.[20]

At first, the Soviets remained cautious and even somewhat hopeful that Reagan's bluster was an act. (Ideology chief Mikhail Suslov, not unexpectedly, was an exception, warning in early 1981 that the ideological struggle between the United States and the USSR was heading into a genuinely new phase.)[21] For much of 1981, this was reflected in the fact that their criticism of Reagan did not consistently rise to the sort of direct insults Reagan himself had used after taking office. But the president's prominent and personal role in leading the rhetorical charge against the USSR did not go unnoticed. The head of the Ukrainian KGB unleashed an attack on Reagan in late 1981, warning that there seemed to be a kind of contagiousness to the new president's rhetoric.

> It is worth noting that recently, especially in connection with events in Poland, anti-Soviet propaganda in the USA and several other capitalist countries has assumed an unprecedented level of fury and mendacity. This has been promoted to a great extent by the numerous anti-Soviet statements of the current president of the USA, R. Reagan. Whereas previously anti-Soviet propaganda was, in the main, handled by bourgeois hacks, today such high-ranking persons very close to the American president such as U.S. Secretary of State A. Haig and Pentagon chief C. Weinberger, many congressmen, and also members of the parliaments and governments of several NATO countries have directly joined in the campaign of malicious lies and slander.[22]

Due to their proximity to Poland, the Ukrainians had plenty to worry about. What the KGB might have suspected (or even known) is that Reagan was not going to leave the matter of the crushing of Solidarity at the level of rhetoric and would soon sign an order giving covert assistance to the Polish rebels.[23] But this criticism of Reagan was built around an unavoidable fact: American political attacks on the Soviet Union were no longer the province of fringe-right anticommunists, but official policy that emanated from the Oval Office.

THE PROPAGANDISTS SOUND THE ALARM

Even if there had been no material assistance or military spending to buttress Reagan's fiery attacks on communism, the message itself was regarded as deadly by Soviet propagandists. The opening into Soviet society provided by détente, a risk Soviet leaders assumed they could manage under Nixon and even Carter, was now seen as explosively dangerous when exploited by a figure like Reagan. The predictable response was to try to head off further intrusions, and it is hardly surprising that Moscow took steps to limit contact with the West. (The Kremlin wisely did not take Reagan up on his mid-1982 challenge that he and Brezhnev should address each other's nations on television.)

Like white cells swarming to the site of an infection, the Soviet ideological establishment went on high alert to try to contain the damage. The analogy of illness was one used by the Soviets themselves: a

1983 Central Committee plenum on ideological work even spoke of the need to help Soviet citizens develop an "immunity" to "hostile ideas and views."[24] The Soviets rapidly came to understand that their system was under direct attack and that countermeasures were needed. In October 1982, a national meeting of Soviet ideological workers was called in Tallinn that included exhortations by the leadership to involve Soviet cultural and artistic figures more intimately in ideological work. The explicit warning sounded in Tallinn was that the West was now contesting the moral high ground with the Soviet Union and that to fail to fight back was to risk further bourgeois infection of the weakest groups in the communist bloc, particularly among Soviet youth and the subject populations of the Warsaw Pact nations.[25] In the Soviet armed forces, especially, this infiltration of "bourgeois" ideas was considered so dire a threat to young Soviet men that special counterpropaganda groups were set up within the Soviet military in 1983.[26]

Some of this, to be sure, predated Reagan, particularly the worry about the influence of Western culture on Soviet children. A KGB report in the 1970s was among many to excoriate rock music, for example, with Michael Jackson and Pink Floyd high on the list of "potential threats to the Soviet system."[27] Rock, according to the report, gave Soviet youth "a distorted idea of Soviet reality, and led to incidents of a treasonable nature"—ironic concerns given how many American conservatives probably thought the same thing about the influence of rock and roll on the United States.

Still, the near panic about Western ideological infiltration was, to some extent, justified: the Americans were in fact intentionally using ideological differences as public bludgeons against the legitimacy of the Soviet system. The insistence on religious freedom, for example, agreed to at Helsinki and pursued by both Carter and Reagan, was seen as an especially powerful strain of ideological warfare, and in fact it was. (Pope John Paul II's dramatic 1979 visit to Poland was regarded by the Politburo as an act of "ideological subversion" that marked the beginning of a Vatican campaign of "ideological struggle" against the socialist countries, an overheated but essentially accurate description of the Polish pontiff's efforts to bolster the faith and hopes of his countrymen.)[28] What might have been dismissed as Soviet paranoia about secret deals between the White House and the Vatican to aid Poland and in general to raise the visibility of religious organizations would turn out to be true, a fulfillment of Moscow's worst fears. While cooperation between the Vatican and the United States may not have been the "Holy Alliance" that some have suggested, the American attempts to use channels established by Catholic clergy to smuggle things like fax machines and copiers to Solidarity activists could hardly be seen as anything but a direct attack on Soviet rule in Poland.

But the Kremlin overreacted against the Vatican, in the process doing more harm than good to its own attempts to counter growing Western criticisms. (It is a peculiar characteristic of insecure authoritarian regimes to respond to charges of repression by engaging in more repression.) Moscow flooded the Soviet press with warnings about the seductive power of religion, engaged in increasing coercion of religious groups, particularly Catholics and Baptists, and in general acted in ways that confirmed the very worst charges being made about Soviet oppression.

Propaganda in this period suggests a panic that led to self-defeating, even silly attempts to undermine Western political and cultural influences. When Reagan met the Pope in 1982, the Soviet press in the heavily Catholic Baltic states warned that religious organizations were in reality nothing but political organizations and in a remarkably clumsy attack on the Vatican argued that John Paul's meeting with the president was a violation of Christ's injunction to "render unto Caesar" and thus to keep politics and faith separate.[29] (The writer, tone-deaf to Christian sensibilities, somehow failed to see that to use Scripture against the Pope was merely to increase the overall offensiveness of the whole attack.) American pressure on matters like freedom of religion, particularly in Eastern Europe, was having an effect; although the regime correctly understood that a growth in religious belief was a direct threat to centralized political control, its attempts to limit the influence of faith were so odious as to be worse, in terms of alienating ordinary Soviet bloc citizens, than benign neglect.

Even romance fell victim to the increasing vigilance of the Soviet authorities in this period. Although marriage to foreigners was illegal under Stalin, it was relegalized after his death. But this was a formality, since in fact such relationships were ever more harshly discouraged as East-West relations deteriorated in the late 1970s. In a legalistic outburst that even the angriest father would recognize as ludicrous, a recalcitrant Soviet woman who had the misfortune to fall in love with a French citizen in 1981 was excoriated by a Soviet official who said: "By falling in love with a foreigner, you have violated the rules of behavior of a Soviet citizen living outside the USSR."[30] The net effect of such harassment, like the campaign against religion, was to increase the alienation of ordinary Soviet citizens from their government, as heavy-handed countermeasures against Western influence made daily life in the USSR more irritating and more dispiriting than it already had to be.

There were other moments of paranoia on the part of Soviet officialdom that were no doubt outright laughable even to Soviet citizens themselves. A 1982 Soviet review of the movie *Superman II*, for example, found all sorts of ideological messages hidden in the story of the Man of Steel's attempt to save Earth from three supervillains from his own planet bent on destroying everything in sight, including the White House. At the end of the movie, Superman repairs the flag-bearing cupola over the Oval Office and apologizes to the President for having let him down. (In the movie, he had been incommunicado at the North Pole, distracted and unaware of the trouble back home while he shared a mylar bed with Lois Lane, but details need not detain us here.) *Pravda's* correspondent agreed with a radical French critic's interpretation that found the movie permeated with the spirit of "revanche" and added that the final scene represented not only the restoration of the cupola, but "presidential power," an apparent reference to the new, more robust presence in the White House.[31] (The fact that the screenplay actually was developed in the mid-1970s and parts of the sequel were shot during the filming of the original in 1978 did not stop *Pravda* from assuming a connection to Reaganism in the 1980s.)

The charge that Superman was just a lackey for imperialism was only one of a slew of Soviet criticisms of American popular culture in the 1980s. Much of what Moscow saw on Western televisions and movie screens touched a raw nerve of insecurity, as evidenced by the huffy reactions of Soviet propagandists even to harmless fluff like the British comedy "Comrade Dad" (set in "Londongrad" in 1999 after Britain falls to the USSR).[32] But they were right to suspect that there was in fact a trend in the culture that seemed to track with the new mood in Washington, with the Soviets or their allies showing up increasingly as the heavies in any number of films and television programs. Most of these films were not available in the USSR, but it is not difficult to imagine why the Soviet reaction to them was so intense. In part, there was a concern that a steady diet of anti-Soviet entertainment was preparing Americans for war, and more than once Soviet ideologists wondered aloud about whether masterminds in the Reagan administration were behind movies like *Red Dawn* (a camp classic in which high school students run around the mountains of Colorado taking on Soviet special forces commandos) that only the most humorless Soviet could take seriously.[33] Always more aware than the democracies of the power of popular culture in forming character and shaping beliefs, the Soviets apparently worried that the new turn in Cold War culture was actually part of a campaign aimed at shoring up the resolve of the American public.

The concern that President Reagan and the American people were now seeing eye to eye on the Soviet threat was a reasonable one, but again, it was due as much to Soviet actions as it was to Reagan's steady drumbeat of anti-Soviet statements, much less to Hollywood's sudden rediscovery of the Soviet Union. The Soviets were right to believe that they had now gained top billing as the most reliable bad guys both in Washington's rhetoric and in Western entertainment, but they failed to grasp the causal relationship behind it: rather than drawing the conclusion that their own behavior was driving an anti-Soviet mood in the popular culture, they instead assumed that the popular culture (at the instigation of the country's most powerful former actor) was creating anti-Sovietism from thin air.

In any case, Reagan's public castigation of the Soviet Union reached an apocalyptic crescendo in 1983. Speaking to a conference of evangelical Christians, Reagan delivered one of the most famous lines of the Cold War.

> Yes, let us pray for the salvation of all of those who live in that totalitarian darkness—pray they will discover the joy of knowing God. But until they do, let us be aware that while they preach the supremacy of the state, declare its omnipotence over individual man, and predict its eventual domination of all peoples on the Earth, they are the focus of evil in the modern world.

"I urge you to beware the temptation," Reagan continued, "of pride—the temptation of blithely declaring yourselves above it all and label both sides equally at fault, to ignore the facts of history and the aggressive impulses of an evil empire."[34]

The effect of the "evil empire" speech is debated even now in Russia, with some observers arguing that it was taken by the Soviet leadership as only so much sloganeering (with an impact in the Kremlin "close to zero" according to a former Soviet Foreign Ministry official) while others contend that it genuinely stung some of the more thin-skinned men in the Kremlin.[35] One retired general has suggested that the statement had different impacts on different parts of the Soviet system: "The military, the armed forces, more than the politicians or the diplomats, really used this declaration. They used this statement as a reason to begin a very intense preparation inside the military for a state of war."[36] At the least, the term stuck in the Soviet craw and undermined the confidence of a particular generation of leaders, as Anatolii Cherniaev would later recall:

> We could have expected anything from America, our main adversary and the main danger for us, including these sorts of statements. So as a matter of principle in the political climate at the top of the Soviet government, this label, this nickname, I don't think changed anything. On the other hand, in our circles, those people who were later called the *shestidesiatniki*, the people in their 60s, this term and this propaganda was perceived as punishment for what we did in Afghanistan. In other words, we felt that we deserved it.[37]

Whether dismissed as American propaganda or taken seriously as a sign that the United States was gearing for war, the message behind the speech was hard to miss. Reagan had raised the kinds of concerns once voiced by Carter to a level unseen in American politics, in what amounted to a declaration that there could be no compromising with the Soviet system in its present form.

THE AMERICAN STRATEGY CODIFIED: NSDD 75

Initially, the American attack on the Soviet system was more a matter of the deeply held beliefs of the president and his advisors than of a grand strategy. But while Reagan was publicly raining a storm of invective on the Soviets in 1981 and 1982, the administration was in fact drawing up a long-term strategy against the Soviet Union, a process that resulted in a January 1983 "National Security Decision Directive" from the president, NSDD 75.

The contents of the document itself are less striking than the fact that the document existed at all. It represented an attempt to bring coherence to U.S. Cold War strategy, to think through the problem of how to deal with the Soviet Union, and to imagine what outcomes the United States would find desirable. As one Reagan administration official later pointed out, NSDDs are common documents, and it would be overstatement to say that any one of them is the rudder of foreign policy.[38] If nothing else, however, NSDD 75 captured the administration's strategy of "overdoing it" and confirmed that American policy toward the Soviet Union would no longer rest on the personalized diplomacy of the Nixon-Kissinger years, nor upon the lurching, bifurcated policy of confusion that characterized much of the Carter administration.

Perhaps most important is that NSDD 75 was infused with a sense of American advantages, rather than vulnerabilities, and saw the American objective as doing significant and lasting damage to the USSR as an enemy state rather than "managing" it as an abstract problem. The thrust of U.S. policy would be "to contain and over time reverse Soviet expansionism by competing effectively on a sustained basis with the Soviet Union in all international arenas—particularly in the overall military balance and in geographical regions of priority concern to the United States."[39] The point, however, was not just to alter Soviet behavior in the international arena but to strike the Soviet empire directly, and here NSDD 75 broke with the realist assumptions of Reagan's immediate Republican predecessors and aimed, in language reminiscent of NSC-68, for the heart of the Soviet system itself.

> [U.S. tasks include:] To promote, within the narrow limits available to us, the process of change in the Soviet Union toward a more pluralistic political and economic system in which the power of the privileged ruling elite is gradually reduced. The U.S. recognizes that Soviet aggressiveness

has deep roots in the internal system, and that relations with the USSR should therefore take into account whether or not they help to strengthen this system and its capacity to engage in aggression.

This only codified, of course, what Reagan was already doing. The propaganda offensive begun in 1981 was more than just so much "red meat" thrown to conservative audiences; rather, it was the beginning of "an ideological thrust which clearly affirms the superiority of U.S. and Western values of individual dignity and freedom, a free press, free trade unions, free enterprise, and political democracy over the repressive features of Soviet Communism." Following the president's lead, NSDD 75 explicitly envisioned using the open media to prevent "the Soviet propaganda machine from seizing the semantic high-ground" as part of a campaign "wherever possible to encourage Soviet allies to distance themselves from Moscow in foreign policy and to move toward democratization domestically."

Also evident in NSDD 75 was a recognition of the Western coalition's greater economic and technological ability to arm itself. "The future strength of U.S. military capabilities must be assured. U.S. military technology advances must be exploited, while controls over transfer of military related/dual-use technology, products, and services must be tightened." This was to be coupled with an economic policy that was determined "to avoid subsidizing the Soviet economy or unduly easing the burden of Soviet resource allocation decisions, so as not to dilute pressures for structural change in the Soviet system." What this meant, in practice, was that the Americans were determined to regain military supremacy while making any Soviet attempt to match that effort as expensive as possible. It is little wonder that in later years Soviet "reformers" under Gorbachev would complain that Reagan's policies had made their arguments for less military investment untenable through most of the 1980s and that they were only heeded once the Soviet crisis was beyond remedy anyway.

An important point here is that the call to bring the U.S. technological edge to bear in NSDD 75 was not, in the main, aimed at nuclear modernization but rather at the far more expensive proposition of upgrading Western conventional arms. Former Soviet diplomat Valentin Falin, like many Soviet officials, saw in this a conscious plot hatched after 1981, based on a supposed American recognition that conventional arms were "five to seven" times more expensive than nuclear arms and would break the Soviet treasury that much faster.[40] But this is too clever an interpretation, not least because it ignores the reality of the situation in Europe at the time: although NSDD 75 was initially classified as "Secret" and "Sensitive," it was not exactly a deep secret that NATO was in disrepair and needed mending. NSDD 75's authors echoed the concerns voiced about the Atlantic Alliance during the Carter rearmament of 1978 and warned that "the Soviets must be faced with a reinvigorated NATO."

This call to strengthen the alliance was again an instance in which the Soviets had helped to create a situation they had hoped to avert. Atlantic strategists, particularly NATO commander in chief General Bernard Rogers, were already considering how best to counter the Soviet Union's imposing conventional advantage in Europe. NATO's weakness was plain: Western military forces were no match for the numerically superior Warsaw Pact, whose offensive units were eche-loned to attack the NATO lines at concentrated points in Germany in waves, much like a drill that would grind away at the same spot, with fresh drill bits brought up in succession to replace each one that wore out. Without nuclear weapons, there would be no way to hold back the Soviet assault, and the sheer size of an Eastern attack, coupled with special forces raids against NATO nuclear installations, threatened to shatter Western resistance even before nuclear arms could be brought into the fray.

Against this, General Rogers and his colleagues suggested an overall strategy that came to bear his name. The "Rogers Plan" sought to use NATO's technological edge to engage in "deep strikes" against the waiting Soviet echelons, using long-range aviation and high-precision weapons to disrupt or destroy Warsaw Pact command and control nodes, airfields, supply depots, staging areas, and other targets. The idea was to create havoc in the enemy rear and to ensure that the forces coming to the front would nearly be as ragged as the ones they were supposed to relieve. The third world war in Europe would then threaten to become a drawn-out affair, in which the combined economic might and tighter cohesion of the Western alliance would eventually bear down on a Soviet war machine that had neither the material nor the political capacity to sustain a protracted conflict—especially on a bat-tlefield where Soviet commanders would be surrounded by unhappy Poles, Czechs, and East Germans. Moreover, by removing the Soviet option of a quick conventional victory, the Rogers Plan carried an inherently greater risk of eventual nuclear use by one side or the other, precisely the outcome Moscow hoped to avoid with a blitzkrieglike conventional attack in the first place.

Like all the plans for Armageddon, the Rogers Plan seems now almost to be science fiction in a world where Europe is united, former Warsaw Pact enemies are now NATO members, and the greatest threat to the peace comes from civilian terrorists rather than Soviet marshals. (The idea of striking deep into enemy territory and collapsing command and control systems, however, became a central feature of the way the United States fights, as Saddam Hussein can attest.) Whether the Rogers

Plan would have worked in a European battle is an open question; certainly, to judge by the massive outpouring of vitriol directed against it in the mid-1980s, the Soviet military thought the idea had merit.[41] As Mastny has noted: "Perhaps the most startling discovery to have come out of the Warsaw Pact archives so far has been the deep impact on the communist assessment of the military balance of the high-tech precision weapons the West developed and deployed from the 1970s onward.[42] Senior Soviet military commanders no doubt feared that NATO was trying to do exactly what *they* were trying to do: win without the use of nuclear weapons and then dictate terms to the defeated coalition under the threat of nuclear blackmail.

The important point about NATO's material and intellectual reinvigoration was that it represented, as did NSDD 75, a renewal of Western will at a time when Moscow hoped that the United States and Europe were losing their belly for further competition. The Soviets were beginning to realize the growing vulnerability of their own global position, as did the authors of NSDD 75. The Americans could now see that the Soviet fall from the pinnacle of its powers in the mid-1970s was underway and that the United States was now in a position to bring particular Western advantages to bear in order to accelerate that decline.

WE CANNOT ALLOW U.S. MILITARY SUPERIORITY, AND WE WILL NOT ALLOW IT

Whether the Soviets were aware of the existence of NSDD 75 is unknown, but they clearly understood the thrust of the approach to the USSR. With Reagan's election, *Pravda* complained, "wholesale ideological sabotage against the socialist countries was openly elevated to the rank of U.S. state policy (previously it was at least covert)."[43] Dobrynin affirms that "two features of Reagan's policy toward the Soviet Union upset [the Kremlin] most. One was his apparent determination to regain military superiority; the other, his determination to launch an ideological offensive against the Soviet Union and foment trouble inside the country and among Soviet allies."[44]

In the wake of one of Reagan's speeches in May 1982, the Soviet ministers of defense and foreign affairs, along with the head of the KGB (Gromyko, Ustinov, and Andropov), sent the Politburo a joint memorandum "vividly illustrating the real feelings of the core of the Kremlin toward Reagan's proposals and his presidency."

It angrily accused him of creating "a propaganda cover-up for the aggressive militarist policy of the United States" and trying to break the détente agreements of nuclear parity. The speech as a whole, they said, "is satu-

rated with gross, unadulterated hostility toward the Soviet Union" and
was aimed at splitting the socialist countries and liquidating our system.[45]

This reflected Soviet rage over Reagan's direct attacks on the legitimacy
of Soviet rule in Eastern Europe, specifically his continuing criticism of
martial law in Poland. (Indeed, both Carter and Reagan had reaped
dividends by keeping international attention focused on Soviet moves
on Poland. Suslov, in late 1981, told the Politburo point-blank that
public scrutiny had limited Soviet options: "We are carrying out a great
deal of work for peace, and it is impossible for us to change our position
now. World public opinion wouldn't understand us. . . . That is why we
must not change our position [i.e., to refuse to intervene militarily] with
regard to Poland.")[46] A month after the Politburo report, Reagan used
the word "crusade" in a 1982 speech in London calling for an increased
effort to foster democracy around the globe; the Soviets, seeing another
confirmation of their fears, seized upon it immediately, calling it a holy
war against communism "led by the President of the USA himself and
his closest assistants."[47]

Yuri Andropov laid out the situation to Soviet allies in a grim
January 1983 speech in Prague. "It would not be an exaggeration,"
he told a closed meeting of the Warsaw Pact leadership, "to say that
we are faced with one of the most massive efforts of imperialism to
slow down the process of social change in the world, to stop the
progress of socialism or even to roll it back, at least in some areas."[48]
Referring to the U.S. president as a "political boor," Andropov
wondered aloud about the origins of the "phenomenon of Reagan,"
and he found answers in the reverses suffered by imperialism in the
Third World: "The revolutionary changes in Angola, Ethiopia, Nicaragua, and other countries . . . were seen by Washington, and not
without reason, as a defeat of American policy." As a good Marxist,
Andropov also pointed to internal economic dislocations in the West,
including "a decline in production, inflation, [and] mass joblessness,"
that have propelled the "bourgeoisie" to seek "solutions in foreign
policy adventures."

Andropov's instincts, however, were too sharp to accept the renewed
American offensive as just a knee-jerk reaction to domestic unemployment, and he directly warned his audience that the enemy was trying
to exploit *Soviet* problems as well.

But this, as we believe, is only one side of the problem. The other side is
that the United States and NATO saw an opportunity in the difficulties,
which all of us encountered in our economic development to some extent.
I am referring to the growing hard currency debts, the food situation, the
technological lagging behind in some sectors of the economy, and a num-

ber of other difficult issues. They assess the internal political difficulties in some socialist countries in a similar fashion. We are not going to close our eyes on that—as long as these problems exist, the class enemies will make efforts to turn them to their favor; that it is why they are the class enemies.

In other words, Andropov recognized the American strategy for what it was. He almost could have been reading from a draft of NSDD 75, except that his speech predated it by a month; still, it was reminiscent of Sestanovich's description of the Reagan strategy of "overdoing it" when Andropov added, "The struggle is unfolding practically in all directions."

If Andropov realized the Americans were trying to force the Soviets into an arms race, however, he was nonetheless willing to meet them more than halfway. Washington, he said, had set itself "a goal to break the [military] equilibrium."

The challenge that has been presented to us in the military sphere is especially dangerous. . . . The new round of the arms race, which is being imposed by the United States, has principal qualitative features that distinguish it from the previous ones. If in the past the Americans, when speaking about their nuclear weapons, preferred to emphasize the fact that those were, first of all, means of "deterrence," now, by creating improved missile systems, they are not trying to conceal the fact that those are realistically designed for a future war. This is where the doctrines of a "rational" or "limited" nuclear war come from, this is the source of the arguments about the possibility to survive and to win in a protracted nuclear conflict. It is difficult to say which part of it is nuclear blackmail, and which part represents readiness for a fatal step. In any case, we cannot allow U.S. military superiority, and we will not allow it. The equilibrium will not be broken.

Despite America's "explicitly destructive" positions, Andropov pledged to continue to negotiate with the United States, not least in the hopes of isolating Washington from what he saw as the more "rational" NATO allies. Nor did Andropov envision a strictly military response to the American buildup; in a telling miscalculation, Andropov suggested that the international peace movement, along with nuclear freeze supporters, might be of use. The antinuclear movement "is becoming more powerful in Western Europe and in the United States itself. The idea of freezing the nuclear arsenals enjoys wide support in the Democratic Party of the United States. [The] Labor party supports nuclear disarmament of Great Britain. These are not just little things."

The support of liberal U.S. senators for a nuclear freeze may not have been a little thing, but it was not nearly enough to blunt the overall impact of Reagan's military revitalization of U.S. and NATO defenses.

Andropov, like Brezhnev, found himself facing mounting pressure from the Soviet military to respond. (Even Gorbachev later called such Soviet faith in the peace movement "more than naive.")[49] In his speech in Prague, Andropov seemed resigned to the fact that something would have to be done, but he warned that the lopsided economic balance between the superpowers would take its toll.

> Probably, the Soviet Union feels the burden of arms race into which we are being pulled, more than anybody else does. It is not an easy task for anybody to appropriate additional resources, to strengthen their military forces. *It is not a big problem for Reagan to shift tens of billions of dollars of appropriations for social needs to the military industrial complex. Meanwhile, we cannot stop thinking about the well-being of the workers. But unfortunately, today we do not have any other alternatives, except to respond to NATO's challenges with our countermeasures*, which would be persuasive for the present American politicians. Our peoples would not understand it if we showed carelessness regarding the threats from NATO [emphasis added].

The hope that Westerners would rise up and put a stop to this challenge was misplaced. Andropov and other senior Soviet leaders apparently came to believe that Reagan and other conservative NATO leaders were vastly more unpopular than they actually were, a fundamental misunderstanding of the Western public that probably reflected a certain amount of wishful thinking. KGB defector Mitrokhin reports that "ensuring that Reagan did not serve a second term . . . became Service A's [the "active measures" and disinformation section] most important objective," with KGB residencies in the United States ordered in 1983 to begin such active measures, including contacts with the staffs of presidential candidates.[50] Reagan's 1984 landslide re-election was, according to Russian scholar Vladimir Batiuk, a "shock" to the Soviet leadership, even if it was a foregone outcome to everyone else.[51]

Any lingering illusions about Reagan or the Americans in general were shattered in September 1983, when the Soviets shot down a Korean Airliners 747 that had strayed off course into Soviet airspace. By all accounts, Andropov was taken aback by the "stormy anti-Sovietism" that followed the shootdown, a reaction that Arbatov says turned his "doubts" about dealing with Reagan to "certainty"; other Russian historians suggest that the KAL incident finally convinced Andropov to give up any hope of engaging the Americans diplomatically.[52]

Even without the Korean airliner disaster, Soviet-American relations would still have worsened in late 1983 as Washington escalated its offensive. Lesser members of the Soviet coalition were strung around the globe, and the administration soon made plain it intended to attack as many of them, by various means, as possible. Although Reagan himself did not openly articulate a strategy of overthrowing communist regimes in peripheral areas until 1985, its premises were set forth as early as the president's 1981 inaugural speech.[53] Robert Gates, too, notes that

> from the outset, the Reagan administration targeted covert action, foreign assistance, diplomacy, and even direct military intervention on Third World battlefields in opposition to the Soviets, Cubans, Libyans—and anyone else perceived to be a surrogate of the Soviet Union. . . . But [as opposed to the Carter administration policy of covertness] the surrogate wars in the Third World under Reagan were not just visible, but openly characterized as the cutting edge of a broader challenge to the Soviet Union.[54]

The 1983 invasion of Grenada in particular convinced some in Moscow that Reagan was serious about eradicating Soviet clients. Grenada was a small place with a big impact: as Brian Crozier has argued, previous Soviet reverses had been tactical, not strategic, and while "the imperial drive may have been thwarted . . . no territories that had already been incorporated into the Empire were lost. The first *strategic* reversal would come with the U.S. occupation of Grenada in 1983" [emphasis original].[55] A Soviet commentator concluded that Grenada showed the president meant what he said: "*Gospodin* Reagan's 'crusade' isn't just rhetoric or an expression," but rather an actual strategy hatched by the Pentagon and the CIA, aimed at the eventual "destruction of the socialist social system."[56]

The Soviets were seeing more coherence than there actually was. The Grenada operation took place two years before journalist Charles Krauthammer would give a name to the "Reagan Doctrine," a term Reagan and his advisors apparently never thought to use in any formal way. The Reagan administration's determination to undermine Soviet clients was more a guiding principle than it was a set of well-defined plans, but the Soviets were nonetheless right to believe that a worldwide assault on their system and their weaker coalition partners was now underway.[57]

By late 1983, Reagan's initial challenges, at the level of both propaganda and concrete military preparations, were showing results. While Reagan's rhetorical attacks had galvanized a network of protest in both the United States and Europe, the Soviet Union still ended up on the defensive in the international arena, not least due to self-defeating actions like the Korean shootdown and the war in Afghanistan. No matter how much the Kremlin wanted to take heart from mass demonstrations by the nuclear freeze movement, the fact of the matter was that by 1983, NATO's confrontational policies were supported or at least tolerated by its various populations. Although Soviet leaders recognized that the USSR was ill-prepared to match the American military buildup, they also felt that the audacity and explicit menace behind U.S. efforts demanded a response. Indeed, until the arrival of Mikhail Gorbachev in 1985, the Soviets would concentrate on arms at the expense of repairing their damaged prestige, leading one Russian analyst later to conclude that one of the great ironies of the Cold War was that the Soviets almost won the arms race, while still losing the overall ideological competition.[58]

The charge that Reagan was actively seeking the destruction of the Soviet system become a staple of public propaganda, with the added worry that the president did not much care how that was accomplished—even if it meant apocalypse. "Never before," one Soviet daily wrote in 1982, "have plans for nuclear war against the socialist nations been discussed so candidly in the West as now."[59] Even some of Reagan's nominal supporters began to wonder if the whole thing was not going too far. Richard Nixon, for one, voiced concerns about his Republican successor: "We've got to make [the Soviets] understand," he said in 1982, "that we're not out to get them."[60]

It was about to get worse: Mutual Assured Destruction, the cornerstone of the Soviet-American strategic relationship for over two decades, was about to come under attack, as President Reagan served notice to the Soviets (and to the world) that the United States no longer intended to accept the inevitability of the threat of ballistic missiles.

SDI AND THE REJECTION OF MAD

Soviet leaders concerned about Reagan's fulminations could content themselves with the notion that, whatever Reagan's threats, there was nothing the Americans could do, short of launching a suicidal nuclear war, to destroy their system. Nuclear arsenals on both sides numbered tens of thousands of warheads, and Mutual Assured Destruction remained enshrined at the center of the Soviet-American strategic relationship. MAD, as a fact, was undeniable: the redundancy of nuclear delivery systems and particularly the sure retaliation from ballistic missile submarines meant that there was no way to launch a first strike without taking cataclysmic damage in return. Elaborate scenarios developed by defense thinkers on both sides could not hide the essential fact that a nuclear exchange meant, in all likelihood, the end of Western civilization—and all life in the Northern Hemisphere.

Reagan was evidently haunted by this realization, and his approach to nuclear weapons was simple: either the world would rid itself of the danger by abolishing nuclear weapons or the United States would keep the peace with an absolute superiority in such arms. In his first few years as president, Reagan alternated direct attacks on the Kremlin with statements that reflected his desire to reduce the risk of nuclear war. Speaking to the British parliament in 1982, for example, he said,

> We see around us today the marks of our terrible dilemma—predictions of doomsday, antinuclear demonstrations, an arms race in which the West must, for its own protection, be an unwilling participant. At the same time we see totalitarian forces in the world who seek subversion and conflict around the globe to further their barbarous assault on the human spirit. What, then, is our course? Must civilization perish in a hail of fiery atoms? Must freedom wither in a quiet, deadening accommodation with totalitarian evil?[61]

The Soviets, understandably, were less than reassured about Reagan's commitment to keeping the nuclear peace, in part because the administration was playing—as Moscow had for so many years—a double game and sending competing messages. Even as the president was wondering aloud about the fate of humanity, U.S. Defense Department official T. K. Jones was telling the *Los Angeles Times* that in a nuclear war, "everyone's going to make it if there are enough shovels to go around. The idea is to dig a hole, and cover it over with a couple of doors and then throw three feet of dirt on top. It's the dirt," Jones added helpfully, "that does it."[62] While the idea was to convince the Soviets that the United States wanted peace but was serious about fighting and winning a nuclear war, in Moscow, it seemed as if the Reagan administration was serving the peaceful line for foreign consumption while girding Americans for an actual nuclear war.

Soviet suspicions about Reagan's views on nuclear war were confirmed in March 1983, when the president did the unthinkable and attacked the underpinnings of MAD itself. Speaking to the American nation, he said,

> Let me share with you a vision of the future which offers hope. It is that we embark on a program to counter the awesome Soviet missile threat with measures that are defensive. Let us turn to the very strengths in technology that spawned our great industrial base and that have given us the quality of life we enjoy today. What if free people could live secure in the knowledge that their security did not rest upon the threat of instant U.S. retaliation to deter a Soviet attack, that we could intercept and destroy strategic ballistic missiles before they reached our own soil or that of our allies?[63]

Reagan proposed, in other words, to use America's technological advantage—and here, he called upon the scientific community specifically to aid him—to neutralize the Soviet missile arsenal. If Carter with

Presidential Directive 59 had begun the conceptual turn away from MAD, Reagan now abandoned it decisively.

Of course, the Strategic Defense Initiative (enshrined in the popular consciousness as "Star Wars" after it was so dubbed by detractors) could not conceivably alter the Soviet-American military balance in the short term. But the president's new commitment to defenses exploited several Soviet weaknesses simultaneously. First, because the Soviet strategic arsenal was heavily tilted toward land-based missiles, SDI threatened, even if only in the far future, the one clear area of Soviet advantage. Second, the whole notion of defenses negated everything Soviet diplomacy had tried to achieve in arms negotiations with the United States; indeed, the American position represented a philosophical reversion to a position the Soviets themselves had held in the 1960s and thus not only presented Soviet diplomats with a defeat, but suggested that there was no longer common ground on which to negotiate the issue.

Finally, the investment in defenses represented a massive infusion of resources in both pure science and engineering. While the Soviets were always strong in "blackboard science," they were paralyzed by the woeful state of their applied sciences, and so SDI meant that the military-technological competition had now shifted to the area of greatest Soviet weakness. In truth, most of the improvements in American weapons since the 1970s were viewed by the Soviets as threatening in this regard, but the sheer scale and scope of SDI made a technological arms race seem especially daunting. As Kissinger has put it, "with a single technological stroke, Reagan was proposing to erase everything that the Soviet Union had propelled itself into bankruptcy trying to accomplish."[64]

The reaction in Moscow to the announcement of the SDI effort was, by many accounts, was one of near panic, particularly among older members of the leadership who understood that any attempt to match the American missile defense project would only worsen the crisis engulfing the already desperate Soviet economy.[65] This generational difference may have been rooted in a long-standing Soviet sense of technological inferiority not shared by younger Soviets, or it may simply have been that the older men better understood the monumental expense of the effort that would be demanded of the regime by the military and scientific communities. Those demands in fact materialized in short order: some elements of the military, in one account, "were initially put into a state of fear and shock because we understood that this could be realistic due to the economic and financial capabilities of the United States."[66] According to two former Politburo advisors, despite the fact that "the commitment of resources needed to run the arms race at all was already crushing . . . the high command refused to consider 'quick fix' responses to the SDI threat. Their determination to have a full-blown strategic defense of their own dramatized the internal price of the arms race and made clear the need to shake the system up."[67]

At the least, there was a broadly shared concern that even if SDI did not create a missile shield in the short term, there was the unpredictable problem of what the Americans might discover along the way, and this led to demands from the Soviet scientific community (which reacted strongly as well to Reagan's announcement) joining those of the military.[68] As former Soviet general and arms negotiator Nikolai Detinov later described it,

> [A committee of Soviet scientists] presented its conclusions at the end of 1983, the beginning of 1984. It agreed that during the next 15 to 20 years it would be unrealistic to expect the SDI program to produce any results. But at the same time, another result of this program could actually be the development of a whole line of new technologies in the United States that were not completely devoted to defending against a strike from the Soviet Union but to a certain degree still constituted an antimissile defense. This was the danger of the program. . . . The danger of the SDI program was that it would lead to the development of new kinds of weapons.[69]

By most Soviet accounts, this initial sense of urgency began to abate as Soviet researchers became more confident that they could defeat an American defense. (Russian military historian Aleksandr Orlov has cleverly described the initial panicking effect of SDI as akin to a successful exercise in "socialist realism," presenting fantasy as reality.)[70] But it is also clear in retrospect, as one Soviet general later admitted, that "SDI did harm us," both in terms of money spent and Soviet energies wasted.[71] In the end, SDI convinced many in the leadership that further military competition with the United States would be, in the words of one Russian scholar, "too fantastically expensive" and drove home the realization that "[Soviet] resources were not unlimited."[72]

It should be noted that some former Soviet officials have taken issue with the idea that SDI or any other military program was the spur to more spending. Some, for example, have argued that bloated military budgets were a long-term result of the German surprise attack in 1941, a painful memory that Soviet military leaders could resurrect at will to pressure the leadership for more money. This is evident in a conversation between Anatolii Dobrynin and Marshal Sergei Akhromeev. "Do you indeed believe the United States and NATO could attack us some day?" Dobrynin asked. "It's not my mission to believe," the marshal answered, "or not to believe. I can't depend on you diplomats and all your conferences or whatever you call them." Akhromeev then raised the issue of the 1973 nuclear alert issued by the White House during the Yom Kippur War, and he turned the question back to Dobrynin.

> Now, does President Reagan inspire more confidence [than Nixon]? That is why my motto as chief of the General Staff is "National security along all azimuths." We proceed from the worst conceivable scenario of having to fight the United States, its West European allies, and probably Japan. We must be prepared for any kind of war with any kind of weapon. Soviet military doctrine can be summed up as follows: 1941 shall never be repeated.[73]

Gorbachev aide Cherniaev, speaking to an American audience in the late 1990s, confirmed that "the military-industrial complex was pressuring our politicians so much that when Defense Minister [Dmitrii] Ustinov would get in the Politburo and ask for a few billions for something, nobody would say anything against it. This . . . is a complex result of 1941, gentlemen, and it worked independently of any politics and independently of relations with the United States or the West."[74]

Dobrynin, in fact, dismisses the entire line of reasoning about arms races and sums up the effect of the military competition this way:

> Sadly for the ardent followers of Reagan, the increased Soviet defense spending provoked by Reagan's policies was not the straw that broke the back of the evil empire. We did not bankrupt ourselves in the arms race, as the Caspar Weinbergers of this world would like to believe. The Soviet response to Star Wars caused only an acceptable small rise in defense spending. Throughout the Reagan presidency, the rising Soviet defense effort contributed to our economic decline, but only marginally as it had in previous years. The troubles in our economy were the result of our own internal contradictions of autarky, low investment, and lack of innovation.[75]

While this may appear to be difficult to reconcile with Soviet accounts that decried the ruinous economic effects of American policy in the early 1980s, Dobrynin may well be correct but misleading here. If the Soviet economy had already reached a dead stop by 1976 (as many Russian economists believe it did) while military expenditures grew, then it stands to reason that there was not much room for dramatic increases in military spending.[76] But the pressure from the United States, as so many other former Soviet officials have since admitted, prevented any serious consideration of reallocation of resources or experimenting with reform. The problem was not that the military budget *grew* but that it became impossible to *shrink* it. The net effect of keeping Soviet military spending high to the detriment of the economy would be the same to the ailing Soviet system.

In any event, in the immediate atmosphere of hostility, it was the political message of SDI that was more frightening to the Soviets than any eventual system it might produce or what it might cost. The Kremlin felt that the Americans had engaged in an unconscionable escalation of the military competition, and at least some in the leadership came to believe that these actions could only mean one thing: that Washington was serious about launching a nuclear war. Even before SDI, in 1981, all KGB foreign stations were placed on alert to watch for signs of a nuclear first strike, an order that reflected a belief on the part of then KGB chief Andropov and Defense Minister Dmitrii Ustinov that Reagan was actively preparing the United States for war.[77] Although the alert was a secret, the thinking behind it was not. A widely cited March 1982 article in the leading journal *Kommunist* directly charged that "the system of propaganda measures undertaken by U.S. imperialism today are nothing other than psychological preparation for nuclear war," a judgment in which KGB analysts concurred.[78] The announcement of SDI, the KGB reported to the leadership, was "part of the psychological preparation of the American people for nuclear war."[79] Public propaganda on this theme became ubiquitous and, at least inside the Soviet Union, somewhat effective.[80]

But the war scare was more than propaganda. In November 1983, NATO held an exercise called "Able Archer," meant to test procedures for the release of nuclear weapons in Europe. (This, as Beth Fischer notes, was only a week after the United States forcibly removed Grenada's communist "thugs" from power, and the Soviets were already somewhat tense.)[81] Warsaw Pact units, to the surprise and alarm of NATO observers, began to go on alert, apparently fearing a possible sneak attack during the maneuvers and preparing for a retaliatory nuclear strike of their own. Soviet rhetoric betrayed Moscow's growing fear; in the midst of the crisis, Politburo member Grigorii Romanov gave a speech to a Kremlin audience, carried on the front pages of the main Soviet dailies, in which he thundered: "Comrades! The international situation is now white-hot, fundamentally white-hot."[82] Although Soviet forces eventually stood down, the whole event was one of the most dangerous of the Cold War and shook even many hardened Soviet cold warriors. Vasili Mitrokhin claims that after the Able Archer alert, veteran Soviet intelligence agents were "more concerned by the alarmism at [KGB headquarters] than by the threat of a Western surprise attack."[83]

The Americans were at first incredulous, with many senior leaders refusing to believe the Soviets could so easily think that Washington had lost its collective mind.[84] Gates admits that U.S. intelligence "had failed to grasp the true extent of [the Soviet leadership's] anxiety."[85] Had Reagan's initial strategy backfired and perhaps even increased the risk of a Soviet-American military conflict? Dobrynin seems to think so.

> The impact of Reagan's hard-line policy on the internal debates in the Kremlin and on the evolution of the Soviet leadership was exactly the opposite of the one intended by Washington. It strengthened those in the Politburo, the Central Committee, and the security apparatus who had been pressing for a mirror-image of Reagan's own policy. Ronald Reagan managed to create a solid front of hostility among our leaders. Nobody trusted him.[86]

It could be argued that this, to some extent, was what the Americans had hoped for: to corner the Soviets, to make them second-guess their every step, and to bait them into trying to match the Americans in an expensive arms race that could lead only to a Soviet economic meltdown. But to judge by the international situation at the end of 1983, Reagan's policies could well have been considered a costly mistake, one that had wasted millions of dollars and resulted only in an increased risk of war and the most unstable relations between Moscow and Washington in over twenty years.

BLOWBACK?

Reagan had certainly scared the Soviets, but in a kind of domestic "blowback" effect, he had managed to frighten a lot of Americans, too. While ordinary people were unaware of the nuclear drama of Able Archer, they were nonetheless anxious and on edge. By early 1984, a variety of polls showed that support for Reagan's overall program of rearmament had fallen to an all-time low, with significant majorities of Americans moving toward a live-and-let-live approach to the USSR, not least because most believed that constantly picking fights with the Soviets had simply become too dangerous.[87] The president's strident approach had overshot the mark: in Moscow, Soviet leaders were convinced that the United States wanted not only the diminution of their system, but its actual physical destruction; while at home, Americans and Europeans were losing almost as much sleep as the beleaguered Soviets.

There was a real sense of alarm in America and Europe in the early 1980s, a feeling that nuclear war was imminent. In 1983, 750,000 people rallied in Central Park for a nuclear freeze; a year earlier in Germany, the biggest rally since World War II brought 250,000 Germans protesting nuclear weapons into the streets of Bonn. Again, as in the days of Sputnik, Western leaders were trying to formulate strategy in the face of deep anxiety—only this time, at least some of the blame for the uproar had to rest with the intemperate tone set by the president himself. Unlike the Soviets, who tended to domestic and foreign public opinion carefully, the Americans had lost a sense of the effect their own pronouncements were having, even on their own coalition.

Nowhere was this more evident than in the popular culture, which by 1983 was awash with fears of nuclear war. Images of Armageddon literally saturated the airwaves, bookstores, and movie theaters, especially in media directed at the young. MTV music television went on the air in 1981, and soon nuclear war was a staple of its offerings, as young Americans were treated to a steady stream of songs with apocalyptic themes and menacing titles.[88] An imported 1983 German hit called "99 Luftballoons," for example, offered the tale of a girl who releases some balloons she bought for a lover and accidentally triggers a nuclear holocaust. Music videos routinely made reference to a coming nuclear war; one called "Sleeping with the Enemy" showed images of American high school marching bands and the Red Army parading through Red Square as equivalent menaces to mankind, with the obligatory mushroom cloud punctuating the point. In a further sign of how politicized entertainment had become, some songs mentioned Reagan by name, and one immortalized the now forgotten Konstantin Chernenko on video: for their 1984 Cold War themed hit "Two Tribes," the British group Frankie Goes to Hollywood actually hired actors resembling Reagan and Chernenko, who spent the video physically pummeling each other in the midst of a throng of cheering people. (At the end of their fight, the world explodes. Video then, as now, was hardly a subtle medium.)

On television and at the movies even the lightest entertainment often carried deadly serious messages. Movie superspy James Bond, after years of battling a variety of grandiose and utterly improbable lunatics (as well as the mythical terrorist organization SPECTRE), returned in 1983 in *Octopussy* with a more unsettling mission clearly taken from the day's headlines. Instead of the science fiction plots of earlier movies, *Octopussy* found 007 trying to stop World War III from being unleashed by a renegade Soviet general—using stolen nuclear weapons to destroy a NATO base in Europe, no less—who thinks the Politburo lacks the guts to wipe out the West, with an unusually tense climactic moment at a circus full of children that was out of character for the Bond series at the time. On a more serious note, this period also saw the release of more thoughtful but depressing and bleak films like the 1983 *Testament*, in which a nuclear war takes place off screen at the very beginning, leaving suburban housewife Jane Alexander to watch as her small community withers, dies, and finally vanishes. On television, even low-quality, made-for-TV offerings carried grim warnings. In the 1982 two-part movie *World War III*, the grain-starved Soviets invade Alaska;

Rock Hudson's American president tries and fails to negotiate peace. The credits roll before the bombs hit, but there is no doubt about the outcome.

Nothing, however, matched the fanfare that surrounded ABC Television's presentation of *The Day After* in autumn 1983. Coming as it did at a time when the Soviet-American relationship had hit rock bottom—it aired on November 20, less than three months after the outrage over the Korean airliner disaster—Americans were transfixed by the first feature-length film to depict the effects of nuclear war in detail.

As a film, *The Day After* is unremarkable. The script is flimsy, and the characters are wooden, noble caricatures of stout Midwesterners (the film focuses on the destruction of Kansas). There is no plot to speak of, no real explanation of the crisis before the war begins, nor any sense of what started it. Still, the movie carries an impact; ABC warned its audience about its graphic nature, as the more intense scenes of destruction are unsettling. (The 1985 British film *Threads* was far more disturbing, but for its time, *The Day After* was about as grisly as American television was allowed to get.) At times, the movie achieves chilling images, such as the memorable shot of people standing in their yards watching the smoke trails of U.S. nuclear missiles that have left their silos—a moment pregnant with the realization that the Soviet attack (or retaliation, the movie will not say who fired first) will arrive in moments. Whatever its failings as a film, *The Day After* soon became a political event in itself and was eventually shown in over 40 countries.

The American public was noticeably shaken by *The Day After*: it was one thing to talk tough to Moscow, another entirely to see Americans incinerated in a flash and Kansas City reduced to smoking rubble. Antinuclear activists, predictably, wasted no time in capitalizing on this anxiety. The then ubiquitous (if now largely forgotten) Helen Caldicott, for example, used the movie's showing to opine on a New York talk radio station that it was time to take heed of the danger that Reagan's re-election the following year would make nuclear war with the Soviet Union "a mathematical certainty."[89]

The fear of war hit home with one American in particular who watched *The Day After* and agreed that things had escalated out of control: Ronald Reagan. Beth Fischer has convincingly argued that a series of events, including the "near miss" of Able Archer, the Korean airline disaster, and *The Day After* (which Reagan saw privately on October 10, less than one month before Able Archer), convinced the president that he had let things go too far and that the world was edging toward an unintended nuclear showdown.

To Reagan's shock and disbelief, the Soviets believed that he would initiate a nuclear war against the USSR. This misperception, Reagan realized, had brought the world to the edge of a nuclear conflict. Consequently, in order to guard against an accidental nuclear exchange in the future, Reagan needed to correct Soviet misperceptions about American intentions. It became imperative to engage in a dialogue with the Soviets. At the same time it was essential to reduce the number of nuclear arms in the world.... In late 1983 Ronald Reagan took the reins and began to redirect U.S. Soviet policy. A tragedy had narrowly been avoided, he believed, and changes needed to be instituted quickly.[90]

Although historians have tended to trace the thaw in Soviet-American relations to the arrival of Mikhail Gorbachev, it appears that the Americans and President Reagan in particular were reassessing U.S. strategy as early as 1983 and looking for ways to soften the effects of the administration's hard-edged policies. In a sense, the Reaganites were victims of their own success: the effort to hem the Soviets in, to isolate and to weaken them, had worked so well that there was now a danger of provoking a final and violent death rattle from a system that was in far more trouble than even its most severe detractors realized.

Even if Reagan himself were not convinced of the danger of an accidental war, the growing difficulty of keeping the American public committed to the showdown with the Soviets was itself a good reason to improve the tone of American rhetoric. Maintaining long-term public support for confrontational policies is a challenge, not only because it requires a democratic society to endure long periods of tension with no evident signs of success, but also because it is difficult to gauge just how much propaganda and confrontation can be directed at an enemy before threats designed to contain an opponent accidentally end up terrifying the domestic population as well. Reagan had created a dilemma for himself in 1983, one that left him trying to hold together a democratic coalition that was frightened—as he now was—by images of war that had been intended only to warn the enemy of Western resolve, not of Western malice.

Reagan tried in 1984 to reach out to the Soviet leadership, but the Kremlin was for the time being locked in geriatric stasis. Chernenko, a complete nonentity and already dying, had been the compromise choice to warm the General Secretary's seat while the heir apparent, Gorbachev, negotiated and networked among the more senior men who would have to approve his accession. This was just as well: Reagan's initial efforts to soften his tone were sentimental and misdirected, and it is probably for the best that the Soviets were likely not paying attention to them. In his characteristic way, the president assumed that representing the Soviet-American dialogue as a kind of discussion among ordinary people would make clear to the Soviets that he meant them no harm. It was Reagan himself who inserted the story of two hypothetical Soviet and American couples—Jim and Sally, Ivan and Anya—and the common interests they might share over the kitchen table into his 1984 State of the Union address. For once, the Great Communicator bombed onstage; the story was so sappy it even prompted one of Reagan's own National Security Council staffers to exclaim, "Who wrote this shit?"[91]

In early 1985, Chernenko died and was buried with unseemly but understandable haste. For many observers of the Cold War, Chernenko's passing and Gorbachev's arrival marked the beginning of a hopeful time, not least because so many Western academics, like so many Soviets, were filled with hope that Gorbachev could rescue socialism from its Soviet shame. Others in the West hoped that Gorbachev would tame the Soviet war machine and force the USSR to look inward, rather than outward. Ordinary Americans and Europeans, for their part, were relieved to encounter a Soviet leader who seemed, on camera, more human and animated than his glowering predecessors and was able to communicate in something other than the Marxist-Leninist duckspeak of official Soviet rhetoric. In both superpowers, there was a sense that the clouds of war might be dispersing. As will be seen, the partnership between Reagan, Gorbachev, and Thatcher and later, the efforts of other leaders such as Helmut Kohl and George H. W. Bush would bring the Cold War and the Soviet Union itself to a quieter end than anyone dared dream possible.

Nonetheless, by 1985 there was still work to be done. The object now would not be to continue to press the Soviets against the wall, but to take Gorbachev at his word and test his commitment to peace.

THE VALUE—AND RISKS—OF CONFRONTATION

What can be learned from the experiences of the early 1980s? President Reagan's admirers point to the obvious revitalization of the Western coalition that took place during his watch, and the consequent clutch of insecurity and fear that enveloped the Kremlin, as evidence that his instincts were correct, as proof that the only way to cage and eventually to defeat the Soviet Union was by force. The president's critics would contend that the whole period was one of incredible luck and that the eventual breakthrough in Soviet-American relations was due not to Reagan's hard line—which nearly sparked a war—but rather to his change of heart after 1983. Others would argue that Reagan was more or less irrelevant and that real change in the Soviet Union was inevitable once Mikhail Gorbachev and other new, more flexible leaders supplanted the older generation of mediocrities who had risen to power after World War II and admitted that the Soviet experiment was in deep trouble, if not an outright failure.

All of these interpretations have something to recommend them, particularly the issue of generational change. There was in fact a new spirit afoot among the younger leaders in the Soviet Union. These men, most of whom were in their fifties during the late 1980s, had seen the promises of earlier generations amount to little in the lives of ordinary Soviet citizens and were unable to deny the achievements of the West; unlike their fathers, they had not experienced the Revolution, Stalinism, or World War II (at least not as grown men) and therefore did not have the same visceral and unyielding attachment to previous dogmas that many of their elders shared.

But generational change was no guarantee of peace: there were men of Gorbachev's generation (as will be seen in the next chapter) who were far more bellicose than Brezhnev or Andropov would ever have dared. Some of the younger leaders of the Soviet Union wanted détente and cooperation with the West; others, however, wanted confrontation, expansion, and even a kind of revenge for the USSR's ongoing impoverishment. To say that Gorbachev was a member of a new generation is true but uninformative, for it says nothing about why he was chosen as that generation's representative in the halls of power, as opposed to some of his far more dangerous contemporaries.

But even before Gorbachev came to power, the Americans were changing course, and this raises a blunt question: Did Reagan go too far? The war scare of 1983 suggests that he did. Whatever satisfaction there may have been in the immediate situation of obvious Soviet anxiety, even Reagan and his closest advisors would never have argued that the point of their policies was to make the Soviet Union think that an American nuclear strike could occur out of the blue at any moment. (This is not to say that the Americans wanted to encourage complacency in the Soviet defense establishment; U.S. Air Force jets were routinely ordered to trespass Soviet air space to keep Soviet radar operators jumpy.)[92] Moreover, Reagan's rhetorical attacks on the USSR produced undesirable consequences at home, as the worsened international situation undermined U.S. public support for programs he valued and made it that much more difficult for him to maintain the mandate he had been given by the voters in 1981.

But does this then lead to a dismissal of the value of the confrontational strategy of 1981–1983? The answer is no, with some important caveats.

First, whatever the public's fears about Reagan, the fact of the matter is that within one year of that dark autumn in 1983, the president would win re-election with the second largest electoral landslide in history. Voters who might have wanted a return to the pre-1978 Carter era had the chance to do so by voting for Carter's avowedly liberal vice president, Walter Mondale. American elections, of course, are rarely decided

on foreign policy, and 1984 was no exception: Mondale's bizarre promise to raise taxes during the economic recovery of 1984 had more to do
with his defeat than his stance on the Soviet threat. It is important to
bear in mind that the economy, more than Reagan's rhetoric, may also
have been behind the deflation of support for more military spending
in 1983, when the United States was in the depths of a recession and
unemployment was heading toward the ten percent mark. In any case,
if the voters were concerned about the state of relations between Moscow and Washington, their worries did not displace their concern over
jobs, and ultimately they were not inclined to remove Reagan from
office over the newly intensified Cold War.

Perhaps even more revealing is that they were not even moved to
press their representatives to make a less stark, but nonetheless important, gesture of protest: the nuclear freeze. The measure died in the
Senate in October 1983, never to return, while funding for SDI research
and for the creation of the Strategic Defense Initiative Organization in
early 1984 continued apace, despite Soviet warnings and domestic
protests. Although there can be no question that Americans were, by
1984, deeply apprehensive about the course of the Soviet-American
conflict, it is less clear that Reagan's stance crippled public support for
his strategy.

Still, the confrontational approach was flawed, primarily by the fact
that it took such little notice of the effect it was having on the opponent.
The Americans engaged in a static modeling of the enemy's strategy:
they assumed that increased pressure on the Kremlin would lead to a
mechanical Soviet attempt to pursue previous strategies at greater cost.
This was not all that unreasonable an assumption, but it did not look
ahead to ask whether or how the Soviets might reassess the nature of
the conflict in the circumstances of renewed hostilities. How would
they regard the effort to spend them into oblivion, and how would they
react once their ability to respond was so compromised that they were
faced with surrender in the arms race? No empire until this point in
history had ever seen fit to go gently into the night, and it was a
tremendous risk for the Americans to assume that the Soviets would
not, once they saw the the game was lost, lash out in desperation.

The genuine shock with which the Able Archer incident was greeted,
for example, arose from an optimistic American belief that no rational
Soviet leader could really believe that the United States of America
would ever launch a nuclear first strike, despite repeated Soviet warnings that many in Moscow in fact did believe just that. This represented
a failure of intelligence, as Gates and others later admitted. The Reagan
administration assumed that the Soviets were possessed of a far greater
self-confidence than they actually were and missed important signs,
such as the level of anxiety revealed even in open Soviet sources, that

might have flagged rising Soviet paranoia. (To be fair, it was the Kremlin's intent to mask its growing fears, but it is precisely the task of national leadership, supported by the intelligence community, to see past such ruses.)

The Reagan administration did attempt to add some concessions, such as canceling the grain embargo, among its attacks, but these were not enough to overcome the conflicting and mostly hostile signals being sent from Washington. Moscow understandably chose to focus on the sticks rather than the carrots. The sluggishness of the Soviet response—which contributed to the sense in Moscow that the Americans were plowing ahead with their plans heedless of anything the Soviets could say or do—was complicated by a situational problem that the Americans could not control but that they needed to take into account, namely the terrible physical condition of the Politburo. During Reagan's first term, the Kremlin saw three changes of leadership, as Brezhnev, Andropov, and Chernenko all died within three years of each other. Soviet successions were messy affairs, as full of uncertainty and tension for the participants in Moscow as they were for observers abroad. Thus, not only were the Americans pressuring a country at the end of its economic rope, but they were doing so during a period of ongoing instability and insecurity.

With all of this said, however, it is fair to ask what other options the Americans had available to them by 1980. Years of *realpolitik* maneuvering produced an era of "détente" that had served Soviet interests while doing little to alter the nature of the Soviet regime or the aggressiveness of its policies. Nothing, it seemed, was enough to restrain Soviet ambitions. In this light, a dual program of ideological challenge and military revitalization were obvious choices to all but the most dedicated proponents of arms control or even of outright appeasement.

It is reasonable to wonder, however, whether a tougher American military stance needed to be coupled with such inflammatory rhetoric. One answer is to point out that only such rhetoric could give meaning to changes in military expenditures and foreign policy priorities. A program of rearmament could not have been undertaken in a vacuum; if the strategy was to cow the Soviets and regain the high ground for American values while baiting the Soviets into defending their own, it is difficult to see how a more moderate stance would have done much beyond muddling Washington's intended message.

In any event, although many of Reagan's critics found the president's harsh tone shocking, it was no worse than similar language that was directed against the United States and it allies even during the most friendly periods in Soviet-American relations, and it is difficult to argue that the Soviets were not due for a taste of their own medicine. Every nation, including the United States, occasionally needs to remember the important truism that words have consequences, but no regime needs such a lesson more than an ideological state, whose entire existence is, in a sense, premised on words. Reagan's initial attack on the Soviet Union was a bracing reminder to Moscow that Soviet claims of support for the eventual destruction of the capitalist system might be taken seriously and that at some point making those claims may mean having to defend them. In effect, the Americans were forcing a choice on the Soviets: either they would embrace their own ideological rhetoric, with all that such a public reaffirmation of Marxism-Leninism would entail, or they would have to step back from the very beliefs on which their own state was predicated. It was an unenviable dilemma and one that would fall to Gorbachev at a time when there would be few Soviet options to resolve it.

The American military buildup has to be viewed in light of this renewed ideological struggle: if the rhetoric was intended to give meaning to military policies, those policies in turn were needed to give weight to the rhetoric. Had the Americans, in the absence of a visible attempt to gain military superiority, merely lambasted the Soviets for being inhumane, the effect probably would have been much the result Jimmy Carter experienced when he engaged in exactly that tactic. Carter's complaints were seen as annoying, on occasion even infuriating, but they were not taken seriously in Moscow. The Americans could fulminate at length about Soviet policies, but because there was no sense of threat to Soviet interests, there was no motivation for Moscow to do much about such complaints beyond trying to repair the public relations damage. The Reagan administration, building on measures taken at the end of the Carter years, added that sense of threat and made clear that the Americans might inflict a price for Soviet actions (including, perhaps, the outright overthrow of Soviet client states) that would be a bit more painful than the occasional tongue-lashing from the U.S. State Department.

Among the lessons to be drawn from the experience of the Carter and Reagan years is that confrontational strategies are most effective when an ideological enemy is pressed to live with the consequences of its actions. Whether it is Moscow's claim that capitalism must inevitably fall to revolution or Osama bin Laden's proclamations of holy war against American infidels, such stark ideological pronouncements should never be allowed to stand unchallenged. Silence, in the international community, is assent, particularly in the eyes of smaller or more uncertain coalition partners; it was not until Reagan took the many strands of criticism of the USSR (including some pioneered by Carter) and wove them into a coherent ideological case against communism that the West again found its voice and the Soviet ideologists began to falter in the face of a sustained counterattack.

Although explicit ideological confrontation is central to such a strategy, rhetoric needs to be bolstered by visible measures. As Carter learned and Reagan verified, changing the tone of debate is not enough; entities like the Soviet Union, who already have a firm belief that Western polities are decadent and weak, will watch actions even more closely than pronouncements. More to the point, merely railing about Soviet crimes while avoiding taking the military measures that could press the exposed nerve of Soviet economic vulnerability might have been a way to conduct the Cold War on the cheap, but it was not effective. Nixon presided over a large military establishment (and even a foreign war), but he was loath to draw the Soviets into an ideological competition. Carter, by contrast, was relentless in his criticism of the USSR, but his concurrent fixation with arms control betrayed to the Soviets a lack of seriousness. Reagan wedded a dramatic increase in military capabilities to a clear exposition of purpose, and it was only at that point that the Soviets became genuinely apprehensive about the new turn in the Cold War.

However, another lesson to draw from the early 1980s is that while it is undeniably important to know when a confrontational strategy (or any other, for that matter) is failing, it is just as important, if not more, to know when it is *succeeding*. The major shortcoming with the strategy of "overdoing it" was not, as its critics claim, that it hardened Soviet attitudes and prolonged the Cold War, but rather that it worked too well in creating a sense of genuine fear in Moscow. The goal was to destroy Soviet self-confidence by challenging their every move in the eyes of the world, to destroy, more tangibly, the USSR's economy by luring the Kremlin into an unwinnable arms race, and to undermine a framework of mutual deterrence that had allowed Soviet mischief to go unchecked as a result of the nuclear standoff. The Soviets leaped to the reasonable conclusion that the Americans were seeking the complete annihilation of the socialist bloc, by means of nuclear war if necessary. This was a step too far, and it is the world's good fortune that President Reagan was, at the ultimate moment, suddenly aware of the unintended impact of his own policies (and that the Kremlin was in any case too plagued with illness and age to respond more aggressively). It is easy to launch a strategy of confrontation, but it is another to be able to control its effects once it is underway.

Finally, it is important to bear in mind that a strategy of confrontation depends heavily on timing. Confrontation is expensive, and not just in expenditures on arms. It requires a healthy economy, a stable polity at home, and a willingness to transfer resources to allies and clients who are being asked to join in the fight. But it also requires an opponent that has been properly softened up for the attack; Henry Kissinger—certainly no admirer of the ideological hard line—is right when he suggests,

> Reagan had transformed what had been a marathon race into a sprint. His confrontational style linked to a risk-taking diplomacy would probably have worked at the beginning of the Cold War, before the two spheres of interest had been consolidated, and immediately after the death of Stalin. . . . Once the division of Europe was frozen and so long as the Soviet Union still felt confident, the attempt to force a settlement would have almost certainly produced a major clash and strained the Atlantic Alliance, the majority of whose members wanted no unnecessary tension. In the 1980s, Soviet stagnation made a forward strategy appropriate again.[93]

It is of no use to invite an opponent into such a conflict if the enemy is capable of bearing its costs. The Soviet Union of the early 1970s could have better afforded to match a strategy of confrontation; worse, it might have been able to use the proximity of the Vietnam conflict to convince the international community of the irredeemably aggressive nature of the United States. Whether more could have been done in the 1970s to weaken the USSR is debatable—certainly, that has been a contention of this study—but engaging in a Reaganite frontal attack against communism was not among American options until the Soviets themselves took the inadvertent steps that in turn ensured that such a strategy would have maximum impact.

In the late 1980s, the Americans made an abrupt turn back toward cooperation with the Soviet adversary, scaling back talk of "evil empires" and instead inviting the Soviet Union to prove itself anew in the international system. This was an invitation to drink a cup of hemlock: the Soviet Union could not logically be part of the system it was sworn to overthrow, and any attempt to accept a challenge that required reconciling the Soviet revolutionary identity with a new commitment to the international status quo was doomed to end in ideological self-destruction. But with all other options in ruins (save the horrible alternative of war), it was a challenge Mikhail Gorbachev was forced to accept. By the time the implications of his choice were clear, it would be too late to reverse course.

NOTES

1. "The Russians, Bialer reported from Moscow...were about to teach Reagan a lesson." See Walter Laqueur, *The Dream That Failed* (New York: Oxford University Press, 1994), p. 126.

2. Seweryn Bialer and Joan Afferica, "Reagan and Russia," *Foreign Affairs*, Winter 1982/83, p. 263.

3. Robert Conquest, *Reflections on a Ravaged Century* (New York: Norton, 2000), p. 173.

4. George Kennan, "The GOP Won the Cold War? Ridiculous," *The New York Times*, October 28, 1992, p. A21.

5. Raymond Garthoff, *The Great Transition* (Washington: The Brookings Institution, 1994), p. 753.

6. See Richard Ned Lebow and Janice Gross Stein, "Reagan and the Russians," *The Atlantic Monthly*, February 1994.

7. Peter Schweitzer, *Victory: The Reagan Administration's Secret Strategy That Hastened the Collapse of the Soviet Union* (Boston: Atlantic Monthly Press, 1994), p. 101.

8. See Peter Rodman, "How the West Won (Cont'd)," *National Review*, August 29, 1994, p. 61.

9. Georgii Arbatov, *The System: An Insider's Life in Soviet Politics* (New York: Random House, 1993), p. 313. (This is the English translation of his earlier Russian version and differs slightly in places from the original.)

10. Stephen Sestanovich, "Did the West Undo the East?," *The National Interest* 31, Spring 1993, p. 28.

11. Robert Gates, *From the Shadows* (New York: Touchstone, 1996), p. 195.

12. See John Newhouse, *War and Peace in the Nuclear Age* (New York: Knopf, 1989), p. 333.

13. Dan Caldwell, "The Demise of Détente and US Domestic Politics," in Odd Arne Westad, ed., *The Fall of Détente: Soviet-American Relations during the Carter Years* (Oslo: Scandinavian University Press, 1997), p. 108.

14. Caldwell, p. 102.

15. Lee Lescaze, "Reagan Denounces Soviets But Speaks Gently of Iran," *The Washington Post*, January 30, 1981, p. A4.

16. Russian analysts point to this speech as the first and most immediate disappointment in the new Reagan administration. Interview with Vladimir Batiuk, Moscow, February 4, 2000.

17. Later Soviet leaders made reference to the defense of proletarian internationalism and the furtherance of global revolution, but in more careful terms. Reagan's rhetoric, in any case, evenly matched Brezhnev's charge in 1971 that, "There are no crimes to which the imperialists have not resorted in trying to maintain or renew their rule over the peoples of the former colonies or other states trying to escape the grip of capitalist exploitation." *Materialy XXIV s"ezda KPSS* (Moscow: Politizdat, 1971), p. 16.

18. Batiuk, interview.

19. Gates, p. 195.

20. Batiuk, interview.

21. "Povyshat' kachestvo i effektivnost' ideologicheskoi raboty," *Pravda*, April 21, 1981, p. 2.

22. Roman Solchanyk, "Ukrainian KGB Chief Warns of Ideological Sabotage," *Radio Liberty Research* RL 422/81, October 22, 1981, p. 3.

23. See Michael Nelson, *War of the Black Heavens* (Syracuse, NY: Syracuse University Press, 1997), p.159, and Alvin Snyder, *Warriors of Disinformation* (New York: Arcade, 1995), p.153. In 1982, Reagan signed NSDD 32, which established a range of measures to aid Poland, including increased propaganda via Radio Free Europe and the smuggling of shortwave radios (and later, VCRs) into Poland and other parts of Eastern Europe via channels established by priests, agents, and representatives of American trade unions.

24. "Burzhuaznoi propagande—aktivnyi otpor," *Krasnaia Zvezda*, July 26, 1983, p. 3.

25. "Nepokolebimoe torzhestvo sotsialisticheskoi ideologii," *Pravda*, October 14, 1982, p. 2.

26. "Burzhuaznoi propagande—aktivnyi otpor," p. 3.

27. Christopher Andrew and Vasili Mitrokhin, *The Sword and the Shield: The Mitrokhin Archive* (New York: Basic Books, 1999), p. 548.

28. Andrew and Mitrokhin, p. 513.

29. B. Nosovich, "Religiia i politika," *Sovetskaia Estoniia*, August 8, 1982, p. 2.

30. Elizabeth Teague, "Anniversary of Stalin Law Prohibiting Marriages with Foreigners," *Radio Liberty Research* RL 73/82, February 15, 1982, p. 3.

31. Georgii Kapralov, "Korolevskii maneken i prigovor istorii," *Pravda*, July 19, 1982, p. 6.

32. "Russians not amused by TV's comrades," *Daily Telegraph*, Subject File "Ideologicheskaia bor'ba," Soviet ("Red") Archives, Records of Radio Free Europe/Radio Liberty Research Institute, Open Society Archives, Budapest, Hungary.

33. I personally heard Soviet colleagues make this charge repeatedly in the 1980s.

34. The full text of this and other Reagan speeches is available on *The Soviet Union Fights the Cold War: Official Documents of the Reagan Administration*, a CD-ROM issued by the American Foreign Policy Council in 1999.

35. See comments by Sergei Tarasenko in Nina Tannenwald, ed., *Understanding the End of the Cold War, 1980–1987: An Oral History Conference* (Providence, RI: Watson Institute for International Studies, 1999), p. 252; and Anatolii Dobrynin, *In Confidence* (Seattle: University of Washington Press, 1995) p. 527.

36. Tannenwald, ed., p. 264.

37. Tannenwald, ed., p. 251.

38. Rodman, p. 61.

39. All references to NSDD 75 are from *The Soviet Union Fights the Cold War: Official Documents of the Reagan Administration*.

40. Valentin Falin, *Bez skidok na obstoiatel'stva* (Moscow: Respublika-Sovremmennik, 1999), p. 365

41. This campaign reached astonishing proportions in the military press. See Thomas Nichols, *The Sacred Cause: Civil-Military Conflict over Soviet National Security, 1917–1992* (Ithaca, NY: Cornell University Press, 1993), pp. 115–118.

42. Vojtech Mastny, "Did NATO Win the Cold War," *Foreign Affairs*, May/June 1999, p. 186.

43. V. Bol'shakov, "Vashingtonskie 'krestonovtsy' na marshe," *Pravda*, January 31, 1983, p. 6.

44. Dobrynin, p. 495.

45. Dobrynin, p. 503.

46. Quoted in Brian Crozier, *The Rise and Fall of the Soviet Empire* (Rocklin, CA: Forum, 1999), p. 708.

47. Iu. Nalin, "'Krestonovtsy' antisovetizma," *Agitator*, April 1983, p. 46.

48. This and all references to this speech are from "Speech of General Secretary Comrade Yu. V. Andropov of the Central Committee of the Communist Party of the Soviet Union," available at the National Security Archive online, http://www.gwu.edu/~nsarchiv/NSAEBB/NSAEBB14/doc19.htm.

49. Gorbachev, *Memoirs* (New York: Doubleday, 1995), p. 444.

50. Andrew and Mitrokhin, p. 243.

51. Interview with Vladimir Batiuk, Moscow, October 3, 2001.

52. Georgii Arbatov, *Zatianuvsheesia vyzdorovlenie* (Moscow: Mezhdunarodnye Otnosheniia, 1991), p. 323; interview with Ilya Gaiduk, Moscow, February 3, 2000.

53. Mark Lagon, *The Reagan Doctrine* (Westport, CT: Praeger Publishers, 1994), pp. 2–3.

54. Gates, p. 197.

55. Crozier, p. 249.

56. Vadim Zagladin, "Uroki Grenady," *Sovetskaia Rossiia*, November 17, 1983, p. 1.

57. Many Reagan officials deny there was anything well-thought out behind the Reagan Doctrine (a term coined by itself coined by journalist Charles Krauthammer). See Joseph Shattan, *Architects of Victory: Six Heroes of the Cold War* (Washington, D.C.: The Heritage Foundation, 1999), p. 256, and Lagon, p. 2.

58. Batiuk, interview.

59. Vadim Nekrasov, "Leninskim kursom razriadki," *Komsomol'skaia Pravda*, February 2, 1982, p. 3.

60. Quoted in Shattan, p. 248.

61. *The Soviet Union Fights the Cold War.*

62. Newhouse, p. 297.

63. *The Soviet Union Fights the Cold War.*

64. Henry Kissinger, *Diplomacy* (New York: Simon and Schuster, 1994), p. 778.

65. Interview with Vladimir Matiash, Moscow, February 3, 2000.

66. Tannenwald, ed., p. 51.

67. Quoted in Sestanovich, p. 29.

68. Interview with Viktor Laptev, Moscow, February 4, 2000.

69. Tannenwald, ed., pp. 40–41.

70. Interview with Aleksandr Orlov, Moscow, February 4, 2000.

71. Tannenwald, ed., p. 41.

72. Laptev, interview.

73. Dobrynin, pp. 524–525.

74. Tannenwald, ed., pp. 21–22.

75. Dobrynin, p. 611.

76. See Nichols, p. 103.

77. Dobrynin, p. 523; see also Nichols, pp. 113–114.

78. L. Tolkunov, "'Psikhologicheskaia voina'—priznak iadernoi patologii," *Kommunist* 4, March 1982, p. 104.

79. Andrew and Mitrokhin, p. 214.

80. During my stay in Leningrad in the summer of 1983, I was continually asked by Soviet citizens why President Reagan was trying to start a nuclear war and whether Americans were really crazy enough to support such an evil intention.

81. Beth Fischer, *The Reagan Reversal* (Columbia: University of Missouri Press, 1997), p. 125.

82. G.V. Romanov, "Velikaia zhiznennaia sila idei i dela oktiabriia," in *XXVI s"ezda KPSS: edinstvo teorii i praktiki*, vol. 4 (Moscow: Politizdat, 1984), p. 425.

83. Andrew and Mitrokhin, p. 214.

84. Details can be found in Fischer's excellent account, pp. 131–135.

85. Gates, p. 273.

86. Dobrynin, p. 482.

87. This and other data from the mid-1980s is taken from the summary of polls presented in Thomas Ferguson and Joel Rogers, "The Myth of America's Turn to the Right," *The Atlantic*, May 1986. Ferguson and Rogers believe that the data show a turn away from Reaganism in general; while that conclusion is debatable, the level of anxiety about foreign affairs indicated by virtually every poll taken in the period is undeniable.

88. Professor Paul Brians of Washington State University has estimated that MTV was showing images related to nuclear war nearly once per hour in the mid-1980s. His website is an excellent source of nuclear pop culture information, at http://www.wsu.edu/~brians/nukepop/na.html.

89. I was living in New York and heard this personally. But this was hardly the silliest or most alarmist of Caldicott's various pronouncements—she wrote a best-selling book called *Missile Envy* whose thesis should be evident—and readers interested in the brief but noisy career of this Australian pediatrician-turned-nuclear activist can find more at http://www.wagingpeace.org/hero/helen_caldicott.html.

90. Fischer, p. 137.

91. Quoted in John Lewis Gaddis, "How Relevant was U.S. Strategy in Winning the Cold War?" (Carlisle, PA: U.S. Army War College Strategic Studies Institute, 1992), p. 15.

92. "It really got to them," Schweitzer quotes one U.S. State Department official as saying of these "psychological operations" flights. Schweitzer, p. 8.

93. Kissinger, p. 784.

8

Managing the End

I've just arrived from Berlin. It is like witnessing an enormous fair.
The frontiers are absolutely open. Without the U.S. this day would
not have been possible. Tell your people that.

—Helmut Kohl to George H. W. Bush,
November 10, 1989

The euphoric excitement in the U.S. runs the risk of forcing unforeseen action in the USSR . . . that would be very bad. We will not
exacerbate the problem by having the president of the United States
posturing on the Berlin Wall.

—Bush to Kohl, one week later

MAKING PEACE

If the experiences of the early 1980s make a strong case for the uses of
confrontation during a cold war, the late 1980s provide equally useful
lessons in the careful termination of such a conflict. The renewed war
that began with Jimmy Carter's human rights criticisms in 1978 and
continued with Ronald Reagan's all-fronts offensive through 1983 had
left the Soviet Union beaten but not destroyed, a mortally wounded
superpower that might yet be more dangerous in defeat than at the
height of its powers. The effort to cripple the Soviet ability to conduct
the Cold War struggle had met with unimaginable success, but unless

the Western coalition could accomplish the difficult transition from making war to making peace, it would be a short-lived victory.

The American shift toward a more conciliatory relationship was embraced by Mikhail Gorbachev, but the new Soviet leadership soon learned that their counterparts in Washington were willing to de-escalate the conflict only gradually. The more cordial tone between Moscow and Washington did not mean that the Americans were conceding anything that had been at issue earlier; Reagan aide Stephen Sestanovich rightly points out that,

> in contrast to the détente of the early 1970s few agreements were reached, there was no mutual acceptance of the status quo, and the idea of resolving disputes by splitting differences never took hold. In fact, Western demands tended, if anything, to escalate, and the criteria for believing perestroika to be "serious" grew stricter.[1]

Soviet leaders complained, then and now, that each concession from Moscow led to greater demands from the West. Anatolii Cherniaev described Gorbachev and his circle as "not just surprised but upset" that the Reagan administration seemed unwilling to match Soviet moves: "We were constantly being provoked [after 1985], constantly being tested. We felt there were no elements of trust in place."[2]

Still, the Americans in this period refrained from directly challenging Gorbachev as they had his predecessors. Western leaders now came as something like friends, to offer advice and even a certain limited sympathy. Sestanovich elaborates:

> Reagan, Thatcher, Bush, and the other Western leaders who dealt with Gorbachev had only limited leverage over him. What they did, in effect, was hand him a gun and suggest that he do the honorable thing. As is often true of such situations, the victim-to-be is more likely to accept the advice if it is offered in the gentlest possible way and if he concludes that his friends, family, and colleagues will in the end think better of him for going through with it. For Soviet communism, the international environment of the late 1980s was a relaxed setting in which, after much anguished reflection, to turn the gun on itself.[3]

The point was to make Gorbachev realize the hopelessness of the situation he had been left by the men who had tried, in the previous half decade, to wage the Cold War on American terms and to accept as inevitable the eventual abandonment of the Soviet struggle against the West. In return for Soviet acquiescence in quitting the global revolutionary struggle and accepting a place for Moscow as a regional or hemispheric power, America and its allies would welcome the Soviet Union into the ranks of civilized nations and forego the relentless military and ideological assault of the early 1980s.

Eventually, the United States would in effect become the sponsor for the USSR's continued position as a great power. As Foreign Ministry official Sergei Tarasenko later admitted, at the 1989 Malta summit between Gorbachev and President George H. W. Bush, "We felt that the Soviet Union was in free fall, that our superpower status would go up in smoke unless it was reaffirmed by the Americans."[4] In the end, there was no way to maintain that status, but there was also no reason to make things worse. After 1988, the U.S. approach would be to allow the Soviet position to erode, rather than to try and destroy it outright. By the time Reagan left office, the Soviet Union was well along the path to complete collapse, but there were dangerous waters yet to be navigated. The Cold War would end, for all practical purposes, during the Malta summit, but it would fall to Bush to ensure that nothing—not even dramatic moments like the reunification of Germany or the tense 72-hour coup against Gorbachev—would reopen it.

GORBACHEV: A SIGN OF THE END

It has become a habit among some Western observers to attribute the end of the Cold War to Mikhail Gorbachev, with many writers eager to place those laurels upon Gorbachev if only to forestall them being given to Reagan instead. But the experience of the Carter and Reagan years should make plain that by the time Gorbachev arrived, the most important moves in this final phase of the conflict had already taken place. As Tarasenko later put it,

> it is very hard to find another period in history when there were so many negative things coming together [for us] . . . we lost Egypt, we had the Korean airliner incident, we lost—if I may say—the "game" with the United States over deployment of the Pershing and medium range missiles in Europe. There was also the problem of human rights . . . and the issue of [emigration] from the Soviet Union. As a result, there were always demonstrations wherever we'd go abroad. So the image of the country at that point, when Gorbachev came to power, was actually the worst it has ever been in the eyes of international society. And we all felt that our image was very poor in the eyes of international society. I think that one of the first concerns of the Gorbachev administration was to repair this image so the Soviet Union wouldn't be viewed as "the evil empire."[5]

From a commanding position astride the world in 1975, the Soviet Union ten years later was on the brink of bankruptcy, reviled as widely as it was once admired, embroiled in an endless Third World military adventure, and barely able to hold together what was left of its own restless "coalition," most obviously in Poland. Gorbachev may have sincerely wanted to reform the Soviet economy and put the USSR back on its feet, but the events of the previous decade ensured that his agenda would of necessity be a reactive one, aimed at shoring up the damage and leaks in the Soviet ship of state rather that charting a new course for it.

Still, Gorbachev at first came to power with a great optimism about reform, certainly greater than the situation warranted, and this was central to his later missteps. The Soviet Union in 1985 was an exhausted power; telling Soviet citizens to drink less and work harder, while telling the United States in an almost patronizing way that Moscow was willing to reopen discussions, was hardly going to stop Soviet economic and political implosion. Despite the Western adulation of the last Soviet president, many former Soviet officials of various persuasions depict Gorbachev as a leader who never really understood the processes he unleashed domestically or politically, a man quickly overtaken by events rather than controlling them.

This is an opinion shared by friend and foe alike, at least in Russia: Gorbachev's former press secretary Andrei Grachev has referred to him as "President Lear," uncomprehending of the maelstrom swirling about him, while former prime minister (and 1991 coup plotter) Valerii Boldin has charged that Gorbachev, in denial about the state of his nation and his role in creating it, curtailed his travels in the USSR rather than face the reality that the Soviet Union was disintegrating in front of him.[6] *Perestroika*, to this day a term more admired in the West than in Russia, became a kind of shorthand among Soviets for the rudderlessness of their last leader.[7] Despite ongoing attempts since the Soviet collapse by Gorbachev and his admirers to impose some sort of coherence on his career as the last Soviet leader, it is difficult to escape the conclusion that in both the domestic and foreign arenas Gorbachev ended up more as an observer than a motivator of the changes that destroyed the USSR.

But Gorbachev is hardly irrelevant to the end of the Cold War, not least because of how the Soviet Union's final years might have played out under a different leader. It is here, in the ascension of Gorbachev, that American policy may have scored one of its most important victories by making any other choice of a Soviet leader almost impossible. Gorbachev's rise to power was a response to the horrid economic condition of the Soviet Union, a state of affairs for which the United States could take a reasonable amount of credit, and his appearance itself was a sign of the accelerated Soviet decay brought on by the intensification of the Cold War, rather than a successful response to that increasing decrepitude.

While we still do not know all of the inner machinations that brought Gorbachev to power, it is important to consider a major step that the Soviets did *not* take: rejecting the candidacy of the reformer Gorbachev for General Secretary and choosing someone else, such as the representative of the military-industrial complex, Grigorii Romanov. (Moscow party chief Viktor Grishin was also supposedly an option, but he was already elderly and promised to be no better than the now discredited Brezhnev.) Gorbachev's later gulling of Western academics about how Reagan prolonged the Cold War conveniently sidesteps the fact that his own election as leader of the Communist Party was itself an act by the Politburo that indicated an unwillingness to continue a pitched struggle with the Americans. Romanov, brought into the Soviet leadership personally by Andropov, was intensely anti-American—he was the leader who had warned, during Able Archer, of the "white hot" international situation—and a clear advocate of meeting Reagan's challenges head-on come what may. If the Politburo was as angry as it seemed and was looking for someone to champion a strong response to the Americans (and thus to fulfill Seweryn Bialer's dire 1984 prediction that the Soviets were girding for more battle with the White House), they needed to look no further than Romanov.

Romanov's candidacy, like any other, found no takers in the Politburo. This was partly because Romanov himself was deeply disliked ("odious," according to Arbatov, and "narrow-minded and insidious, with dictatorial ways," according to Gorbachev) but also because any return to aggressive policies would have solved nothing, even if there had been any money left to fund them.[8] Moreover, the Soviets had been badly burned in the renewed propaganda war; Reagan's challenges, bolstered by the efforts of Margaret Thatcher, Pope John Paul II, and even less likely allies such as French president Francois Mitterrand, had met with a great deal of public support in both America and Europe. Some in Moscow, as we saw in the previous chapters, had already begun to consider the possibility that their own actions had played a role in creating the uncomfortable situation in which they found themselves by 1985, and with the Soviet military and diplomatic position in tatters not only in Europe but even among some of Moscow's traditional friends elsewhere, the last thing the Soviets needed was a fire-breather like Romanov as General Secretary.

Of course, Gorbachev's successful candidacy also rested on the fact that he told his colleagues what they wanted to hear by promising he could find a way out of the looming economic disaster that was now obvious to the entire leadership. Moreover, it was understood that solving the economic crisis—Soviet leaders in the 1980s still refused to understand that the problem was structural and clung to the hope that it could be somehow fixed—meant dealing with military spending.

Even Gorbachev's eventual opponent in the leadership, conservative Politburo member Egor Ligachev, is reported to have said: "How long will our military-industrial complex keep devouring our economy, our agriculture, and our consumer goods? How long are we going to take this ogre, how long are we going to throw into its mouth the food of our children?"[9] The other possible contenders for power were too old (like Grishin and Gromyko) or too despised (like Romanov), and in the end there was no real alternative to Gorbachev: the competition with the United States had blighted Soviet diplomacy, placed the Soviet military in a position of increasing technological inferiority, undermined Soviet self-confidence, and drained the Soviet treasury. Although the old men of the Politburo were able to stave off Gorbachev's accession for a last hurrah of Brezhnevism under the ailing Chernenko in 1984, by 1985 only the most obtuse Soviet leader could argue that the Kremlin should indulge itself in business as usual.

The heavy-handed diplomacy and threatening military policies of Brezhnev and Andropov had helped to create Reaganism; now, the burden of the dealing with the American challenge was straining the Soviet system to the point where the Kremlin would have to turn to Gorbachev out of desperation if nothing else. This is not to say that American policy was directly responsible for Gorbachev's election as General Secretary, but rather only to point out that American moves had helped to make other options less plausible. The strategy of pitting U.S. economic, ideological, and military strengths against Soviet expansion had not solely caused Soviet bankruptcy or been at the root of discontent in the Soviet empire, but it did lure the Soviets away from measures that might have staved off, at least for a time, the eventual reckoning. Far from producing a more determined Soviet foreign policy, the strength of the Western response led Moscow to realize that the only hope of Soviet economic and imperial survival lay in finding a way out of the ongoing confrontation with the United States.

DISENGAGING

To end the Cold War struggle with the Western coalition, Gorbachev would have to disengage from combat, both rhetorical and actual. Critical to this attempt to undo the damage of previous Soviet policies would be to deprive the Americans and their allies of an enemy by opening the Soviet Union to the world and showing it had nothing to fear from the kind of contacts begun during détente. The propaganda war had outlived its usefulness: once an area of Soviet advantage during the late 1960s and early 1970s, when the world's televisions were saturated with images of U.S. bombers pounding Vietnamese villages, the propaganda weapon was now being used with similar effectiveness against the USSR, particularly regarding the plight of dissidents, Soviet living standards, and the war in Afghanistan. In any case, whatever Gorbachev's loyalties as a communist, neither he nor his closest advisors were old guard ideological fighters like the late Mikhail Suslov, and they had no real inclination to return to the dogmatic language of their elders.

While this was admirable, disengagement from the propaganda conflict was also unavoidable. There was now no way to insulate the Soviet public from Western sources of information and entertainment; it was now relatively easier to counter the Kremlin's agitprop and disinformation, and the Americans were literally barging into the Soviet Union electronically. By the time Gorbachev arrived, the cultural assault on the closed Soviet system included things like videocassette players loaded with Western films, with over two million VCRs in the entire Soviet bloc (some 30,000 of them in Leningrad alone) by 1987. Soviet efforts to compete in propaganda were pointless—did anyone really take Radio Moscow seriously?—as well as terrifically expensive: in 1986, the Soviet Union spent $3.2 billion on radio and television broadcasting, while the entire budget of the U.S. Information Agency came to only $600 million.[10] As a former USIA official later recalled,

> by 1986 hundreds of millions were being plowed into the projects for new and more powerful [Voice of America] stations. If jamming was expensive for the Soviets now, it would only get much worse. There was no way out. Soviet accommodation with American propagandists had to be reached.[11]

Neither Gorbachev nor any other Soviet leader could stem the growing flow of images and information, and it is to his credit that he realized it would be pointless to continue trying.

Aside from the inability to control this flow of information, there was also a certain amount of curiosity about the West among the new Soviet leaders, not to mention a streak of envy and a growing sense of self-doubt. While it may have been possible for someone like Gromyko to go to New York dozens of times and see nothing but poverty and misery, other men in the Kremlin were, as Paul Hollander writes, increasingly demoralized by what they saw of the West.

> Learning about the West weakened the capacity [of the Soviet elite] to dismiss as unimportant the failures of their own system, supposedly made on account of the great vision it sought to realize....those who came to (or near) power in the 1980s, differed from their predecessors in that they were no longer capable of ignoring or repressing politically or morally problem-

atic evidence or disregarding information; their skill in handling cognitive dissonance was greatly diminished.[12]

Flooding the Soviet empire with the images and sounds of life in the West (and tourists, for that matter) sharpened this sense of contradiction and dissonance. Cherniaev describes something similar happening to Gorbachev himself upon meeting President Reagan in Geneva in 1985: "Gorbachev, for the first time . . . got the sense that there is something deeply wrong in our general evaluation of the American administration and American life, that our class analysis is failing and does not give us an answer that would provide a good basis for any kind of realistic politics and achieve any result."[13] The years of combat with the Americans, during which the West had become more prosperous than ever and the Soviet Union yet more impoverished, had taken their toll on the confidence of the new leaders and left them seeking answers not in the outdated formulas of their forefathers, but in looking more closely at the comfortable and happy lifestyle of their enemies. Essential to this was that the West, led during the 1980s by optimists such as Reagan and Thatcher, had never wavered in their public insistence of the moral and material superiority of the Western way of life.

But there was more to this than just toning down the official rhetoric and allowing Soviet citizens greater access to the West (and vice versa). The reduction of political hostilities would have to be followed by action in three areas. First, any improvement in relations would mean scaling back the Soviet menace to NATO. This would require, at the least, removing the European nuclear threat that Brezhnev had so foolishly allowed the Soviet marshals to put in place in the 1970s. (As Cherniaev later admitted, "[Gorbachev] learned that in order to pursue some sort of transformation, to improve socialism, nothing could be done unless you stop the arms race, because it is the only way to change the image of the Soviet Union in the eyes of the western world.")[14] Second, in order to make peace not only with the Americans, but even more neutral states, he would have to bind the Soviet "bleeding wound" in Afghanistan, if anything he said about his commitment to the peaceful rights of the members of the socialist bloc was to have any meaning. But to do any of this, he would have to detach the Soviet Union from its revolutionary moorings—an ideological abandonment of Soviet principles that Gorbachev called the "new thinking" but that many loyal Soviets saw as nothing short of heresy—and give up the global struggle that was central to the Soviet ideological identity. Gorbachev himself did not see it this way, but he was facing a retreat from Europe, an abandonment of the struggle in the Third World, and the eventual junking of revolutionary ideology. It was an agenda for surrender.

SEEKING PEACE IN EUROPE: FROM REYKJAVIK
TO THE INF TREATY

Gorbachev, like many other Soviet civilian leaders, saw the SS-20 deployments as an "unforgivable adventure," and it took no leap of brilliance for him and his advisors to grasp that to remove them would yield far more diplomatic benefit than stubbornly leaving them in place.[15] "With the help of a variety of intermediate proposals," Cherniaev wrote in a 1986 memo to the Foreign Ministry,

> we have sought to induce Reagan toward concessions [on arms]. Nothing has come of this. He will change his position only in the event that we succeed in pulling Western Europe to our side and if we further skillfully set world opinion against Reagan. Leaving the SS-20s in Europe will not bring Western Europe to our side.[16]

If any progress was to be made in ameliorating the East-West competition (an effort that necessarily including mending fences in Europe), the SS-20s would have to go.

Still, the Soviet high command was determined to gain its pound of flesh for letting go of an entire weapons system. At the 1986 summit at Reykjavik, Reagan again suggested the "zero option," the complete removal of both American and Soviet intermediate range weapons. (Reagan and Gorbachev were so taken with the idea of de-nuclearizing Europe that they nearly agreed to ban *all* nuclear arms, a dramatic but ill-considered leap that understandably worried aides on both sides. When National Security Advisor John Poindexter protested to the president that he could not possibly have agreed to do that, Reagan said, "John, I was there, and I did.")[17] From the Soviet point of view, this breakthrough between Reagan and Gorbachev should have been a golden opportunity to get rid of the dreaded Pershings while trading off a Soviet system that had caused Moscow nothing but heartburn. But for some reason—almost certainly pressure from the Soviet General Staff—Gorbachev insisted that any acceptance of the zero option be linked to limits on the testing and development of SDI.

This, for the Americans, was a trap. As Cherniaev wrote before the summit, "the chief task of Reykjavik . . . is to 'stun' [*oshelomit'*] Reagan with the boldness or even 'riskiness' of [our] approach to the major problem of world politics [and particularly disarmament]."[18] The idea, apparently, was to offer a sweeping agreement on nuclear arms in Europe and then hope the Americans were so caught off balance by the possibility of bringing home a treaty from Iceland that they would finally dump their plans for strategic defenses. Had Reagan wavered at this point, it is difficult to imagine that more concessions would not have been demanded by a General Staff emboldened by the payoff at Reykjavik, and the whole INF deal might have vanished into a thicket of linkages.

As it turned out, Reagan's flat refusal to deal with an SDI-INF package deal left the Soviets, rather than the Americans, stunned. A senior Soviet official later told Henry Kissinger: "We had thought of everything except that Reagan might leave the room."[19] For the third time in seven years, Moscow's attempts to use the promise of an arms agreement as leverage against the West had blown up in its face (the other two being NATO's 1979 refusal to halt the deployments of the Pershing and cruise missiles and Reagan's willingness in late 1983 to let the Soviets walk out of the Intermediate-range Nuclear Forces talks in Geneva). This blundering attempt to get rid of both the Pershings and SDI had failed and managed instead only to cloud the new U.S.-Soviet relationship. The director of the U.S. Arms Control and Disarmament Agency, Kenneth Adelman, was present at the summit, and he later described Reagan as "steaming." When Gorbachev, as he was getting into his limousine to depart, protested that he did not know what else could have been done, Reagan shot back: "Well, you could have said yes!" Furthermore, Adelman claims that this was the moment when Gorbachev and the Soviet leadership realized there would be no compromise with Reagan. When asked, years later, what the turning point was that set the USSR on a course for oblivion, Adelman reports Gorbachev as answering without hesitation: "Oh, it's Reykjavik."[20]

This might be too much to claim for one summit, but the fact remains that Soviet diplomacy never recovered the initiative on European security affairs after it. Rather than excoriate the Soviets for trying to spring the trap at Reykjavik, the Americans continued to offer the complete removal of U.S. and Soviet intermediate-range nuclear weapons, a deal that was too good for the Soviets to pass up—even if it meant accepting that it signaled the beginning of a Soviet withdrawal from Europe. Besides, the delay in reaching an agreement was hurting Moscow more than Washington in the eyes of the world: as Cherniaev later confirmed, "Gorbachev started to suspect that . . . [the Americans] saw his very strong interest in disarmament, that they were trying to use this and pressure us on the issues of human rights and so on, to discredit us and our image as a state. . . . He had some very bitter words on the negotiations. 'They have a good laugh' [Gorbachev said], 'they are drinking whiskey, they have a good time, they are ready to negotiate for decades.' "[21]

In 1987, the Soviets abandoned their attempts to restrain SDI— Gorbachev later claimed not to care about it, telling Reagan that if he wanted to waste his money to go right ahead—and signed the INF Treaty, a document that codified the "zero option" of 1981 that had been so cavalierly dismissed by Gorbachev's predecessors.[22] Although the Pershings were never fired in anger, they did their damage, as Gorbachev later attested.

> By signing the INF treaty we had literally removed a pistol held to our head. Not to mention the exorbitant and unjustifiable costs of developing, producing, and servicing the SS-20—funds swallowed up by the insatiable Moloch of the military-industrial complex. . . . Hence I deemed it my duty to avert the deadly danger to our country and to correct the fatal error made by the Soviet leadership in the mid-1970s. In a sense, I believe this to be as important an achievement as the withdrawal of Soviet troops from Afghanistan.[23]

Although some critics at the time worried that Reykjavik was a lost opportunity, in fact it was an important step toward a treaty that was far better than any of the deals considered up to that point. Previous "walks in the woods" taken by U.S. and Soviet negotiators would not have resulted in removing the entire class of weapons from Europe; more important, they would not have forced the Soviet Union to admit, even implicitly, the magnitude of the strategic error represented by the SS-20s. Reagan's intransigence in 1986 paved the way for a more dramatic success in 1987.

The treaty represented a concrete Soviet attempt to seek an exit from the punishing superpower competition in Europe, a process that Gorbachev had been trying to galvanize without much success at home. In May 1987, six months before the treaty was signed, Gorbachev met with Warsaw Pact representatives in Berlin and pushed through a program that called for, among other things, reductions of forces in Europe to the point where neither side could begin offensive operations against the other.[24] The idea that NATO could successfully attack the Warsaw Pact was laughable, of course, but the reality that NATO could now vigorously defend itself was not. If Gorbachev was going to scale back military influence on the budget—the "Moloch" he described in his memoirs—he would have to remove both the threat of the SS-20s and the sense that Eastern forces were poised for a major offensive. He could accomplish the first by treaty (and Russian sources later confirmed that he committed the USSR to the INF Treaty publicly in order to outflank military objections voiced in private), but to restructure conventional forces in Europe would take more time and effort.[25] In this, Gorbachev was helped by the fact that a young German was landing a Cessna in Red Square even as the Berlin meeting was taking place, an appalling breach of security that allowed him to start sacking some of the high command. Reagan, for his part, welcomed the more cordial relationship that grew after the disappointment of Reykjavik but did not let up the pressure on Gorbachev in Europe: in June, one month after the Berlin meeting, the president also went to the same city and dared his Soviet colleague to tear down the Berlin Wall.

In this light, the INF Treaty, coming on the heels of the Berlin meeting, should be seen as part of Gorbachev's attempts to undermine Soviet opposition—primarily among the military—to remove the Soviet threat to Europe and to exit the diplomatic quagmire that his predecessors had bequeathed to him. It was a situation that Brezhnev and Andropov had created, to be sure, but it was one exploited by Reagan; although earlier Soviet leaders had created the problem, the price was exacted from Gorbachev. The new Soviet leader's efforts to gain control of his own defense establishment were, up to this point, only partially successful, and after tussling with the high command through 1988, Gorbachev again simply plowed ahead by announcing unilateral cuts in Warsaw Pact forces at the United Nations at the end of that year. The chief of the general staff, Marshal Sergei Akhromeev, resigned in protest after the speech; when the marshal later tried to call Gorbachev in his capacity as "the president's military advisor," Gorbachev is said to have told Akhromeev that he had no such advisor and then hung up on him.[26] Three months later, he purged the leading ranks of the Communist Party of its most senior (and most conservative) military members in an attempt to shore up his control of defense affairs. But by the spring of 1989, the Cold War in Europe was already over, and the Soviet Union, even on its own terms, had lost it.

The Soviets thus began a withdrawal that continued through 1989, when Gorbachev confirmed that the USSR would not resort to force to keep the Warsaw Pact intact. Nothing less would suffice: as Sestanovich points out, "acceptance of East European revolution became the test Gorbachev had to pass to preserve good relations with the West."[27] Gorbachev, boxed in by Western pressure, and having affirmed loudly and repeatedly that the Warsaw Pact (and, for that matter, the Soviet Union) was a voluntary association, could not then turn and subdue it by force and thus admit that the entire Soviet project itself was a lie and a failed lie to boot. The challenges, even the taunts, of Western leaders forced Gorbachev into choosing to preserve either the Soviet empire or his own credibility as a new type of Soviet leader. He chose the latter hoping to regain the former and in the end lost both the empire and his position as its ruler.

It is no accident that Gorbachev described the Pershings and the Afghan problem in similar terms. Both were misadventures initiated by his predecessors, and both were costly in diplomatic and economic terms (and in Afghanistan, of course, in terms of blood). They were similar in another way as well: they were both areas in which the United States inflicted defeats during the endgame with Moscow. The INF

Treaty, however, could at least be sold at home as a success, even if more savvy elements in the military and ideological establishments saw it as something less benign; the Americans had helped Gorbachev in that regard by making the transition from the acrimony at Reykjavik to the signing of the treaty in Washington a relatively smooth business. Gorbachev would be less fortunate with regard to Afghanistan.

THE PRICE OF AFGHANISTAN: ARE WE GOING TO FIGHT ENDLESSLY?

The invasion of Afghanistan in 1979—like the brutalization of "fraternal" allies Hungary and Czechoslovakia in 1956 and 1968—was a result of the tension between the revolutionary optimism of official Soviet ideology and the stark reality of the actual geopolitical situation around the USSR. (The USSR, a common joke of the 1970s ran, was the only state in the world surrounded by hostile communist powers.) The Soviets invaded Afghanistan against their better judgment, but they felt they had no better option. Perhaps the greatest irony in the Afghan disaster is that ideological considerations at first seemed to be keeping the Soviets *out* of Afghanistan. In March 1979, then KGB chief Andropov told the Politburo:

> We know Lenin's teaching about a revolutionary situation. Whatever type of situation we are talking about in Afghanistan, it is not that type of situation. Therefore, I believe that we can suppress a revolution in Afghanistan only with the aid of our bayonets, but that is for us entirely inadmissible.[28]

Gromyko agreed, adding that once the Soviet Army enters Afghanistan, it "will be an aggressor. Against whom will it fight? Against the Afghan people first of all, and it will have to shoot at them." Yet, by the end of the year, the Soviet leadership would come full circle and embroil the USSR in a conflict so consuming it led Gorbachev to exclaim in 1986: "We have been fighting in Afghanistan for six years. . . . What, are we going to fight endlessly, as a testimony that our troops are not able to deal with the situation?"[29]

Another reason Soviet involvement in Afghanistan is in retrospect so surprising is that apparently everyone in the Kremlin in 1979 seemed to think the whole business was a quagmire best avoided. This cautious instinct was sensible. The various species of communists in Kabul at the time were hardly people on whom the Kremlin could count, ideologically or politically, and initial Soviet estimates of the situation suggested a pox on all houses. But Moscow was still smarting from Anwar Sadat's recent and embarrassing defection as a Soviet client, and whatever their concerns about the ideological purity of the various Afghan revolutionaries, Soviet leaders were growing anxious that whoever won the struggle in Kabul might "pull a Sadat" and they would then lose Afghanistan to the West as they had Egypt some years earlier. The Afghan comrades might be incompetent communists, but they were communists nonetheless, and this made them worth keeping.

The invasion itself represented a head-on collision of political interests and ideological precepts, and the pernicious and distorting effect of ideology on Soviet policy began to show itself almost immediately. Soviet leaders could hardly make a nakedly political case to themselves, to their public, or to the world that Afghan civilians had to be slaughtered and Soviet boys killed in order to keep revolutionaries of questionable vintage from allowing Kabul to fall under Western influence. Something more had to be placed at stake. As Odd-Arne Westad has pointed out, as early as June 1980, Brezhnev had recast the conflict "into a standard Cold War context"; by 1983, Yuri Andropov would be telling the Politburo in private that the Soviet Union was "fighting against American imperialism, which well understands that in this part of international politics it has lost its positions. That is why we cannot back off."[30] The Soviets could not stand to be perceived, or to perceive themselves, as an aggressor and so imbued the Afghan intervention with an ideological dimension that not only forced them to keep fighting a hopeless struggle, but actually created the situation they claimed they were trying to prevent, as the war in Afghanistan really did become a struggle between East and West.

There is an unmistakable parallel here with the United States and its efforts to preserve South Vietnam. The Americans had invested themselves in a crusade to stop communism in Southeast Asia, seeing Vietnam as one more battlefield in the ongoing struggle with Moscow, just as the Soviets persuaded themselves that Afghanistan was part of the fight against American imperialism. But there is a significant, even crucial, difference between the two wars: there actually *was* a communist army trying to take over South Vietnam. There were no "American imperialists" in Afghanistan. The chaos in Kabul in 1979 was the result of communists fighting communists, an internecine conflict among Afghan leaders that threatened to create a power vacuum.

But if the Soviets wanted to see the hand of Washington behind events in the mountains of Afghanistan, the Americans were willing to oblige them, and the Reagan administration set about to increase the costs of the conflict. In 1984, military aid to the Afghan resistance increased dramatically, and in 1985, U.S. policy moved onto the offensive by making plain Washington's intention to drive the Soviets from Afghanistan completely. By one estimate, just providing the Afghan resistance with British and U.S. anti-aircraft weapons alone resulted in the destruction of some 270 Soviet aircraft, at a cost of well over two billion dollars.[31] Soviet diplomat Oleg Grinevskii later complained that this made it impossible for the Soviets to disengage, and prolonged the fighting:

> You know, back in Andropov's time there was a clear understanding that we needed to leave Afghanistan. I'm not saying that it was right, but let me tell you what the understanding was in Moscow: that the Americans would not let us leave Afghanistan, that this was a calculated U.S. policy to keep the Soviet Union in Afghanistan and draw blood and weaken the Soviet Union.

Former U.S. Ambassador to Moscow Jack Matlock was present when Grinevskii made this comment and answered: "Our Russian colleagues keep asking the question, 'was it your policy to keep us in Afghanistan?' It absolutely was not. . . . We really wanted the Soviets out of Afghanistan, and we couldn't understand why they weren't leaving, unless they were determined to stay."[32] The American effort to drive up the costs of Afghanistan, however, had run directly into a Soviet ideological preconception about "imperialist" efforts to capture a Soviet client; as Tarasenko later noted, given all the loss of blood and treasure in the war, "how could we leave if the CIA was there? If the Americans are attempting to hurt our national security by being there, how could we justify leaving?"[33]

By 1986, it was unmistakable, as one Reagan official put it, that "Soviet body language suggested a yearning to get out," even if the least astute student of Marxism-Leninism and Soviet history had to know that for the Soviets to withdraw without victory would be an ideological defeat of the first order.[34] Such a defeat would force the Soviets to abandon a "revolutionary" regime in time of need and in effect to rescind the Brezhnev Doctrine. The Soviet Army, so vaunted and feared during the Cold War, would also suffer the humiliation of losing the only major engagement it ever fought after World War II.

Turning Afghanistan into a crusade, even if only rhetorically, meant that the Soviets had effectively delegated initiative in the conflict to the Americans, who could keep raising the costs of the conflict by pressing that raw ideological nerve at will. As a result of this needless Soviet infusion of ideology into the conflict, Gorbachev could not later close what he acknowledged as a "bleeding wound" without paying an ideological price, since a loss in Afghanistan had now been defined by the Soviets themselves as a loss to the Americans. Although he initially tried to present the whole mess as the legacy of his doddering predecessors, he nonetheless understood the damage that was about to be done to the Soviet Union's identity as a revolutionary power, and he therefore tried to prepare the ground for a withdrawal by trying to pare away the ideological baggage the war had been saddled with by the Brezhnev leadership.

Soviet intellectuals and writers allied with Gorbachev tentatively began to suggest that the days of viewing the Third World as an arena for ideological struggle between the superpowers should come to an end and that Soviet-American disputes on the periphery should be resolved within a framework of traditional state-to-state relations.[35] This was nothing less than Gorbachev and his advisors rescinding a public Soviet commitment to revolution and internationalism. As former Reagan Administration official Peter Rodman put it, it was clear to the Americans that the Soviets had come up "with an elaborate new intellectual construct, with appropriate quotations from Marx and Lenin to back it up, but the essence of the matter was the virtual dismantling of much of the traditional ideology."[36] By any reckoning, the end of the war had to be considered a Soviet failure in the face of American intervention. Gorbachev could rationalize the withdrawal however he wanted, but the Soviet military and hard-line Party loyalists knew it for what it was: defeat at the hands of the imperialists.

In later years, some military leaders tried to be stoic about the defeat in Afghanistan, but their accounts of the war are still suffused with bitterness. In 1996, retired senior general M. A. Gareev blamed the Afghan defeat on an overall failure of civilian policy, noting that the Soviet military "fulfilled every task they were given. . . . By order of their government, Soviet forces came and left in an orderly fashion. In any case, they didn't leave the way the Americans did in Vietnam."[37] The commander of the Soviet "contingent" in Afghanistan also took a swipe at the Americans in his evaluation of the end. While he admitted that some people believed the USSR had suffered "utter defeat" [*sokrushitel'nyi razgrom*], General Boris Gromov argued that it was impossible to say that there was either victory or defeat, but only that "Soviet forces fulfilled their tasks—unlike the Americans in Vietnam—and made an orderly return to the Motherland."[38] But Soviet ground forces Commander in Chief Valentin Varennikov (later to hold the distinction of being the only man tried—at his own insistence—for complicity in the 1991 coup) would have no such equivocation and would complain that Gorbachev's unilateral surrender in Afghanistan was of a piece with his unwillingness to stop the collapse of the Warsaw Pact and the Soviet Union itself. "Gorbachev . . . accepted capitulation on the West's terms. . . . If I and my compatriots in '45 had ever thought that such a fate awaited us, that such a monolith, such a fortress, as our great state [*derzhava*] would be overthrown without a battle" [ellipsis original].[39]

Adding insult to injury, the Americans were not content to claim victory in the wake of the Soviet pullout. During a 1988 press conference, President Reagan pointedly retracted what few concessions he had already made about future aid to the Afghan rebels and affirmed that American policy would remain unchanged even after the Soviets were gone: how could the United States do any less when innocent people were fighting to throw off communist rule? Gorbachev was, in his own words, "embarrassed and incensed" at this, but by that point there was nothing he could do about it.[40] It could be argued that this was a needless slap in the face of an already defeated enemy, but it was also risk free: there was no possibility that Gorbachev could renege on the withdrawal. And the Americans, in fairness, could hardly be faulted for indulging themselves in one of the clearest victories of the Cold War only fourteen years after the U.S. defeat in Vietnam. Brezhnev and Andropov had foolishly turned Afghanistan into an ideological test of wills: it was Gorbachev's misfortune to be in power when the Reagan administration inflicted the full measure of humiliation for their rigidity and recklessness.

THE ABANDONMENT OF IDEOLOGY

When the Soviets offered to make the struggle in Afghanistan an ideological issue, the effective strategy was to take them at their word. Thus, the American refusal to allow Gorbachev a graceful exit forced him either to admit an ideological defeat—or to try to remove ideology entirely from the equation. Gorbachev tried to take the latter approach, oblivious to its dangers. But even if he was aware of the risk he was incurring, there was little room to maneuver. The West, on one side, was demanding to know if Gorbachev was willing to defend the faith of his Soviet fathers and to continue defining the Soviet state as one necessarily opposed to the international status quo. On the other side, ideologues within the Soviet government (particularly among military and ideological cadres) were increasingly attacking Gorbachev as an apostate from that faith, a charge with the sting of truth to it.

Ideology had become too costly. To stem Western criticisms, open an escape hatch from the increasingly pointless competition in the Third World, and outflank domestic critics, it would have to be removed from its central role in the Soviet political identity. Foreign affairs, an unsigned editorial in *Pravda* proclaimed in early 1987, had been rendered "soulless by the cult of force"—this was almost certainly a rebuke aimed at the Soviet high command—"and the militarization of consciousness" and would have to be rehumanized and deideologized if true international security were to be achieved.[41] A year later, Foreign Minister Shevardnadze declared point-blank that international relations were no longer characterized by the struggle of two opposing systems—a direct abandonment of a core belief on which the Soviet state had been founded.[42]

The turn away from ideology begun in 1987 marks the final phase of the Soviet descent, a moment that some Russian scholars feel has been "grossly underestimated" by Western historians.[43] To renounce an arms race with the West is one thing—Soviet leaders did so rhetorically on a regular schedule—but attempting to outmaneuver Western pressure and trump Communist Party ideologues by removing ideology from the East-West competition was quite another. If the Soviet Union was not to be a revolutionary state committed to the support of like-minded movements around the world, what point was there in being a "Soviet Union" at all? But once Gorbachev committed the USSR to that position, the rest of the world took him at his word, and he could hardly now turn and claim, in Eastern Europe as well as in Afghanistan, that he had not been serious all along.

As an aside, it should be noted that since the fall of the USSR, Gorbachev has tried to have it both ways, presenting himself as a Western-minded reformer in one venue and a loyal Soviet communist who had tried to save the empire in another. At a 1992 conference in San Francisco, according to Professor Anthony D'Agostino (who was present), Gorbachev "blithely took credit for the end of Communism, explaining that, as he had got further into the process of Soviet reform, he had come to realize that the problems in the Soviet system were greater than he thought!" But in 1994, at the trial of 1991 coup plotter Varennikov, Gorbachev hotly denied that he intended to bring down the USSR, instead laying the blame on internal power struggles that crippled the Kremlin. D'Agostino rightly asks: "Well, which was it? Did he knowingly preside over the changes of 1985–91 or were they done against his best intentions? Both of Gorbachev's lines of argument cannot be correct," and he sensibly concludes that the latter explanation makes far more sense. It is "at least better than trying to prove that Gorbachev intended the liquidation of the state that he was chosen to rule" or that "Gorbachev at some point turned against the Communist idea, which he was in fact still defending the day before he resigned his position as head of the party on 24 August 1991."[44]

Whatever Gorbachev may have really believed, he was in an ideological bind that he needed to escape if he was to silence his critics and relieve the pressure from the West. His political maneuvering in this period, while innovative, was something like a priest avoiding a charge of heresy by claiming there is no God: it might catch one's opponents off guard for a moment, but explaining it to the faithful (who quickly will become accustomed to living without the burdensome rules of strict religious belief) can be something of a chore, especially once they all flee the church.

Some Soviet friends and clients saw Gorbachev's move for what it was, prompting Georgii Arbatov to say, rather defensively, in 1990: "We need to explain our foreign policy to well-intentioned circles who argue that the Soviet Union has turned its back on them."[45] But there was little to explain. The fact of the matter was that the Soviet Union, exhausted from the pressure that competition with the West had placed on its malfunctioning system, had indeed turned its back not only on its traditional friends, but even on its own imperium in Eastern Europe. Whether Gorbachev or anyone else wanted this was irrelevant: the once mighty Union of Soviet Socialist Republics could no longer maintain its own fragile existence, much less its commitments around the globe.

Gorbachev could conceivably have stopped the momentum of that decline by reversing himself and using force to prevent further erosion of Moscow's authority at home and abroad. To do so, however, would have required admitting that he was wrong about *perestroika*, reigniting the Cold War with a Western coalition that was not disinclined to fight it, and essentially handing over a great deal of his own power to the men he had fought for dominance in the Communist Party. In abandoning ideology and accepting the Western view of international life as the status quo maintained among nation-states rather than classes, Gorbachev publicly foreclosed to himself the coercive instruments that kept the Party barely in power, the Soviet economy barely running, Soviet nationalities barely under control, and Soviet allies barely loyal.

As the Soviet alliance system crumbled, the situation inside the USSR itself worsened. The Soviet Union by 1990 would be in the grip of what Russian sociologists later called "full social disintegration," as the paralysis of the central government in Moscow became ever more apparent.[46] Abroad, the question was not whether the Warsaw Pact would be torn apart, but rather a matter of when; Gorbachev's inability to use force—or rather, his inability to use force without completely destroying everything he had hoped to achieve in escaping the Cold War's burdens—meant that there was nothing to stop the Eastern Europeans from doing what they had wanted to do for forty years: to overthrow their Soviet-appointed masters. Gorbachev, according to Helmut Kohl, later turned his back on his hapless fellow leaders in the socialist bloc: "He seems to be preoccupied with the USSR," Kohl would tell Bush in mid-1990, "and seems to have little interest in the situation of some of his colleagues."[47]

The Soviet coalition, by the late 1980s, was doomed. Gorbachev's task would be to salvage what he could of the Soviet Union itself, and this in turn meant taking the final step in the Cold War: surrender.

SURRENDER AT MALTA

In December 1989, Gorbachev and Bush met near Malta, in a summit that was supposed to be conducted at sea aboard the Soviet and American ships *Gorky* and *Belknap*. (In retrospect, there was an echo of history in meeting an embattled leader aboard a U.S. warship—only sending the *Missouri* might have been more symbolic—but as it turned out, poor weather and rough seas led to most business being conducted on the more stable *Gorky*.) It was the last time a U.S. president and his Soviet counterpart would ever meet with any pretense of equality. Indeed, it was less a summit than a careful negotiation of a Soviet surrender, in which Bush laid out America's willingness to help the Soviet Union continue the path away from communism—this included an offer of assistance on things like setting up a banking system and a stock market, institutions that were anathema to the Soviet system—but also made clear that the price of American forbearance was a continued Soviet disengagement from global competition with the United States.

Neither leader had arrived with the idea of outright surrender in mind, of course, but the desperate Soviet situation dictated that discussions would take on that undertone. Although it was Gorbachev who initially tried to seize the agenda at Malta, it was Bush who ended up laying down terms. This probably came as a surprise to both men, who by all reports liked each other well enough and were not seeking an adversarial encounter. On the recommendation of Secretary of State James Baker, the Americans decided to head off any Soviet agenda with one of their own. As National Security Advisor Brent Scowcroft recalled:

> Whatever Gorbachev had in mind for his initial comments remained a mystery, for the President had obviously upset his game plan. He appeared nonplussed after having been buried in the avalanche of U.S. proposals. He recovered fairly quickly and made a creditable presentation, but any fears we had of emerging from this initial exchange on the defensive were laid to rest.

This blitz of proposals led Gorbachev to pause and then to comment on the obvious implication for the summit: "This has been interesting. It shows the Bush Administration has already decided what to do."[48] Malta made clear to Bush and his advisors how limited Gorbachev's options in dealing with the Americans really were. Shortly after the summit, Bush reflected on the fact that Gorbachev had tried to complain about U.S. aid to the Philippines, which at the time was fighting an insurrection. "He's really got a problem with anything that makes it look like we're on the march while he's on the retreat, doesn't he?" Bush mused. "I sort of knew that, but hearing from *him* was somehow different."[49]

Clashes over Soviet involvement in Central America and naval arms control arose during the meeting, but the real issue was the future of

Europe in the wake of a Soviet power vacuum, particularly the status
of the Baltic states and the looming question of German reunification.
Any unseemly American celebration over the German situation or any
American intervention to hasten what was by now the inevitable independence of the Soviet Baltic republics could serve as the deal-breaker
in terminating the Cold War, not least because further Soviet humiliations could undermine Gorbachev to the point where his own position
as Soviet president could become unviable. American concerns about
Gorbachev's stability were more farsighted than much of academic
opinion on the subject; into the last days of the USSR, many American
sovietologists, rapt with admiration for Gorbachev, confidently declared that he was firmly in control and that it was mere alarmism to
think he could be deposed. (Professor Stephen Meyer of MIT even went
so far as to tell the Senate Foreign Relations committee that "hints of
military coups are pure flights of fancy" in testimony he gave on June
6, 1991—just nine weeks before Gorbachev's temporary ouster).[50]
Bush's advisors, however, as well as the CIA, were far less sanguine
about the Soviet leader's future, and Bush was determined not to make
Gorbachev's situation any worse than it had to be.

There is a time to make peace with a desperate enemy, and the arrival
of President Bush was a fortunate marriage between the man and the
moment. Had Bush been elected when he first challenged Reagan in
1980, the Cold War would have taken a very different turn, perhaps
even a return to the policies of Nixonian accommodation for which
Moscow was so fervently wishing at the time. A sudden turn away from
Carter's ideological attack back toward détente would have been a
disaster and probably would have accelerated the political decline of
NATO. But in 1989, the Reaganite approach (or at least what Georgii
Arbatov called the "early" Reagan) would have been equally, if not
more, dangerous. Even before Reagan left office in 1988, the Soviet
Union was beaten; but that does not mean Moscow was completely
without resources—or without tens of thousands of nuclear weapons
pointed at the United States and NATO and hundreds of thousands of
soldiers scattered across Europe.

As it turned out, Bush's cautious—one might even say, prudent—instincts served him well in the last days of the Cold War. "We will do
nothing to recklessly try to speed up [German] reunification," the
president told Gorbachev. Noting pressure from Senate Majority Leader
George Mitchell to be less "timid" about the issue, Bush nonetheless
reassured an evidently relieved Gorbachev that he would not be stam-
peded into doing anything dangerous. "This is no time for grandstanding or steps that look good but could prove reckless."[51] Regarding the
Baltics, Bush and Gorbachev carefully felt their way to something like
a deal: the United States would not press the question of independence,

and Gorbachev would not use force in the region. Bush warned that violence against the Baltics would create "a firestorm" of anti-Sovietism in the West, but if Gorbachev abided by his promise to pursue the problem by negotiation, the U.S. position would be one of restraint because, in Bush's words, "we don't want to create big problems for you."[52]

Toward the end of the meeting, Gorbachev reports that he "decided to outline some aspects I deemed fundamental."[53] What followed was as close to a tendering of surrender as the Cold War would see.

Gorbachev began by declaring: "The United States should take as a starting point that the Soviet Union will never, under any circumstances, start a war with the United States, and what is more, is prepared not to regard it as an enemy." Other witnesses recall this being stated more strongly, with Gorbachev explicitly surrendering Europe in the bargain: "We don't consider you an enemy anymore," one account quotes Gorbachev as saying. "Things have changed. We want you in Europe. It's important for the future of the continent that you're there. So don't think we want you to leave."[54] Whatever the wording, the effect was the same, with the USSR retracting an identification of the United States as an enemy regime and welcoming U.S. help in stabilizing what was soon to be a much rowdier and disorganized Europe. Gorbachev also proposed more progress on disarmament and to "join efforts to ensure mutual security," which probably reflected an attempt to head off any incipient U.S. unilateralism (although under the elder Bush, this was less of a danger than the Soviets might have feared). Finally, in keeping with his speech to the United Nations a year earlier, Gorbachev assured Bush that the Soviet Union had now developed a defensive military doctrine and was restructuring its forces in Europe so as reduce their offensive capabilities.

Taken as a package, what Gorbachev offered was a Soviet exit from the Cold War. Whether Bush and his aides fully realized this is unclear; certainly, the former president does not describe Malta in those terms in his own recollections of it. But the fact is that as 1990 wore on, the usual items on the agenda of Soviet-American relations—human rights, regional conflicts, and arms control among them—gave way to the pressing business of reordering the world in the wake of a Soviet defeat. Bush's great care in not pressing for an unconditional Soviet surrender from Gorbachev laid the foundation for Gorbachev instead to offer a more gradual Soviet capitulation, with better terms and a better outcome than any final American thrust to the Soviet heart could have gained. Indeed, Bush was so intent on heading off a more explosive end to the Cold War that he traveled to Ukraine in the summer of 1991 and gave what was later derided as the "Chicken Kiev" speech, an address in which he warned the Ukrainians not to indulge in "suicidal nationalism." The message was ill-timed—by 1991, there was no way to keep the Soviet Union intact, and Bush could only succeed in antagonizing leaders he would later have to speak to as fellow presidents—but the impulse to avoid a sudden and convulsive end to the already dying USSR was a reasonable one.[55]

Given the failures of the realist aspirations of the Nixon and Ford administrations, there is no small irony that Bush's brand of patient realism would be the approach best suited to the final days of the Cold War. That the end of the Cold War was in sight should have been evident as early as 1987, but how it would end was less clear. There was no reason to expect that it would grind to a slow halt as the Soviet republics abandoned the Union rather than in some terrifying explosion of violence. Had the United States attempted to inflict a Carthaginian peace on Moscow—perhaps by vocal support of independence movements, increased economic pressure, relentless propaganda, and demands for one-sided concessions on arms—the end of the Cold War might have looked very different indeed. President Reagan's unyielding ideological campaign showed great promise as a strategy for fighting a Cold War, but it was President Bush's sober and restrained offer of partnership to the defeated Soviets that provides a model for ending one.

On Christmas Day 1991, some four months after a group of bureaucrats and thugs deposed him for three days and set the USSR on the final course to oblivion, Mikhail Gorbachev faced reality and resigned. He gave a speech on Soviet television, handed the codes to the Soviet nuclear arsenal to Boris Yeltsin, and left the Kremlin. President Bush, in keeping with his temperament, did not gloat. Instead, he announced the end simply and directly. "For over 40 years," Bush said in his Christmas address to the nation, "the United States led the West in the struggle against communism and the threat it posed to our most precious values. This struggle shaped the lives of all Americans. It forced all nations to live under the specter of nuclear destruction."

"That confrontation," the president told the American people, "is now over."

NOTES

1. Stephen Sestanovich, "Did the West Undo the East?," *The National Interest*, Spring 1993, p. 30.

2. Nina Tannenwald, ed., *Understanding the End of the Cold War, 1980–1987: An Oral History Conference* (Providence, RI: Watson Institute for International Studies, 1999), p. 259.

3. Sestanovich, pp. 30–31.

4. Quoted in Michael Beschloss and Strobe Talbott, *At the Highest Levels* (Boston: Little, Brown, 1993), pp. 153–154.

5. Tannenwald, ed., p. 75.

6. These comments and a discussion of Gorbachev's loss of control over his own policies can be found in Thomas Nichols, *The Russian Presidency*, rev. and exp. ed., (New York: Palgrave, 2001), pp. 25–27. The best and most complete account of Gorbachev's inconstant and contradictory approach to the reform process is in Anthony D'Agostino, *Gorbachev's Revolution* (New York: New York University Press, 1998). D'Agostino convincingly argues that Gorbachev was more concerned about holding onto power rather than initiating fundamental change and to this day does not understand the degree to which his own incompetence brought down the Soviet Union.

7. See Nichols, p. 25.

8. Mikhail Gorbachev, *Memoirs* (New York: Doubleday, 1995), p. 145, and Georgii Arbatov, *Zatianuvsheesia vyzdorovlenie* (Moscow: Mezhdunarodnye Otnosheniia, 1991), p. 304. Arbatov claims that Yuri Andropov was a poor judge of character and that Romanov was proof of it.

9. Quoted by Cherniaev in Tannenwald, ed., p. 33.

10. Alvin Snyder, *Warriors of Disinformation* (New York: Arcade, 1995), p. 166.

11. Snyder, p. 167.

12. Paul Hollander, *Political Will and Personal Belief: The Decline and Fall of Soviet Communism* (New Haven, CT: Yale University Press, 1999), p. 286.

13. Tannenwald, ed., p. 115.

14. Tannenwald, ed., p. 79.

15. Gorbachev, p. 443.

16. A. S. Cherniaev, *Shest' let s Gorbachevym* (Moscow: Progress, 1993), p. 107.

17. John Newhouse, *War and Peace in the Nuclear Age* (New York: Knopf, 1989), p. 396.

18. Cherniaev, p. 110.

19. Henry Kissinger, *Diplomacy* (New York: Simon and Schuster, 1994), p. 783.

20. Ken Adelman, "The Real Reagan," *The Wall Street Journal*, October 5, 1999, p. A26.

21. Tannenwald, ed., p. 155.

22. Newhouse, p. 404.

23. Gorbachev, p. 444.

24. See Thomas Nichols, *The Sacred Cause: Civil-Military Conflict over Soviet National Security, 1917–1992* (Ithaca, NY: Cornell University Press, 1993), pp. 178–180, for details on the Berlin meeting.

25. Interview with Aleksandr Orlov, Moscow, Russia, February 4, 2000.

26. Orlov, interview.

27. Sestanovich, p. 30.

28. "The Soviet Union and Afghanistan: Documents from the Russian and East German Archives," *Cold War International History Project Bulletin* 8–9, Winter 1996–1997, p. 141.

29. "The Soviet Union and Afghanistan...," p. 178.

30. Odd Arne Westad, "Concerning the Situation in 'A': New Russian Evidence on the Soviet Intervention in Afghanistan," *Cold War International History Project Bulletin* 8–9, Winter 1996–1997, p. 132.

31. Brian Crozier, *The Rise and Fall of the Soviet Empire* (Rocklin, CA: Forum, 1999), p. 397.

32. Tannenwald, ed., pp. 83, 97–98.

33. Tannenwald, ed., p. 84.

34. Peter Rodman, *More Precious Than Peace* (New York: Scribner's, 1994), p. 341.

35. Some analysts have suggested that more farsighted Soviet thinkers began testing this line even before Afghanistan, but I would argue that it did not reach the major Communist Party journals and did not reflect policy until Gorbachev was committed to it after 1986. I am indebted to Dr. Linda Titlar for her comments on this section.

36. Rodman, p. 306.

37. M. A. Gareev, *Moia posledniaia voina* (Moscow: Insan, 1996), p. 376.

38. Boris Gromov, *Ogranichennyi kontingent* (Moscow: Progress-Kultura, 1994), p. 331.

39. Varennikov was later acquitted of treason. See Valentin Varennikov, "My srazhalis' za Rodinu," *Zavtra* 17 (22), May 1994, pp. 1–2.

40. Quoted in Rodman, p. 346.

41. "Za bez'iadernyi mir, za gumanizm mezhdunaronykh otnoshenii," *Pravda*, February 17, 1987, p. 2.

42. Quoted in Linda J. Titlar, "Image and Perception in Soviet and Russian Foreign Policy," unpublished doctoral dissertation, University of Maryland, 1995, p. 96.

43. Interview with Vladimir Batiuk, Moscow, October 3, 2001.

44. D'Agostino, pp. 6–7.

45. Quoted in Titlar, p. 172.

46. For a discussion of the social situation in 1989 and 1990, see Nichols, *The Russian Presidency*, Chapter 2.

47. Ken Olsen, "As Wall fell, leaders talked," *Philadelphia Inquirer* online, November 6, 1999.

48. George Bush and Brent Scowcroft, *A World Transformed* (New York: Knopf, 1998), pp. 163–164.

49. Quoted in Beschloss and Talbot, p. 167.

50. Stephen M. Meyer, "Testimony Before the Senate Foreign Relations Committee," in Theodore Karasik, ed., *Russia and Eurasia Armed Forces Review Annual*, Vol. 15, 1991 (Gulf Breeze, FL: Academic International Press, 1999), p. 348.

51. Bush and Scowcroft, p. 167.

52. Beschloss and Talbott, p. 164.

53. This and the following passages taken from Gorbachev, p. 514.

54. Beschloss and Talbott, p. 163.

55. Scowcroft later derided the idea that Bush was arguing for keeping the USSR intact, but given the timing and location of the speech, it would have been something of a reach to ask his audience to reach a different conclusion. Bush and Scowcroft, pp. 515–516.

9

Lessons of the Cold War

"There are some people," Smiley declared comfortably, favoring with his merry smile the pretty girl from Trinity Oxford whom I had thoughtfully placed across the table from him, "who, when their past is threatened, get frightened of losing everything they thought they had, and perhaps everything they thought they were as well. Now I don't feel that one bit. The purpose of *my* life was to end the time I lived in. So if my past were still around today, you could say I'd failed. But it's not around. We won. Not that the victory matters a damn. And perhaps we didn't win anyway. Perhaps they just lost. Or perhaps, without the bonds of ideological conflict to restrain us any more, our troubles are just beginning. Never mind. What matters is that a long war is over. What matters is the hope."

— John LeCarre, *The Secret Pilgrim*, 1991

WE HAVE SEEN THEIR KIND BEFORE

In his address to Congress in the wake of the 2001 terrorist attacks on New York and Washington, President George W. Bush warned that America's new enemies were not in spirit so different from those of the previous century.

These terrorists kill not merely to end lives, but to disrupt and end a way of life. With every atrocity, they hope that America grows fearful, retreating from the world and forsaking our friends. They stand against us,

because we stand in their way. We are not deceived by their pretenses to piety.
We have seen their kind before. They are the heirs of all the murderous
ideologies of the 20th century. By sacrificing human life to serve their radical
visions—by abandoning every value except the will to power—they follow
in the path of fascism, and Nazism, and totalitarianism.[1]

The war against terrorism, like the Cold War that preceded it, finds the
West again confronted by forces that seek its destruction, an enemy with
whom there can be no compromise and a conflict in which there is no
alternative to complete victory.

But the war on terror is a "hot" war, with U.S. and allied forces
deployed directly in combat against the primary enemy in Afghanistan.
Both President Bush and British Prime Minister Tony Blair have insisted, in a warning no doubt aimed at Iraq and other state sponsors of
terror, that after Afghanistan there will be other campaigns waged in
other places. This is due to the good fortune of the Western coalition in
2001 that its enemies among the terrorists do not so far possess nuclear
weapons or the means to reliably deliver them. America and Britain are
not held at bay by a promise of immediate thermonuclear destruction,
nor do they need to threaten to inflict nuclear Armageddon to achieve
their goals. This will change, perhaps within five to ten years, and one
benefit—we hope—of a successful campaign against terror is that it will
destroy the nuclear infrastructure of rogue states and the sociopaths
who serve them before they acquire such technologies.

In a sense, however, the situation that developed after September
2001 is much like the Cold War, and in some ways, it is even worse. The
West is explicitly named (and the West has reciprocated in kind) by
terrorist organizations and their sponsors as an enemy whose destruction is ideologically imperative. Indeed, the terrorist war against the
United States is beyond ideology, fueled by a hatred of modernity itself
that makes the differences between capitalism and socialism seem
almost trivial by comparison. "The current situation in Afghanistan,"
Taliban leader Mullah Omar said in November 2001, "is related to a
bigger cause—that is the destruction of America. If God's help is with
us, this will happen within a short period of time—keep in mind this
prediction. The real matter is the extinction of America, and God willing, it will fall to the ground."[2] The Cold War was an internecine conflict
between two offspring of Western civilization; the terror war is a fight
between barbarism and civilization itself. It is only the lack of the tense
deterrent relationship that has allowed the United States to strike rather
than to suffer and to avoid a cold war by igniting a hot one.

The speedy victory over the Taliban must not, however, blind Western
policymakers to the reality that there are more challenges to come. The
world, with all its dangers, that existed before "9/11" is still with us.

For now, states that normally do not wish the United States well, like the People's Republic of China, have declared their solidarity with the West in the fight against terrorism, but such promises of support—like those from terror sponsors such as Syria—may end up collapsing under the weight of ideological and hegemonic aspirations. Chinese assurances of support are probably less telling than the videos produced by China's state-run news agency, in which images of the destruction of the Twin Towers are set to dramatic music while a commentator intones:

> This is the America the whole world has wanted to see. Blood debts have been repaid in blood. America has bombed other countries and used its hegemony to deny the natural rights of others without paying the price. Who until now has dared to avenge the hurts inflicted by unaccountable Americans?[3]

Iran, for its part, has already chosen sides and made it clear that the United States remains the enemy, even as Teheran plows ahead with its ballistic missile programs. And North Korea, while offering platitudes, also made threatening movements along the 38th parallel in late 2001 that suggest that Kim Jong Il, like his father, has not learned the lessons of 1950.

But these are the enemies we know, and they may turn out to be more manageable than the enemies we have yet to meet. As John LeCarre's fictional George Smiley warned in 1991, it may be that without "bonds of ideological conflict to restrain us"—that is, without the Cold War as the bipolar ordering principle of international life—our troubles have only just begun. Certainly, the Soviets seem an almost civilized opponent compared to fanatics using civilian aircraft as cruise missiles, and it is chilling to realize that the future may well be a series of overlapping cold *wars* with groups and states who feel they have far less to lose than the cautious old men in the Kremlin once did. As U.S. State Department official John Bolton said in late 2001, a group that would ram airplanes into the World Trade Center was "not going to be deterred by anything. Had these people had ballistic missile technology, there is not the slightest doubt in my mind that they would have used it."[4] But as awful and fantastic as those opponents may seem, they are, as President Bush rightly charged, still recognizable as the ideological heirs to the tyrants who fought the democracies in World War II and again in the Cold War.

Although American and British leaders have warned that the war on terrorism will be a "new kind of war," it is against an old kind of enemy. The next cold wars, too, will be against the "heirs" of the enemies we have fought before. What can we learn—and just as important, what should we *not* learn—from the Western victory that will help us prevail in a new century of conflict?

THE MEANING OF THE WESTERN VICTORY

First and foremost, it is important to understand why the West won the Cold War, and to appreciate the meaning of that victory, it is imperative to start at the beginning and reaffirm what the Cold War was about in the first place. It was not, as realists would have it, a geopolitical shoving match between two large states; the cordial relations between the United States and the Russian Federation (a relationship that has grown even warmer given Russian support in the wake of the 2001 attacks) should put to rest the idea that two large, nuclear-armed states are inevitably destined to quibble over the map like children arguing over a spilled bag of marbles. Nor was it, as the revisionists would insist, a needless conflict brought on by the rapacious reach of unrestrained global capitalism or the mindless acquisitiveness of American imperialists. Rather, the Cold War was fundamentally a moral struggle between good and evil, between freedom and tyranny. The idea that the Cold War "was really about the imposition of autocracy and the denial of freedom" is, as John Gaddis has pointed out with admirable directness, a "fact that many of us had become too sophisticated to see."[5] When thinking about future cold wars, this realization is supremely important, and we must take care not to fall into the complacent assumption that a cold war is little more than a great power tiff that can be managed on some kind of shared understanding of realist principles.

In fact, it is the worst kind of self-delusion to ask what ideological opponents, whether Islamic terrorists or Chinese tyrants, "want." Understanding the moral and ideological nature of the Cold War should serve as a warning that there is no one issue, no clever realist bargaining or geopolitical palliative, that can avert the conflict—a constant temptation, given that such maneuvers bought the Americans a minor truce in the early 1970s. Likewise, there is no peace to be gained through hand-wringing moral paralysis and a consequent refusal to prosecute the struggle. The Soviets (like the Islamic extremists of 2001) warred on the American coalition because they *had* to, because of what the Western allies represented, and to stay true to the principles of the founding of their own empire.

The nature of the war and the meaning of victory are inseparable. The members of the Western coalition, whatever their occasional missteps, maintained their fidelity to a basic moral choice against compromises with evil—a choice fraught with risk and one that we will face again. Still, it was a choice, rather than a mistake or an accident, and as a result of that choice to resist, even to battle, the enemy's central ideological beliefs, the Soviet Union was defeated on its own terms. World revolution and the subsequent replication of the Soviet system around the globe was not only averted, but the body of ideology on which those overarching goals rested has been so thoroughly discredited that it is unlikely that anyone will ever again take up its banner in the international system.

This is an important and, one would think, obvious point. But many still think the Cold War simply "ended" on its own, like some unfortunate and accidental conflagration that only needed time to burn itself out. There is a disturbing tendency among scholars to view the end of the Soviet Union as a natural process, something brought about by economic or political errors made in a previous generation that in turn planted the seeds of a quiet death. This view denies that it is even possible to speak of "victory" in any meaningful sense or that to do so reflects only mindless American nationalism. A similar view holds that insofar as there is credit to be given for the Cold War's outcome, it must rest with a new generation of Soviets who, after seven decades of mayhem and poverty, somehow had an epiphany and conscientiously tore down the system that their fathers had been willing to risk global annihilation to preserve.[6] There was no Western "victory," only a sudden and sober-minded appraisal by well-meaning Soviet leaders to put the whole silly business to rest so they could remove the nuclear sword hanging over the world and improve the lives of their citizens.

That this view persists in the face of so much evidence to the contrary—it is an explanation that Gorbachev himself happily peddles to credulous Westerners, but can actually provoke cynical laughter from former Soviet citizens today—is bad enough in itself, not least because generations of unsuspecting students will be schooled into believing it. But it is far more distressing in its implications for foreign policy. Sooner or later, this reasoning promises, if only we are patient, cooler heads will prevail in Beijing or Teheran (or in the caves of Afghanistan, for that matter), and in the meantime we should eschew any thoughts of "war" or "victory" lest we make things harder for those Asian or Middle Eastern Gorbachevs struggling, one assumes, so valiantly to dismantle their own systems and beliefs. To accept this passivity in the face of ongoing Chinese and Iranian hostility as well as outright terrorist violence seems far-fetched today, but even at the height of the Soviet war with the West, it is an approach that found support in a great many adherents and one that probably would have found a great many more in twenty-first-century America had the terrorist outrages not reawaked a sense of palpable threat in the United States and Europe.

The Cold War of 1945–1991, then, like the cold wars that will follow it in the twenty-first century, was about ideological beliefs, and the victory at its end was a victory of ideas. A Western coalition forearmed with that knowledge may yet lose sight of that evident fact, as American realists did for a time in the 1970s, but acknowledging the power of ideas and retaining a conviction in the possibility of victory should nonetheless be central in conducting such a conflict.

STAYING IN THE FIGHT

One lesson to be learned from the darker moments of the Cold War is that while there can be respites in the struggle, it is never truly over until one side or the other is defeated outright and capitulates. The history of the Cold War is marked by false endings and disappointed hopes, of optimism and faith in Soviet "change" or "growth" that was subsequently dashed by the violence of Korea, relentless expansion in the Third World, nuclear blackmail in Europe, and other aggressive Soviet moves. Ideological conflict cannot, by its nature, move much beyond temporary truces, for to do so requires accommodation with the enemy that is expressly prohibited as a matter of first principles.

The Soviet Union could find ways to interact with the global economy, and it was able to function in the interstate system. But it could not then approve of and cease the struggle against that set of political and economic arrangements without rendering its own core beliefs incoherent. Even China, which has so far pushed aside some of its former ardor for communism, has only partially displaced it; this is understandable, for without Marxism-Leninism and its theory of one-party rule, Beijing's dictators would lose not only the claim to leadership, but the right to order Chinese society in a certain way. Iranian "moderates" are seeking to restrain their more orthodox colleagues, but even they, too, are finding that there is no compromise with ideological warriors. A "moderate" Iran, like a "capitalist" China, will not be a state with a less virulent form of the official ideology, but one that has abandoned it.

This presents Western leaders with a difficult domestic problem. Citizens of the democracies by their nature are inward-looking people, and they have little patience for a complicated foreign policy that turns their attentions away from home. They are consequently prone to see even minor improvements in relations with a hostile power as "peace," and it is thus a challenge to keep Western populations in the fight over the long haul.

During the Cold War, the Soviets helped to mitigate this desire to drop out of the fight by regularly engaging in alarming policies that kept the communist danger squarely before the Western public. American doubts about Stalin's intentions were laid to rest in the wake of the Korean attack, a senseless adventure that not only solidified a Cold War consensus in American politics that lasted for years but left U.S. troops in Korea right into the twenty-first century. Soviet brutality against

Hungary, Czechoslovakia, and Afghanistan regularly jolted Americans and Europeans with reminders that Soviet rule was imperial, not fraternal. The visible and dramatic increases in Soviet arms, including nuclear arms, in Europe kept the Western coalition together far more effectively than any hollow tub-thumping about the Soviet threat ever could. Only in Vietnam did the Soviets play their cards wisely, allowing the conflict to be perceived as an imperialist intervention in an internal Vietnamese matter, while carefully cultivating European opinion and presenting the USSR as the more peaceable empire.

Even without such missteps by the enemy, the goal of Western policymakers in such circumstances should be to keep public attention focused on the opponent. The Soviet Union in 1970 was no less repressive than the Soviet Union of 1981 and perhaps even more so; what differed was the amount of attention that U.S. and allied leaders fixed on that repression and the language they used to describe it. Nixon and Kissinger sought to calm the American people with businesslike talk of "management," and pointing out that the Soviet system was evil and drawing attention to the corrosive rhetoric that Eastern leaders regularly vented against the West could only have undermined their efforts. The result was a détente that was oversold and of necessity could not deliver on its promises and a Soviet Union that was freed from democratic scrutiny and allowed to expand nearly unhindered. More worrisome was that it also encouraged Americans to think of the Soviet Union and its threats against the Western way of life fatalistically, as a chronic and permanent problem. Jimmy Carter pursued a contradictory course, initially trying to dampen concerns about communism even as he sought support for countering specific Soviet policies. The Americans, their fortitude already worn down by the apparent pointlessness of the war in Vietnam and soothed by the bureaucratic approach of the Nixon and Ford administrations, ignored this hesitant call to action until the 1979 invasion of Afghanistan. Reagan, by contrast, built a domestic and international coalition (with help, to be sure, from plainly stupid Soviet policies) dedicated to more active opposition to the Soviet Union.

Throughout the Cold War, however, no American leader ever declared the struggle "over" before 1991. To their credit, leaders as diverse as Kennedy, Nixon, Carter, and Reagan all maintained an American commitment to fight communism—although their emphasis on the threat posed by the enemy varied, with the result that the public's willingness to counter it varied likewise. Fortunately, at the moment of penultimate danger, both Jimmy Carter and Ronald Reagan chose (in different ways and with different degrees of success) to place the dangers represented by the USSR squarely before the American people, and in time, the Americans responded to that threat. It must be borne in mind that a cold war, for the West, is inflicted rather than chosen, and there is no real recourse but to fight it: an ideological enemy will pursue the battle, whether we respond or not. To do so, however, requires constantly reminding the public of dangers they would rather forget—and that Western enemies would all too gladly present as imaginary.

OVERESTIMATING THE ENEMY: THE VULNERABILITIES OF CLOSED REGIMES

The flaws and warts of a democracy are not only easy to find, but are often put on display in the name of openness, free debate, and public information. Drug addiction in the United States is discussed as a public health concern, not a public relations issue. The size of the prison population and the crimes they have committed are matters of open record rather than private shame. Young Americans who emulate Arab radicals a world away and burn U.S. flags in the public quadrangle of their universities are given headlines and photographs in the newspaper rather than a swift arrest and closed trial. When a new fighter jet crashes or a new antiaircraft weapon annihilates a nearby latrine instead of its target (as one prototype famously did during a test in the early 1980s), it is a subject for open investigation and even for satire, rather than for classification as a state secret.

This open willingness to debate the flaws of a democracy is as it should be. It is also the exact reverse of life in a totalitarian regime, where every accident, every failure, and every act of dissidence are obsessively hidden lest the regime appear to be losing control or even just merely incompetent. No one, of course, seriously believed that the Soviet Union had no drug addicts, no angry dissidents, and no gold-plated lemons in its armory. But over time, the imbalance of information presented many Americans, particularly impressionable younger Americans, with two competing images of East and West: an America plagued by social and economic injustices pitted against a poorer but more equitable and placid Soviet Union. This caricature was only sustained by a willing suspension of disbelief (and the dedicated efforts of many Western intellectuals), especially among Westerners who traveled in the USSR.

More important than the distorted comparisons that resulted from this imbalance of information was the fact that it led to a dramatic overestimation of the power and stability of the USSR. This is an error constantly made by democracies when dealing with authoritarian states and is hardly limited to Western evaluations of the Soviet Union. Even now, there is constant surprise in some policymaking and opinion-leading circles when a dictator like Serbia's Slobodan Milosevic or a group of thugs like the Taliban turns out to be weaker than anyone believed and falls from power. China, Americans are regularly told, is a formidable nation. Yet, this dictatorship of over a billion people is so insecure that it reacts to religious groups like Falun Gong with a sense of near hysteria, bristles at every imagined slight from the international community, threatens to throw a tantrum if it is not handed the Olympic Games, and bares its military teeth with frustration at the evident economic and military strength of Taiwan, a country one-fiftieth its size. The Chinese may indeed be, depending on one's view, single-minded communists or ruthless hypernationalists (just as the Taliban were thought to be hard-bitten, fanatical veterans of years of war), but they are not invincible. They, like all repressive regimes and in particular the Soviets before them, are beset by problems that are often not immediately obvious to the outside world but that are just as crippling as any military shortcoming.

This tendency to overestimate the enemy resulted in the single poorest strategic evaluation made by Western scholars (and foisted on Western policymakers) during the Cold War: that the Soviet Union was a strong and stable nation, one that could barely be contained, much less changed. A generation of young sovietologists—the present author among them—were confidently told by their professors that the Soviet economy, while flawed, worked; that the Soviet government, while oppressive, was popular; and that Soviet minorities, while restless, were loyal.[7] Thus, any strategy that was aimed at undermining the Soviet economy or disrupting the state-society relationship in communist dictatorships was by definition pointless and needlessly provocative. Realists avowed that states cannot reach out and touch each other's internal processes or change each other's natures; mainstream sovietologists warned that such attempts would only provoke the Kremlin to righteous indignation. But this was an image of the enemy that had been warped by propaganda and overly clever social science reasoning. (By the late 1970s, for example, the gray tangle of Soviet bureaucracy mimicked a "normal" state closely enough—at least to those who choose not to look too closely at it—that one of the most commonly used texts on Soviet politics, Merle Fainsod's magisterial *How Russia Is Ruled*, was, in a minor academic scandal, rewritten and tellingly retitled *How the Soviet Union Is Governed* by a revisionist scholar, Jerry Hough.)[8]

But as Stephen Sestanovich later wrote, *pace* Kennan, this was exactly the wrong lesson to draw from our experiences with Soviet communism. "We need to know—because this is what the record shows—that we can in fact influence the internal affairs of rival states, even large and seemingly secure ones."[9] Whatever criticisms might be leveled at Richard Nixon's accommodations with the Soviets or

Ronald Reagan's undeniably expensive military programs, the strategies of détente and confrontation both shared one important characteristic: by exposing Soviet society to Western values, criticisms, and luxuries (either by agreement or by sheer force), they threatened a Soviet regime that was vigilant to the point of obsession about such influences. Every tourist, every Western broadcast, and every smuggled Bible or hidden newspaper was a challenge to the regime that the Kremlin would strive to root out.

This is not, it should be noted, an argument for winning "hearts and minds," nor for providing needless reassurance that the West is benign. In the short term, in fact, Western policies may make life worse rather than better for the captive population of a closed regime. Attacks on the state-society relationship can actually produce more misery, rather than less: the repressive measures undertaken in response to them by the Soviet regime alienated the very citizens the Kremlin hoped to control. But the success of efforts like Radio Liberty lay not in assuring the peoples of Eastern Europe of the friendly intentions of Western governments (for they needed no such convincing) or the relative ease of life in the West, but in confirming to the peoples of the Soviet empire that their governments were indeed as bad as they thought, that the information they were being given about the world around them was flatly a lie, and that the Western nations had not forgotten them and were trying, in whatever way possible, to aid them. It helped, of course, that the Soviet regime constantly allowed itself to be baited into competing with Western views and in the process to make ever more silly and paranoid claims. Even during détente, it is arguable whether greater contacts convinced ordinary Soviets of the superiority of Western political arrangements (and any veteran of late-night discussions in the Soviet Union can attest that to do so was not as easy as it might seem), but one result of détente was undeniable: Soviet citizens were exposed not just to new ideas, but to visitors who were visibly happier, healthier, and wealthier than they were, each one of whom was a living contradiction of Soviet falsehoods.[10]

This dynamic was evident when the Cold War heated up again during the 1980s. Reagan's attacks on the Soviet Union were intended to goad the Soviets into meeting American challenges—in effect, to get them to take an unwise dare—and they struck a nerve in Moscow. Again, observers at the time overestimated the strength of the Soviet state-society relationship and the productive capacity of the Soviet economy, and drastically underestimated the degree of discontent in the Soviet public and the level of insecurity and anxiety among the Soviet elite. The Soviet response to Reagan was not to pull back and to make a liar of him, but instead to dig in their heels and to play every inch the role of the evil empire that Reagan said they were. Some of their mistakes, like the Korean airliner disaster in 1983, were unintentional (although after the public relations fiasco surrounding the shooting down of a KAL flight in 1978, one might think the Soviets would have been less rather than more inclined to be trigger-happy at a time where they were being made out to be international bullies). Some of their actions, like the SS-20 deployments, were born of sheer arrogance. But some, like the unwillingness to reduce military expenditures or the increased restrictions on meetings with foreigners, were a direct attempt to counter Reagan's efforts. These were not only hopeless (the stricture on meeting foreigners actually made many Soviets more curious about Americans than they already were), but also materially affected the daily life of increasingly bitter, depressed, and improverished Soviet citizens.

Recognizing the weaknesses of ideological states and, in particular, their compulsive need to control how their citizens live and think carries certain risks as well. As the Reagan Administration learned, attacking an already paranoid regime can convince its leaders that war is not only likely, but perhaps even the West's goal. Another consideration is a humanitarian one: the human costs of a strategy of direct attack on a regime's control over society will always fall, in the first instance, on the innocent subjects of the regime. It serves little purpose to loosen a dictatorship's grip if the response will be on the order of the 1989 massacre in Tienanmen Square. These are states, after all, that will sacrifice thousands, maybe millions of lives on the altar of their own insecurity, and provoking them should always be undertaken (just as in any act of physical warfare) with a constant concern for proportionality.

None of this is to say that a proper estimation of the enemy should lead to a policy of relentless assault or of ideologically charged combat without quarter. Rather, the goal is to force such regimes to constantly divert resources away from international mischief to internal policing, in hopes both of pressing a retreat from the world stage and an unsuccessful retrenchment at home. As a rule, such states are lacking in wealth and confidence, and a strategy that threatens their stability at home can deplete both of those already scarce resources. But timing is crucial: a weakened West cannot credibly conduct an offensive of the type launched by Carter and Reagan without a solid economic and technological foundation or without careful preparation both of coalition partners and domestic populations for an intensified political struggle.

The Soviet Union was a weak state with a crippled economy, an empire struggling against growing discontent and saddled with an ideology of, at best, uneven appeal. To treat the USSR as a stable superpower was to grant it both legitimacy and breathing space, benefits that are always devoutly desired by authoritarian regimes. In prosecuting a cold war, Western leaders should take as a matter of course that our likely enemies are hobbled not only by economic arrangements that are inevitably less efficient than capitalism, but also by the self-imposed weaknesses and limits that arise from the need to keep their societies captive to their ideology. Exploiting those weaknesses is not only effective, but can be conducted at less cost and with far less danger—again, so long as a careful watch is kept on the opponent's reactions—than arms races or even outright military conflict. To do so, however, requires discarding the myths about authoritarian states that so often led to gross overestimation of the enemy. We must always see the enemy as it is, not as it wishes to be perceived, and certainly never as we *wish* to see it.

THE IMPERATIVE OF CONSTANCY

There is no lesson of the Cold War that is more important or more applicable to the future than that of constancy. In the clash of ideologies that characterized the conflict between the Soviet and American coalitions, both sides at times faltered and fell into self-doubt, but in the end it was only the West's firm adherence to a belief in the superiority of its own values that made it possible for the United States and its allies to endure and to take the measures and make the sacrifices that led to victory.

A West that did not believe in itself could not have effectively made the case, either to the subjects of the Soviet empire or to the world at large, for democracy, for free markets, or for the virtues of the open society. A West that did not believe in itself could not have marshaled a coalition for repeated military conflict with Soviet proxies nor could it have made the economic sacrifices needed to produce the awe-inspiring arsenal that held Soviet ambitions at bay. A West that did not believe in itself would not have been able to resist the twin siren calls of complacency and pacifism and would have ceded the initiative, as it nearly did, of the conflict to the Soviets, eventually ceding the world to communism out of a moral confusion that would have been unable to come up with reasons to do otherwise.

Finally, a West that did not believe in itself could not have been secure enough in itself to bring the conflict to an end by encouraging the enemy to accept, rather than to bow before, our own values. In the end, we did not defeat the Soviet Union by forcing it to accept our way of life; rather, our optimism about and evident satisfaction with that way of life and our obvious enjoyment of its material and spiritual benefits proved more attractive than the grinding moral and economic poverty offered to the world by our enemies.

In short, without a firm commitment to Western values, it would have been impossible to win the Cold War, and if we lose sight of those values, we will at some point lose the next one. Whether the opponent is an increasingly aggressive China, an Iran armed with long-range nuclear missiles, or even a transnational terrorist group with access to weapons of mass destruction, the West should bear in mind the most important lesson of the Cold War: when dealing with those who reject or seek to overturn the basic values of the world's liberal democratic order, there can be no meaningful peace until there is a clear defeat of the opponent's central ideological commitments—something that can only be achieved by maintaining a forceful and uncompromising attachment to our own.

A FINAL WORD: THE CASE FOR CONFIDENCE

Even before war came to America on September 11, 2001, the first decades of the twenty-first century promised to be bleak. The era of complete American supremacy that began with the fall of Soviet communism was destined to be brief; there are too many enemies of liberty and too many weapons at their disposal to think that the United States and its allies would never again face a challenge to their survival. The dramatic end of the Soviet-American struggle created a moment of optimism, even overconfidence—a time when Secretary of State Madeleine Albright would, to the embarrassed winces of U.S. allies, grandly refer to America as an "indispensable" nation—that could only obscure how difficult the fight had been to bring down the Soviet totalitarians and how dangerous the world yet remained. As Vojtech Mastny would later write: "Such happy endings have been exceedingly rare in history. Hence the lessons of the Cold War are not those of complacency and the redundance of force in keeping the world safe."[11]

Still, there is reason for citizens of the Western democracies to take heart as well. We may not yet be at the "end of history," when all other ideologies fall before the irresistible force of personal political and economic liberty. But we may, in fact, be closer to it than we think: the destruction of communism has settled the matter of freedom versus oppression at least in the *civilized* world, and what is left is not, to use Samuel Huntington's phrase, "a clash of civilizations," but rather a fight *for* civilization itself, a series of struggles and unnerving cold wars that will decide whether humanity will live in freedom or under the heavy hand of ideological or theocratic repression.

In this, the West is privileged over its enemies, whether they are dictators in Beijing or terrorist bosses in the Middle East. It is stronger, economically and militarily, than any coalition that has ever existed in human history. It should be no surprise that terrorists as well as repressive regimes are anxiously seeking nuclear arsenals, since the threat of mass murder-suicide is the only trump card such militarily incompetent organizations can play against the immense power of the United States and NATO. It is little wonder that the West's enemies decry globalization even as they seek its riches: they know that the sheer scale of the international capitalist system has made dreams of autarky, of sullen self-sufficiency, completely pointless and that they will feel its influence in the demands of their citizens, whether they want to or not. They also know and fear the productive capacity of the Western coalition. The attacks on New York and Washington led the Americans to appropriate sums for repairs that dwarf the economies of entire *nations*, much less their treasuries. The coming years do not promise a showdown between a decrepit and exhausted Rome and youthful and dynamic invaders, but rather between a global alliance at the very height of its powers and a group of poor, resentful, and weak entities that seek the means and the materials of mass destruction because they have nothing else to offer.

Whatever the awesome scope of the West's military and economic power, the Western advantage is even more decisive in cultural and political strength. Chinese party hacks, North Korean marshals, and Islamic extremists, like the Soviet dictators of the Cold War, fear the United States because they know what the men in the Kremlin knew as well: that given a choice, many of the people they presume to lead would desert them for a better and more enriching life in the West. The Soviets, like the mullahs, tried to crack down on Western influences because they were spiritually "decadent"—that is, because people preferred them to what the regime could offer. This was not a problem with an analog in the West; no one (probably not even a Red-baiter like Joseph McCarthy) seriously worried that if enough copies of *Soviet Life* were passed around or if enough people visited Minsk that there would be a rush to join the Communist Party and that America's best minds and most productive citizens would flee to the open embrace of the USSR. Likewise, terrorists like Osama bin Laden did not hold out the hope, really, of converting Americans to their brand of Islam; it is all they can do to stop other Muslims defecting from it. All of the repressive groups and regimes of the twenty-first century face the same dilemma the Soviets found insoluble: they are competing with a culture that is more attractive and more rewarding, spiritually and materially, than their own.

More infuriating to the West's enemies is that personal freedom means the adoption, rather than the abolition, of competing beliefs, an openness that encourages schisms in the official faith, be it Islam, communism, or anything else. People will always practice Islam in the West, just as some will always adhere to socialism. But it will be by their choice, and it will not be in a form forced on them by madmen in caves or ideologues in Moscow or Beijing. It is this realization—that the West not only offers an alternative, but also is confident enough to allow the practice of opposing ideologies within its borders—that drives communist totalitarians and would-be theocrats to nearly incoherent rage over their inability to stop it.

Cynics, with unrepentant Soviet apologists no doubt among them, will claim that it was only the self-indulgent material rewards of life in the West that led people to brave the guns of East Berlin's border guards, court the wrath of KGB torturers, or risk death in the skies at the hands of Cuba's sadistic air force. Some even now claim that Russia is worse off, that whatever the flaws of the Soviet system, it was better than the unrestrained capitalist frenzy that followed the Soviet collapse in the 1990s. They would also argue that the Soviet Union fell for reasons that had more to do with economic efficiency rather than the natural human craving to escape the smothering anxiety of life in a totalitarian state. This reflects the tendency of the modern social sciences to reduce people to economic abstractions, an intellectual device that avoids unpleasant realities and relieves any need to understand the complex and often conflicting beliefs that motivate human beings. But this confuses the natural hope of a better life (and who would really prefer to raise their child in the repressive squalor of a communist country or an extremist Islamic theocracy than in the West) with the fact that for most people a "better life" is measured in terms more evocative than a bank statement.

Nothing can be clearer at the end of the Cold War than that people, whatever their fears and misgivings, want to be free. They want to associate as they please, to work where their skills and talents may take them, and to worship God as they wish. It is the promise of human freedom that defeated Nazi Germany and the Soviet Union, and it will defeat their heirs, no matter where they reside or what mad ideologies they espouse. There are dangers yet to come, perhaps even more terrifying than the ones we experienced before 1991. Our enemies in the twenty-first century are unrestrained by any shared notion of civilization, and this makes them more lethal than the Soviet Union. It also makes their defeat more imperative. But America's enemies, as before and in the future, will not go to war against a particular type of socioeconomic system, but rather to contest the idea of freedom itself.

Whatever the travails of the future, it is hard to imagine that the fate of these new totalitarians will be any different from their Nazi and Soviet predecessors. They will, as President George W. Bush vowed, "follow that path all the way to where it ends: in history's unmarked grave of discarded lies." Until that moment comes, there can be no alternative to a firm, confident, and public defense of Western values,

backed by the military capacity and willingness to deter or resist even
the most dedicated and ruthless opponents.

But military means in the end will not win our future cold wars. The
commitment to freedom is the single greatest weapon in the Western
arsenal and the one our enemies hope most to destroy; indeed, it is what
motivates them to oppose us in the first place. Freedom, however, is not
the sole claim of a single state or coalition, and its attraction cannot be
undermined by a blow against any one of the many political systems
that espouse and defend it. Freedom is the common aspiration of
mankind; our commitment to it is our promise to preserve it not only
for those who survived the totalitarian horrors of the late twentieth
century, but for all like-minded people and their descendants as well.
If the history of the Cold War of 1945–1991 should teach us anything, it
is that victory over the enemies of liberty is inevitable so long as that
commitment, and that promise, survive.

NOTES

1. George W. Bush, Address to a Joint Session of Congress, September 20, 2001,
available at www.whitehouse.gov.

2. AP international news wire, November 15, 2001.

3. Damien McElroy, "Beijing produces videos glorifying terrorist attacks on
'arrogant' US," *Daily Telegraph* online edition, November 4, 2001, www.tele-
graph.co.uk.

4. William J. Broad, Stephen Engelberg, and James Glanz, "Assessing Risks,
Chemical, Biological, Even Nuclear," *The New York Times* online edition, November 1, 2001.

5. John Lewis Gaddis, "How Relevant Was U.S. Strategy in Winning the Cold
War?" (Carlisle, PA: U.S. Army War College Strategic Studies Institute, 1992), p.
3.

6. "In the end," Raymond Garthoff has written, "only a Soviet leader could
have ended the Cold War because it rested on the Marxist-Leninist assumption
of a struggle to the end of two social-economic-political systems, the capitalist
world and the socialist (communist) world. Gorbachev set out deliberately to
end the Cold War." Raymond Garthoff, *The Great Transition* (Washington: The
Brookings Institution, 1994), p. 754.

7. As a young doctoral candidate in 1984, I was told by one of my professors
that the idea that the Soviet Union could collapse into its constituent republics
was "apocalyptic" and "absurd." He has since retired, but his opinion was the
conventional wisdom and remained so for many academics right up to the fall
of the USSR.

8. For a recounting of this miniscandal, see Robert Conquest, "Academe and
the Soviet Myth," *The National Interest* 31, Spring 1993, pp. 92–93.

9. Stephen Sestanovich, "Did the West Undo the East?", *The National Interest*
31, Spring 1993, p. 34.

10. In 1991, I accompanied a visiting group of Soviet naval officers to New
York. As we stood on Fifth Avenue (packed, as usual, with pedestrians) late on
a chilly November night, one of the officers seemed confused. When I asked what

he was wondering about, he shook his head and said, "We were told no one would be on the streets here after dark, that it was too dangerous." I assured him that the millions of people he was seeing with his own eyes were not actors.

11. Vojtech Mastny, *The Cold War and Soviet Insecurity* (New York: Oxford University Press, 1996), p. 197.

Index

ABOUT THE AUTHOR

THOMAS M. NICHOLS is Chairman of the Department of Strategy and Policy at the U.S. Naval War College, Newport, Rhode Island. He is the author of *The Russian Presidency: Society and Politics in the Second Russian Republic* (1999), and *The Sacred Cause: Civil-Military Conflict Over Soviet National Security, 1917–1992* (1993).